To Dan:

Championship reading inside

Enjoy

Richard L. Shook

LIONS PRIDE

60 Years of Detroit Lions Football

Bob Snodgrass
Coordinating Consultant

Mike Murray
Editor

Dan Hill
Commemorative Specialist

Tom Albert
Photo Editor

Jack Smith
Fine Books Specialist

Dan Arthur
Researcher

Bill Keenist
Lions Consultant

Anita Stumbo
Design and Typography

*Production Assistance by Debra Weld, Stacie Masterson, Jerry Steely,
     Michael Zahn*

Fiber Optic photo Wolf Photography and Chris Dennis

*Hall of Fame Gatefold artwork and photos courtesy
     Pro Football Hall of Fame*

*Contributing Photographers: Tom Albert, George Gellatly, Chris Dennis,
     Vernon Biever, Doug Ashley, Drayton Holcomb, Barry Edmunds*

Remaining photos courtesy the Detroit Lions

Dust jacket design by John Martin and Bonnie Henson

Published by Taylor Publishing Company, Dallas, Texas

ISBN: 0–87833–043–7 (General)
ISBN: 0–87833–044–5 (Limited)
ISBN: 0–87833–045–3 (Collectors)

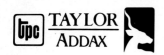

Acknowledgments

There are a great number of great people who helped make this book a reality, and, as editor, I'd like to take this opportunity to extend a brief but sincere "thank you . . ."

To Bill Keenist, the man who got the ball rolling on this project, and who helped give this editor some much-needed advice and direction.

To Tom Gilbert, who spent more hours than he ever imagined gathering and taking photos that would encompass 60-plus years of football. Folks, Tom did a great job and the proof is in the pudding.

To James Petrylka and Barbara Saliba, who were prepared — and maybe wanted — to do more than I asked of them, but helped in more ways than they realize.

To Dan Arthur, for doing his typically thorough job in his typically professional fashion.

To Chuck Klonke, Larry Paladino and Richard Shook, the "go-to" guys who didn't blink.

To Jerry Green and Walter Dell, whose offers came from the heart.

To Bob Snodgrass (no more lists, Bob), Anita Stumbo, Jerry Steely, and the other good people on the Taylor/Addax team. Quite simply, they are the best at what they do.

To Joe Horrigan and Pete Fierle at the Pro Football Hall of Fame — your patience and cooperation made an impossible task easy.

To the *Detroit Free Press, The Detroit News, The Oakland Press*, George Puscas and the long list of photographers whose contributions helped give this book its soul.

To Kent Falb, Dan Jaroshewich, Gene Evans, Jim Pendell, Kim French, and the entire Lions front office staff — Chuck Schmidt is surrounded by the best people in the NFL.

To Joe Falls, whose inclusion in this book is more deeply appreciated than you could know.

Most importantly, to all the Detroit Lions, past and present, for providing more moments, magic and memories than one book could ever capture.

Finally, to the families of those people mentioned here — particularly my own — for all your support.

Thank you.

Mike Murray
Editor

Contents

Introduction

by William Clay Ford
Owner and President
The Detroit Lions, Inc.

There has always been a special relationship between the people of Detroit and the area's pro sports teams; perhaps only people born and raised in these parts can understand that bond.

I grew up here following all the Detroit teams, including the baseball Tigers and hockey's Red Wings, but I always had a special fondness for the Lions. Like many Detroiters, I always felt as if I were a part of the Lions, and the Lions were a part of me.

As a young boy, I attended my first Lions game in 1934 — the club's first season in Detroit. My father, Edsel, took me to the University of Detroit Stadium so I could root for my favorite football team. In later years, I would take my son to see the Lions play at Tiger Stadium.

That's the way it's always been in Detroit. Generation after generation, we've grown up with our heroes of the gridiron. Some of us remember Dutch Clark running for a touchdown at U-D Stadium; some might recall watching Bobby Layne throw a touchdown pass to Cloyce Box at Briggs Stadium; youngsters today know the thrill of seeing Barry Sanders twist and dash to another score at the Silverdome.

The game of football has changed quite a bit in the last 60 years. The players, of course, are bigger and stronger than they were in the early days. The football itself is now sleeker and less round, making it easier to throw but impossible to drop-kick. Specialization has become the vogue, as the two-way player has been replaced by two-platoon football. Halfbacks and fullbacks are out, H-backs and slot receivers are in. And the payrolls . . . well, let's just say that has changed a lot, too.

There are two things, however, that haven't changed over the past six decades. First, we have been fortunate enough to have had a good number of the NFL's most exciting players right here in Detroit. From Dutch Clark, Bobby Layne, Doak Walker and Joe Schmidt to Lem Barney, Billy Sims, Barry Sanders and Chris Spielman, we've been blessed with an array of dazzling stars over the years.

But in addition to the great players, we have been blessed with the greatest fans in the National Football League. Our greatest asset over the past 60 years has come from our friends in the community. Year after year, the support we've received from the good fans in the Detroit area has been tremendous.

Not every day has been sunny. While we've had some successful

seasons, our great fan support has not always been rewarded with victories on the field. To be honest, we have had more than our share of adversity and tragedy. The losses, both on and off the field, have made an impact on this club, at times nearly breaking the team's spirit. But I've been proud of this team's resolve, proud of the accomplishments we've made, and proud of the direction this organization is headed.

For this, our 60th season, we've done everything possible to ensure that Lions fans will have every reason to cheer. Through judicious use of the college draft, we have created the nucleus of a winning team. Trades have brought us a number of talented performers. We have also embarked in a new era of free agency in pro football, and we have improved our team in the span of a few months that otherwise could have taken years.

We have been aggressive in our approach, because we are committed to winning. Winning is our bottom line.

And the same fans who have been so good to the Lions deserve a winner. I hope you enjoy this book. For most Lion fans — myself included — it encompasses a lifetime of memories. ❖

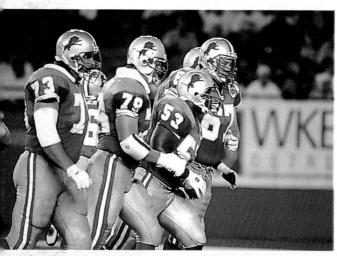

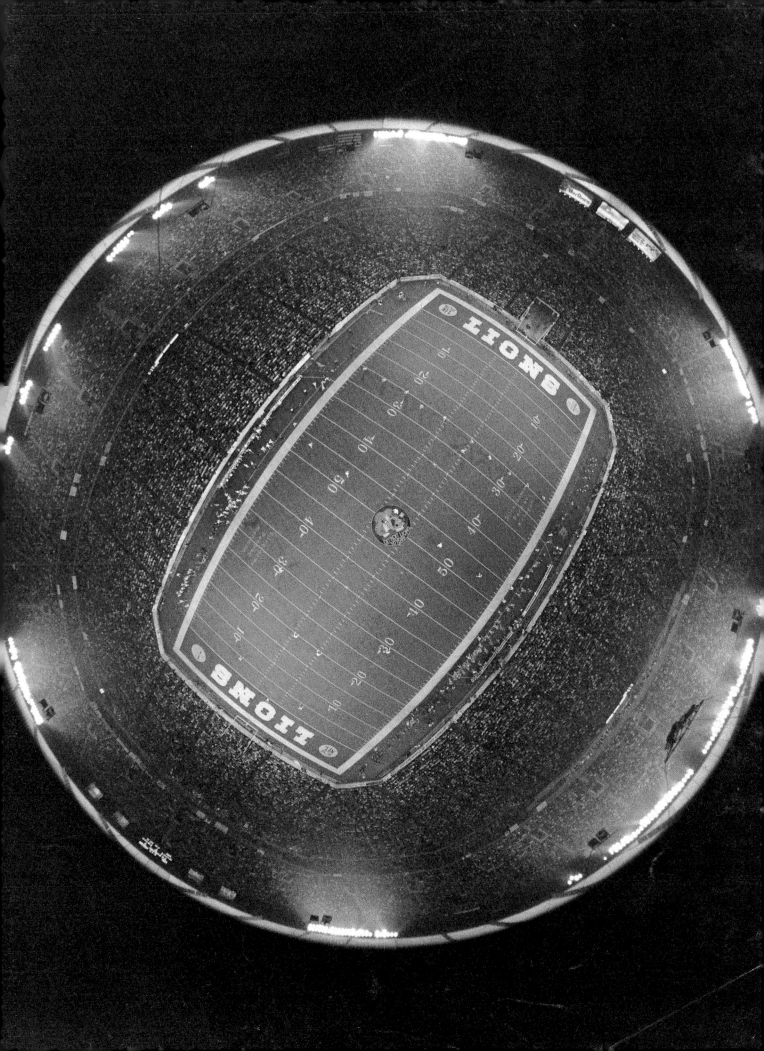

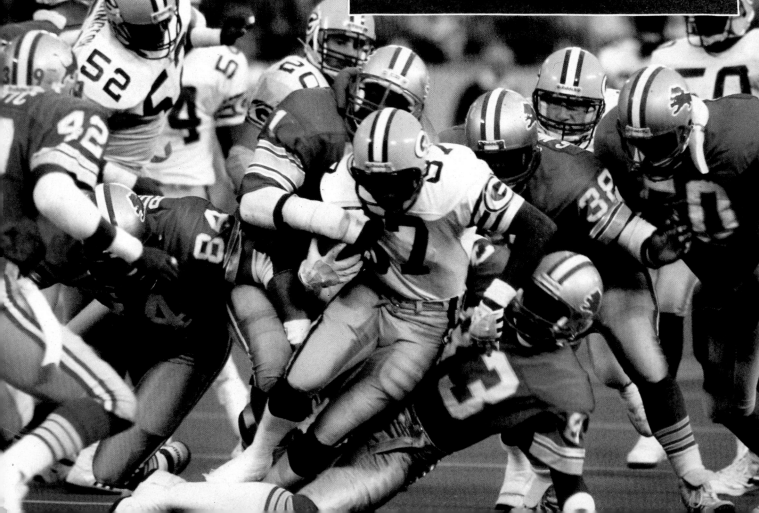

Foreword

by Jerry Green
The Detroit News

Monday afternoon. The saloon. "C'mon, all of you, heah?" says Bobby Layne. His voice was a Texas croak.

"We're all goin' 'cross the street."

Autumn Mondays in Detroit are blue-gray. Smoke pours from the factory chimneys and is visible in the crisp sky above the gray buildings. Detroit is a shot-and-a-beer town, where the people through the generations share passions about their sports teams. And heroes.

"Hurry up, all of ya," says Layne. Detroit is a pro football city where the people on Mondays are consumed by the happenings of the day before on the pro football field.

It has been that way for 60 years now — six decades — three generations — from grandfather, to father, to his son, or daughter.

"I'm buyin'," says Layne. Detroit is the town where Layne was glorified when pro football was young and not complicated, the town where Layne won championships for the Lions. He was the toughest quarterback, on the toughest team.

Forever, it seems, he has been the symbol for this city and the areas surrounding it, and the symbol for this football team. He played without a facemask and he was the finest against the clock.

And just about every Monday through most of the 1950s — until he was traded away, fittingly enough on a Monday — Bobby Layne would assemble his team. These renegades, these spirited champions, assembled in the Stadium Bar, across from Briggs Stadium. Their welts were red, turning blue, and Layne collected the players en mass for a Monday afternoon of revelry and camaraderie.

This was a private team thing — to drink and to talk about the Sunday game. The patrons of the tavern were shooed outside.

They understood. The Lions were that vital in the city. This was the Legend of Layne, and it was real. He was a hero in this town. And ever after, he has been the quarterback against whom all Lions quarterbacks were judged and gauged. It is that way four decades later.

To me — to any of us who go back long distance to the '50s — Layne was that, the hero of heroes, the man whose name can be associated eternally with this franchise. It developed a reputation then for being a different sort of football team. That reputation carries over.

It is a team that has had a multitude of heroes, football players who have qualified for the Hall of Fame down in Canton.

Before Layne, there was Dutch Clark. Dutch arrived with the franchise. He was the link, the connection between the Portsmouth Spartans, when pro football was Small Town America, and the Detroit Lions, when the game left its roots and moved into the larger cities. When George A. Richards, that pioneer, purchased the Portsmouth franchise and its assets — the players — in 1934 for the magnificent sum of $15,000, and moved it all to Detroit, Clark was the prize player.

A year later the Lions won their first NFL championship. It was the pro football club's contribution to the City of Champions. In an unprecedented period of six months from October '35 to April '36 — and never matched anywhere — the Tigers won their first World Series, the Red Wings won their first Stanley Cup championship, and the Lions won in the NFL. At the same time, a young Detroit boxer was knocking opponents stiff on his passage to the heavyweight championship. His name was Joe Louis.

Back then — as now in the '90s — bubble gum cards provided a profound image for young boys attaining their first intimacy with pro football in Detroit. I bought one for a penny, maybe in 1937 or 1938. I have this fond memory of opening the packet and looking at the picture of the solid-looking football player in a pale blue jersey with a silver numeral 7 on it. The athlete's hair was parted down the middle, with a curl covering the forehead. There was the caption: "Dutch Clark, Detroit Lions."

I pictured leather pads on the athletes and roundish footballs being lugged and passed. Many of Detroit's fans obtained their first knowledge of pro football from the reverse side of Dutch Clark's bubble gum card. I know, I did.

Researching a book about the Lions twenty years ago, I came upon a quote, circa the mid-1930s, from a local sports historian: "Until Clark came along, pro football in Detroit was looked upon as a novelty. Its chances of survival were slim

because it was too close to collegiate gridiron centers, but Dutch changed that."

Clark shoveled out the foundation, Layne became the spirit of the franchise — and their accomplishments influence the Detroit Lions today.

Layne was late in his career in Detroit when I started my own career in journalism. I would get to know him through the years. I would get to know Dutch Clark, too. Those Sundays, while Layne was still a Lion, Clark would be one of the first persons to greet me when I arrived in the press box at Briggs Stadium. He was tall, his curly hair was graying, he wore eyeglasses — and my mind always flashed back to that one-cent bubble gum card.

I wish I still had it, it might be worth something. But worth just as much are

(continued on page 25)

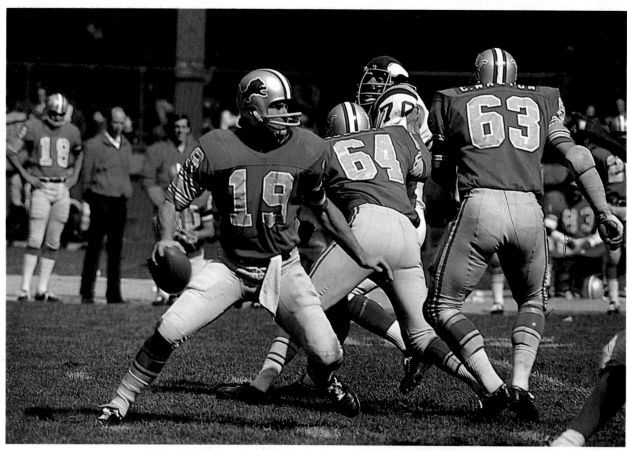

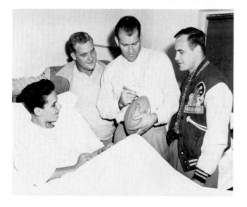

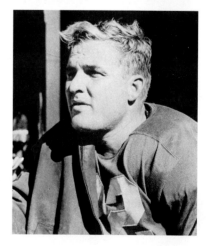

the memories that I carry with me. Memories not only of seeing Clark and of watching and talking to Layne. But of:

Joe Schmidt bobbing like flotsam atop a human mass of joyous fans when the Lions won the championship in '57, then covering him when he coached the team, somehow retaining, most of the time, his sardonic sense of humor.

Lem Barney, still The Supernatural in my mind, playing with so much joy and flash, turning to wave good-bye at his pursuers as he ran for another touchdown.

Mel Farr, who ran so hard, and was concerned so much about the welfare of all athletes when the cheers stop.

Yale Lary, who boomed punts and was so skilled in the defensive backfield, and Night Train Lane, who was so daring, and Doak Walker, who played with so much versatility and style.

Garo Yepremian, who told me "I don't speak English," in flawless English the day he signed, and who knew less about the sport he played than any of us ink-stained wretches who wrote about him.

Steve Owens, who plugged three, four, five yards at a time — until they added up to one thousand.

Alex Karras, who was the best there was pursuing the passer for a hectic, noisy decade.

John Gordy, Wayne Walker, Gail Cogdill, Bubba Baker, Pat Studstill, Doug

English, Dexter Bussey, Greg Landry, Bill Munson, Karl Sweetan — their pictures remain.

Billy Sims and his swirling, slashing style and how, one night, he walked late into a roast at an eastside banquet hall, and everybody in the place stood up to cheer.

Chris Spielman, of the Lions of the '90s, about whom I can pay the ultimate compliment — he's a throwback to Joe Schmidt.

And Barry Sanders, who forty years from now, when this book is rewritten to celebrate the Lions' 100th season, will be the running back against whom all future generations of Detroit football players will be measured.

It all boils down to this — for 60 years of tradition, the Lions have had an undeniably profound impact on this city and its adjoining territories.

And hopefully the words and pictures in this book will come close to describing that impact — or at least allow our hearts to be stirred a bit, like that of a kid opening his first pack of football cards and finding a card of his favorite Detroit Lion. ❖

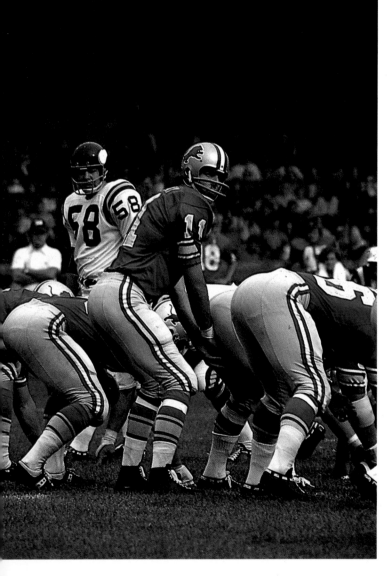

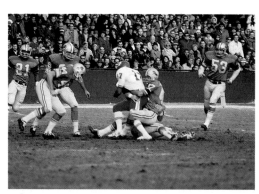

1

"I am interested in the development of the Detroit team. . . . The pro game will be a success here. Detroit is recognized all over the country as a great sports town."

— Joseph Carr
NFL President, 1934

(Above) Green Bay was 10–1–1 when the Packers visited Portsmouth in 1932, but the Spartans bulled their way to a 19–0 win before 10,000 partisans.

Club President G.A. "Dick" Richards (inset), owner of radio station WJR, was primarily responsible for moving the Portsmouth franchise to Detroit.

(Below) In their final season before moving to Detroit, the Portsmouth Spartans posted a 6–5 record to finish second in the Western Division in 1933.

In the Beginning:
Portsmouth to Detroit

George A. Richards
led a group of
Detroit businessmen
who brought the
Ohio-based Spartans
to Motown.

by Larry Paladino

Able-bodied men sold apples or pencils on the corner the year the Detroit Lions first came to town.

Those poor but proud men had frayed collars and worn elbows. When they broke for lunch, many undoubtedly queued up in a line that stretched around the corner at the local soup kitchen. Or maybe in a bread line.

It was 1934, the heart of the Depression. But radio magnate George A. "Dick" Richards and a syndicate of other prominent executives were looking ahead to better times. They felt the time was ripe to gamble on the Lions and reintroduce the still-neophyte game of professional football to a city that had rejected it in better times.

Would Detroiters, many laid off by the auto plants, be willing to pay $1.10 general admission to watch a nearly-bankrupt franchise from 200 miles south in Portsmouth, Ohio, try to regroup?

The new owners, though, knew what it took to satisfy the skeptical: good players, decent prices, and lots of goodwill.

Some 40-cent tickets would be available at the Lions' home, the University of Detroit Stadium, and "rich" folks shouldn't mind parting with $2 for the top-end seats. Programs cost a dime.

And the team would go after a few local college stars to help gain interest, plus do a public relations job worthy of the television age that was still a couple decades away.

Actually, the former Portsmouth Spartans had a lot going for them even before any of press agent Tommy Emmett's hype. They had fielded strong teams in their four years in the National Football League and had a roster that included some top players of the day — plus a big-name coach in George "Potsy" Clark, a rugged former Illinois star who once played in a game despite a broken jaw.

They also had wooed back still-young superstar quarterback Earl "Dutch" Clark from a year of coaching at the Colorado School of Mines, which had paid better than the Spartans. Some newspaper articles deemed him "the greatest quarterback who ever lived" and the caption under a *Detroit Times* photo of him called Clark "the king of professional football players and often called the Ty Cobb of the gridiron because of his daring and spectacular playing . . ."

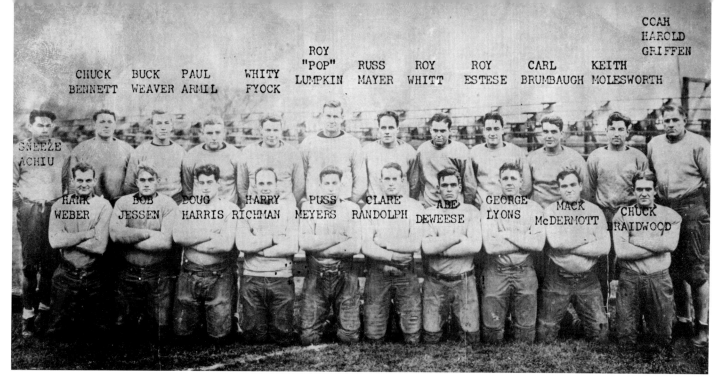

CHUCK BENNETT   BUCK WEAVER   PAUL ARMIL   WHITY FYOCK   ROY "POP" LUMPKIN   RUSS MAYER   ROY WHITT   ROY ESTESE   CARL BRUMBAUGH   KEITH MOLESWORTH   CCAH HAROLD GRIFFEN

SNEEZE ACHIU

HANK WEBER   BOB JESSEN   DOUG HARRIS   HARRY RICHMAN   PUSS MEYERS   CLARE RANDOLPH   ABE DEWEESE   GEORGE LYONS   MACK McDERMOTT   CHUCK BRAIDWOOD

Portsmouth, on the Ohio River some 90 miles south of Columbus on the Kentucky border, had steel mills and a shoe factory closed due to the Depression. It simply couldn't support the Spartans. They had a 12,000-seat stadium — but when 10,000 fans would turn out on Fridays to watch the free scrimmage and then only 3,000 would pay for Sunday's game, the end was in sight.

Players dressed in a shed and hung their clothes on broom handles. A potbellied stove warmed the center of the room and there was one lonely shower in the corner.

On the field, though, the Spartans weren't so shabby. Under Hal "Tubby" Griffen, the 1930 Spartans finished 4–6–3, good for eighth place. In their second season, 1931, Potsy Clark's team had an 11–3 record to finish second behind the 12–2 Green Bay Packers in the Western Conference.

In 1932 they won six games, tied four and lost just two to wind up third behind George Halas' Chicago Bears (7–1–6) — but only after losing a first-place playoff game to them. Curly Lambeau's Packers (10–3–1) then wound up second.

The Spartans closed out their life on the Ohio with a 6–5 record to finish second behind the game's perennial power, the Bears, in 1933.

Richards managed the Firestone Tire and Rubber Co. in Akron, Ohio, in 1914 before moving to Detroit to start an auto dealership. It did so well he wound up selling it to General Motors for $100,000 and became owner of one of America's pioneer radio stations, WJR in Detroit.

"It did not take much persuasion for me to enter the pro game," Richards told a gathering at the Deshler Wallick Hotel in Columbus in October 1934.

The NFL had been eager to get a franchise located in Detroit, which was considered then, as now, a great sports town.

The league president was Joseph Carr, whose main occupation was that of vice president and general manager of the Columbus baseball team in the American Association. Carr turned the franchise over to Richards and his partners on April 9 during a luncheon at Detroit's Hotel Statler, although newspapers had reported that the deal was completed March 24. Officially, the change came on June 30 at the league meeting in New York.

"I am interested in the development of the Detroit team," Carr said. "We

In 1929, the Portsmouth Spartans were an independent pro team. A year later, the club joined the National Professional Football League.

Portsmouth quarterback Earl "Dutch" Clark was one of the league's top players, but left the squad in 1933 for a coaching position at the Colorado School of Mines. G.A. Richards convinced Clark to return to pro ball when he moved the club to Detroit.

have had several offers to place a team in this city, but have waited until the situation was placed in able hands. The pro game will be a success here. Detroit is recognized all over the country as a great sports town. From what I've already learned, it will be represented by one of the best teams in the loop."

Said Richards: "I can assure the fans of Detroit that we will have a high-class team. And by that I mean a winning team . . . I'm not predicting a title for Detroit, but we won't be far behind."

It cost the new owners a $15,000 franchise fee, plus $7,952.08 to their predecessors to cover back expenses. There were so many members of the syndicate, though, that the initial costs certainly couldn't have been that overwhelming.

Besides Richards, these others invested in the Lions:

• Cy Huston, the Lions' new vice president and general manager, who operated billiard halls and bowling centers in Ann Arbor and Detroit.

• W.A. Alfs, who would be another team vice president, as well as its attorney. He was a prominent attorney for the Michigan Central Railroad.

• P.M. Thomas, the Lions' secretary-treasurer, was an executive at WJR.

• Auto company executives L.P. Fisher (president of Cadillac Motor Co.), Ned Fuller (auditor of disbursements for Ford Motor Co.), K.T. Keller (president, Dodge Bros. Corp.), Harry I.

Klinger (president, Pontiac Motor Car Co.), William J. McAneeny (chairman, Hudson Motor Car Co.), and E.F. Roberts (vice president, Packard Motor Co.).

• Department store officials Otto Kern (vice president and treasurer, Ernst Kern Co.), James B. Jones (general manager, Crowley, Milner & Co.), Walker T. Wright (store superintendent, J.L. Hudson Co.).

• Plus, F.B. Ainger (president, Ainger Printing Co.), Mirt L. Briggs (vice president, Briggs Manufacturing Co.), Harvey J. Campbell (executive vice president, Board of Commerce), Maurice J. Caplan (president, Metropolitan Film Co.), William M. Dillon (vice president, Scotten-Dillon Co.), Leo Fitzpatrick (vice president and general manager, WJR), George R. Fink (president, Great Lakes Steel Co.), John H. Kunsky (vice president, Kunsky Trendle Corp.), Dr. William E. Keene, Frederick C. Mattaei (president, American Metal Products Co.), J.E. Moore (president, Kent Moore Co.), and James M. O'Dea (president, Graham-Paige of Michigan).

"Our men play the game clean and hard and all rules are ridgedly enforced, and I am certain Detroit will like the brand of football we serve," Carr said. "I am sure the local team will have a large following because it is a great outfit."

Alluding to all the auto types involved, William F. Fox Jr. wrote in the *Indianapolis News,* "Potsy certainly will have a tough time deciding what kind of car he should own after a few meetings of the board."

Under league rules, Detroit was required to play a home-and-home series with each team in its division, and "it also is at liberty to book the Eastern clubs and intends to do so as far as schedule limitations permit," according to a Sam Greene story in *The Detroit News,* March 25.

In the East were: The Boston Redskins, Brooklyn Dodgers, New York Giants, Philadelphia Eagles, and Pittsburgh Pirates. In the West were: The Chicago

Bears, Chicago Cardinals, Cincinnati Reds, Detroit, Green Bay Packers, and New York Giants.

"The city has had no pro team of major league caliber since Jimmy Conzelman's Panthers used to play at Navin Field Sunday afternoons," Greene said. "Since that time the pro game has advanced rapidly."

The Panthers were Detroit's NFL entry in 1925 and 1926. It failed, as did its predecessor, the Detroit Heralds (1920–21), along with a city-sponsored team in 1928, the Detroit Wolverines, which utilized old players from the area and posted a 7–2–1 record.

The Heralds were a charter member of the American Professional Football Association, the original name of the NFL. They were 1–3 the first year, eighth among 13 teams. In 1921 they had a 1–5–1 record, 14th among 17 teams.

Conzelman, later coach of the Chicago Cardinals, got the Panthers' franchise for $500. They were one of 20 teams stretching from the east coast to Kansas City. Their first year they had an impressive 8–2–2 record (third among 20), then dropped to 4–6–2 (12th out of 22) — then out of existence.

"We simply were ahead of our time in Detroit," Conzelman said. "The town wasn't quite ready for pro football."

But in 1934, it was ready. *The News*, in a March 16 editorial headlined "Let's Have Pro Football," said:

"Detroit has every essential to the success of a pro football team except a team . . . Many feel it (pro football) exceeds the college game in spirit, for only those players take to pro football who are genuinely enthusiastic about the sport . . .

"While the considerations involved in moving an eleven are a little over our heads, we should dislike another year to go by without Detroit representation in a grand sport."

A month later Potsy Clark would be in town already pumping the Lions: "I understand that Detroit demands winners among its athletic teams and we intend to have one."

Clark built his team around Clark — Dutch, that is — former Colorado College star who was an all-pro in Portsmouth in 1931 and 1932.

"For one thing, he knows what plays to call," Potsy Clark said of Dutch (who was no relation) in a *News* column by H.G. Salsinger. "He's one of the most intelligent men who ever played football. He knows the game thoroughly. He rarely makes a mistake. But his main asset is the ability to gain the confidence of players. He makes them absolutely believe in him."

The coach, given a block of stock by Richards as an incentive to take the job, believed in discipline and character. "A playboy can't play on Potsy's team," said *Times* writer Leo Macdonnell.

Among the Portsmouth carryovers were quality players like: halfback Ernie Caddel of Stanford; fullback Ace Gutowsky of Oklahoma City; Nebraska's Glenn Presnell, a quarterback and, like Dutch Clark, a kicker; blocking back Roy "Father" Lumpkin, the original 'Rambl'n'

(Top) Harry Ebding (second from left) led the '35 Lions with nine receptions for 257 yards. He is flanked by fellow ends Bill McKalip (#10), John Schneller (#12) and "Buster" Mitchell (#13).

Backs Ernie Caddel and Ace Gutowsky, tackle Frank Christensen and quarterback Dutch Clark keyed Detroit's vaunted running attack.

Backfield star Ernie Caddel scoots around left end in Detroit's 28–0 win over Boston, the Lions' fifth shutout victory in as many outings. Detroit, in fact, outscored its first seven opponents of 1934, 118–0.

In 1970, the Spartans held a reunion in Portsmouth which featured many of the great players from that era, including (back row) "Pop" Lumpkin, Harry Ebding, Glenn Presnell, "Ox" Emerson and "Popeye" Wager, and (front row) Bill Stern, Cy Kahl, "Ace" Gutowsky, John Schneller and Jack Johnson.

Wreck" from Georgia Tech; George "Tarzan" Christensen, a tackle from Oregon; guard Grover "Ox" Emerson from Texas; Chuck Bernard, an All-America center from the University of Michigan; Big John Schneller, an end from Wisconsin; and All-American end Buster Mitchell of Davis-Elkins College.

Other key players included: ends Bill McKalip and Harry Ebding; tackles Jack Johnson, Sam Knox, Bill Emerick and Ray Richards; guards Russ Lay, Tom Hupke, Joe Gailus and Morry Bodenger; backs Frank Christensen and Bob Rowe; plus centers Clare Randolph and Andy Reise.

Local college players, meanwhile, began coming out of the woodwork hoping to become professionals with Detroit.

"I cannot get over the number of football players anxious to play in the National League," Potsy Clark said, then asked Huston to refuse further tryout requests.

Huston also set out to select uniforms with blue in them. "They had me looking at so many blues I'm blue in the face," he said. "But anyway, it's the kind of blue, I am told, that will match with silver."

The Lions (so-named in keeping with the jungle cat image of the city's baseball team, the Tigers) also got a refurbished team bus, painted blue and silver, and used it to travel to their games —and to practices at Chandler

Park on the east side during the season. Training camp, though, was at Cranbrook School in Bloomfield Hills.

Another purchase was an 11,000-pound tarp for the U-D field. During the season, after seeing a University of Pittsburgh game at which the Panthers had cheerleaders in Panther costumes, Richards ordered four Lions suits for cheerleaders William "Moon" Baker, Gerald Polsin, William Bone and Judy Tosha. But costumes would have to be made to order and it would cost $300. Richards decided on one suit, instead, which went to Baker because, said Bud Shaver, sports editor of the *Times,* "he seemed to have more of the dignity which the role as king of the beasts required and he could roar very convincingly." (Baker, incidentally, was the father of Dan Baker, who now serves as the Lions' mascot.)

The Lions appropriated three official songs: One to the tune of "Barney Google," one using "Man on the Flying Trapeze" music, and a third utilizing the theme song of the group The Vagabonds.

John Millen of the Detroit Zoo, meanwhile, gave the team two Lion cubs as mascots. They were named "Grid" and "Iron" and accompanied the team to its games. Further rapport with the zoo, probably through the efforts of P.R. man Emmett, came in the form of a "signed contract" to play by Jo Mendi, the park's famous chimpanzee.

He was signed "to play roving center on defense and handle the forward passing attack," wrote Jack Weeks of the *Detroit Free Press.* He had a number "0" on his jersey and, coach Clark said, "He looks like good material, but he needs discipline. We don't want any prima donnas on this ball club."

Potsy Clark found himself speaking at the Adcraft Club and on radio shows like WJR's "World of Sport." He also had a column in *The News* entitled, "Fair and Square Club."

By the end of June, the Lions, by their own tabulation, had amassed 624 inches of publicity in newspapers, had three newsreels which each appeared in

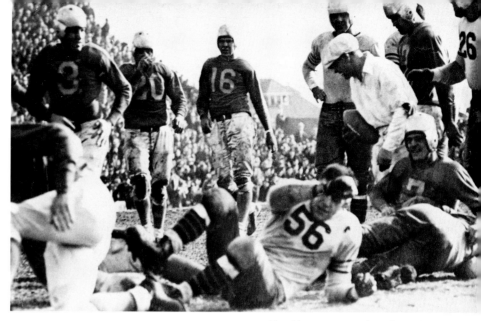

100 theaters, and had gotten air time on six radio stations.

It didn't hurt, either, that the club would hold camps for youngsters and their coaches at U-D. At one such event, the *Times* reported, 12,000 fans came to watch.

The team's "debut" of sorts was an exhibition September 15 away at the Traverse City Athletic Club, a game that was a feature of the American Legion's convention in that northern Michigan resort town.

The opener was just eight days later at home against the New York Giants. Three weeks of two-a-day practices were just about over and Clark had to pare his original 45-man training camp roster down to 25.

Papers reported every detail: 10 Lions were married; players averaged 6-feet-1 inches tall, were 24 years old and weighed 205; linemen averaged 214 pounds and backs 200.

At the team hotel, Webster Hall, players had to use their own money for meals, reported Harry LeDuc in *The News*. "What they eat is their own business," he quoted Potsy Clark as saying. ". . . The player who pays his own money for food can be trusted to eat sensibly and within reason."

Among the NFL rule changes in 1934 was a reduction in the circumference of the ball from 24½ inches to 22½ inches. Presnell said it made it easier to kick, but harder to throw.

Also, added to the officiating crew was a field judge. The others were a referee, head linesman and umpire. They had to wear armbands for the first time. Rules then included a 5-yard penalty for "crawling," a 12-yard infraction for "striking with hands," and a 15-yarder for "pushing."

Nobody was sure what to expect, but everyone wanted to see the Lions. Among the dignitaries at the opening game — some of whom got engraved invitations from Mr. and Mrs. Richards, including an invitation for a post-game get-together — was orchestra leader Paul Whiteman, who canceled his New

York radio show so he could lead the Lions' band in Sousa marches. Also on hand was golf great Walter Hagen; Willie Heston, college football superstar from Michigan's point-a-minute teams; and Detroit Tigers baseball broadcaster Ty Tyson. Doc Holland was the public address announcer.

Detroit shut out New York 9–0 before 12,000 spectators who saw "a serious, conservative team," *The News* said. Dutch Clark's 20-yard drop kick in the third quarter gave Detroit the lead, then Lumpkin wrapped things up with a 45-yard interception return for a touchdown in the closing seconds.

In the weeks to follow came: A 6–0 victory in Chicago against the Cardinals, Clark scoring on a 9-yard run; a 3–0 triumph at Green Bay on a record (which stood for 19 years) 54-yard field goal by Presnell; a 10–0 decision at Philadelphia, as Caddel scored and Clark drop-kicked a 23-yard field goal; and a 24–0 clubbing of Boston at home.

Then, at home against Brooklyn, came a 28–0 triumph, with Clark scoring 21 points (six on a 72-yard run). A 38–0 whipping was next, before 5,000 at Portsmouth against the St. Louis Gunners, who had moved in mid-season from Cincinnati. Potsy Clark started as many former Spartans as possible for the old hometown fans.

Seven games. Seven shutouts. "Ain't

The Lions secured a place in Detroit sports lore with a gutty 1934 Thanksgiving Day effort against the Chicago Bears. Shown here are Lions (left to right) Glenn Presnell (#3), Ox Emerson (#20), Jack Johnson (#16), Clare Randolph (#17) and Dutch Clark (#7).

Twelve thousand fans packed University of Detroit Stadium to watch the Lions sack the Packers, 20–10, on November 17, 1935.

A year after the club's first season in Detroit, the Lions claimed the Ed Thorp Memorial Trophy as the league's 1935 champions.

(Inset) A ticket for Detroit's 1935 championship clash with the New York Giants at University of Detroit Stadium. A crowd of 15,000 saw the Lions claim their first NFL title with a 26–7 victory.

nobody gonna get them Lions out?" asked Georgian Jo Jo White, the former Detroit Tigers baseball star, after the fifth shutout in a row.

No team had crossed Detroit's 22-yard line in the seven-game stretch of whitewashes. That ended at home November 4 against Pittsburgh, which lost 40–7 as the Lions piled up 566 yards (132 rushing by Caddel). Pittsburgh never crossed midfield except for its TD, a 62-yard punt return by Joe Skladany, who caught a cross-field pass from Harp Vaughn, who fielded the punt.

The Cards came to town the following week for a night game and lost 17–13, but five Lions — including Dutch Clark — were injured. Then St. Louis came in for a rematch and fell 40–7 as Detroit tied an NFL record with its 10th straight triumph. Detroit Mayor Frank Couzens and his family were in the stands. The Lions donated profits of that game to the Old Newsboys Goodfellow Fund.

Green Bay ended the euphoria at U-D the next week, 3–0 on Clark Hinkle's 47-yard field goal in the fourth quarter, avenging the Packers' 3–0 loss at home to Detroit.

Next, the Bears came in and won 19–16 on Thanksgiving Day before 26,000 standing-room-only customers in one of the greatest games of all the Lions' 60 seasons. Chicago earned the division title as Bronco Nagurski threw a 2-yard TD pass to Bill Hewitt in the fourth quarter after Joe Zeller returned an intercepted Presnell pass to the 4.

Detroit closed out the campaign a week later in Chicago, losing 10–7 to wind up with a 10–3 record, second in the West. The Bears went on to lose to the Giants 30–13 in the championship game.

To make money, the team had to draw from 8,000 to 10,000 fans a game, Emmett told LeDuc of *The News*. The Lions had to pay visiting teams $4,000,

he said, and club payroll was $2,200 a game. Stadium rental was $400, the four game officials $100, plus $800 in other expenses.

The Lions played before 134,269 spectators, including 79,022 at home. Gate receipts totaled $115,658.46 and expenses were $144,393.98. That left a net loss of $28,753.52 — but for a first-year operation, it had to be viewed as a success. It certainly was on the field.

Dutch Clark finished with 73 points, second-best in the NFL. He was named to the All-Pro team, along with George Christensen. Writers added Mitchell and Emerson to their honor squad. Potsy Clark included Johnson and Ebding to his first team and Schneller, Frank Christensen and Caddel to his second team.

Although a championship would come only one year later, that 1934 team earned the city's everlasting respect, especially after the Thanksgiving Day game against the Bears.

The Lions "collected not only the customers' money, but their wholehearted loyalty, as well," wrote the *Times'* Shaver. "Until the Lions put up their game stand against the Bears, professional football was still just a new enterprise which had most of Detroit's best wishes, but little else.

"In their last home game the Lions won them over. They became Detroit's own team, just as the Tigers and Red Wings are Detroit's own.

"The capture of the fans' loyalty and interest in that one game was worth a great deal more to George A. Richards and his associates than all the coins which clinked into the cash register."

It was clear. The Lions wouldn't emulate the fate of the Heralds, Panthers or Wolverines. In one year, they were a part of Detroit, just as they would be 60 seasons later in their suburban Silverdome home. ❖

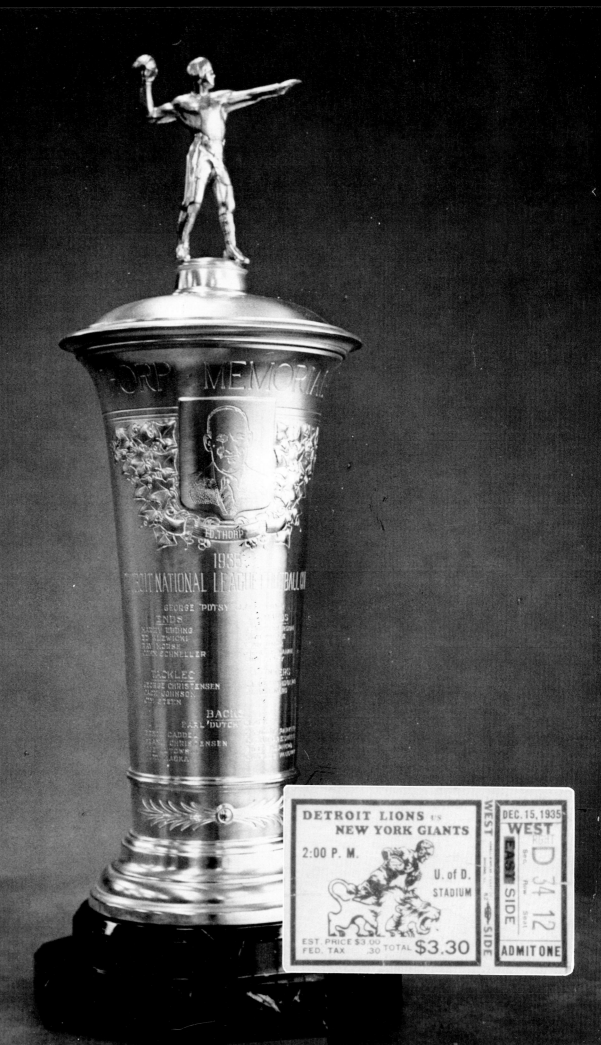

2

"Public support to the Lions has been so generous that University of Detroit Stadium no longer can provide adequate accommodations. . . . The Lions are moving into Briggs Stadium this season to give every football fan the opportunity to see the best football players in the world."

— Bud Shaver
Lions vice president, 1938

The Pontiac Silverdome is the second-largest stadium in the NFL (the Raiders play in the 92,488-seat Los Angeles Coliseum).

A Place to Call Home

From U-D Stadium to
the Silverdome, the
face of pro football
has been lifted many
times in Detroit.

by Richard L. Shook

Home. The word fetches up images: warmth, security, a refuge, a starting out place, where the heart is . . .

And for a professional football team such as the Detroit Lions, it's a whole lot more.

It was easy in the early days. If you played there, they would come. Later, if you built it, they would also come. In very large numbers. But with the proliferation of sports franchises, overlapping seasons, encroachment of non-athletic events into family entertainment budgets, plus expanding media exposure and its salary/ticket price consequences, determining the location of a pro football team's field of dreams can be a nightmare.

Home is no longer just where the heart is. Or where the fans are. It's the closest common point of intersection for delineated graphic components. The components include income maximization, facility financing feasibility, spectator arrival/departure determinants, upgrade possibilities, site acquisition costs and capabilities, environmental impactization and special event suitability.

In other words, it's complex, Newt, it's complex. Where's your fan base? How is the facility going to be paid for? Is there room enough for parking? Can it have practice facilities? Is it easy to get in and out of? Will it generate enough income? How much is enough income? Can it be improved if necessary? Are land costs a problem? Are there environmental considerations?

These are just a few of the questions that need answering, and some may be mutually exclusive. You also have to think 20 to 30 years down the road.

The Lions' current playing place, the Pontiac Silverdome, was in the forefront of new facilities when it became "Dome Sweet Dome" nearly 20 years ago ("on time and under budget" as they like to boast).

The Pontiac Silverdome remains one of the best facilities in the league to watch a game in. It has 102 VIP suites, each with 8–20 seats, in a total of 80,494 seats.

It was the first successful and remains the largest stadium to utilize an air-supported Teflon-coated Fiberglas fabric roof.

It wasn't all that successful on March 4, 1985, when a freak winter storm dumped tons of ice and snow on top to cause its collapse and ultimate shredding by accompanying high winds. However, within 88 days, at a cost in excess of $8 million, an updated 100-piece roof featuring a de-icing system was installed.

Things were a lot easier in the beginning. When George A. Richards, owner of radio station WJR, purchased the Portsmouth Spartans of the National Professional Football League in 1934 and moved the franchise to Detroit, he was probably more worried whether anybody would turn out than wondering how many.

After all, it was the middle of the Depression. And three attempts to establish professional football in Detroit had failed the previous decade.

Richards had reason to be optimistic, though. Interest in pro football was on the upswing, and he owned a radio station which could broadcast games, attract advertising and create more interest.

Richards negotiated a two-year lease with the University of Detroit to use its smaller Dinan Field rather than let crowds of 5,000–10,000 look lost in spacious Navin Field, where the baseball Tigers played. The University of Michigan's cavernous stadium was apparently not even a consideration.

The March 31 issue of *Detroit Saturday Night* reported: "The new syndicate has arranged to lease the University of Detroit stadium for its home games. League contests will be played Sundays. There probably will be some midweek exhibitions under the floodlights. The University of Detroit appears in this arrangement solely as lessor. It has a stadium from which it is willing to derive some revenue other than that accruing from collegiate competition."

The renamed Lions won their first 10 games and averaged a touch above 11,000 fans for their first seven home contests.

The *Detroit Evening Times* of November 15 reported the University of Michigan offered the Lions use of its

stadium for Detroit's Thanksgiving Day game with Chicago. Both teams were undefeated at the time, although the Lions would lose for the first time that day.

Richards politely declined, noting tickets were already printed and arrangements made to play the game. He did say, however, he would be glad to place the second College All-Star game at Michigan Stadium in 1935 "when the Lions win the National League title."

Alas, the injury-depleted Lions dropped their second in a row, 19–16, to Chicago on Thanksgiving, and then were clipped, 10–7, in a December 2 rematch in Chicago. Detroit finished second in the league.

The Thanksgiving Day affair with the Bears drew an estimated 26,000 and the game, which Richards persuaded a national radio network to carry, started an annual tradition.

Attendance figures were not always accurately reported or accounted in that era, but Detroit's inaugural season was a success when it is measured against previous seasons in Portsmouth, where the practices (6,000–10,000) outdrew the games (2,000–3,000) because the practices were free.

The Lions' first season total was announced as 79,022, apparently the figure for the first seven games. The Thanksgiving Day crowd boosted attendance to 105,000, an average of 13,125, and the league announced the Lions' attendance at 85,000.

Total attendance dropped to 82,200 as the Lions finished first in their second season, but with only six home games, the average went up to 13,700. A crowd of 15,000 showed up to watch Detroit beat the New York Giants, 26–7, for the World Championship.

By 1936 the defending World Champions were getting into the 20,000s regularly for their home games (four out of six reached that figure) and the following season they hit 23,000 for an October 31 date with the Green Bay Packers. Their 1937 Thanksgiving Day game with the Bears pulled in 24,173.

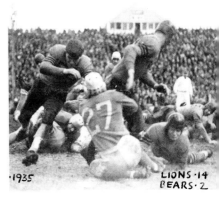

With players such as Dutch Clark leading the way, pro football flourished in Detroit in the 1930s, and it wasn't long before the Lions outgrew University of Detroit Stadium.

A scheduling conflict gave the Lions a return visit to U-D Stadium for the 1950 home opener. Here, Doak Walker connects on a 20-yard field goal with just 2:10 remaining to give Detroit a 10–7 win over the Pittsburgh Steelers.

(Top) Gordon Wilson (seated right), a Detroit auto dealer, negotiates a long-term option to build a new office building for the Detroit Lions across from Briggs Stadium on Michigan Avenue. Completing the deal with Wilson are general manager-head coach Bo McMillin (seated with Wilson), Lions president D. Lyle Fife (standing left), and Lions business agent Lewis M. Cromwell.

(Middle) The Lions' headquarters on Michigan Avenue.

(Bottom) The Lions have had six different office locations in six decades. Those offices, in order, have been at the Fisher Building, Webster Hall, the Book Building, Tuller Hotel (pictured here), 1401 Michigan Avenue, and the Pontiac Silverdome.

Over the years, the Lions trained at many sites during the preseason, including Assumption College in Windsor (top), Michigan Normal (middle) in Ypsilanti, and Cranbrook School in Oakland County (bottom).

It was time to move. The first official report the Lions would shift their home games to newly enlarged Briggs Stadium, home of the Tigers, surfaced on March 2, 1938, following a season where attendance averaged 18,945.

The initial plan by club owner Richards was to hedge his bet with three games in the 55,000-seat baseball facility and keeping three where the Lions had been playing.

But moving completely to the home of the Tigers made too much financial sense. The most the Lions could pack into University of Detroit Stadium, even with temporary bleachers, was about 25,000.

"Public support to the Lions has been so generous that University of Detroit Stadium no longer can provide adequate accommodations," Bud Shaver said on July 3, the occasion of his quitting as sports editor of the *Detroit Times* to become vice president of the Lions. "The Lions are moving into Briggs Stadium this season to give every football fan the opportunity to see the best football players in the world."

The move paid instant dividends —

after the University of Detroit's field got an unexpected swan song.

The Lions' first scheduled game was in Pittsburgh in late September, but the baseball Pirates were drawing a bead on the World Series (they ultimately finished second). So the football Pirates worked a switch.

They consented to play the Lions on the University of Detroit field on Friday night, September 9, which meant they had to return to Pittsburgh to open their own home season two days later. The hastily rescheduled Friday night game still drew 17,000.

The reworked schedule gave Detroit three weeks off. They were then on the road for two games before returning home for their Briggs Stadium debut, where 42,855 welcomed them for a game against Washington.

Detroit also drew crowds of 30,140 and 45,139, as well as 26,200 for its Thanksgiving Day game against Chicago. The average of 30,209 for six home games proved out the thinking behind the move.

Briggs Stadium was the fifth place where baseball and football coexisted. (In the mid-1920s, Coach Jimmy Conzelman's Detroit Panthers played at Navin Field, which was what Briggs Stadium was then called.)

Here's what tickets went for in that inaugural Briggs Stadium season: 55-cents for 10,000 unreserved seats, $1.10 for 19,000 reserved seats, and $2.20 for the balance of reserved seats (all upper deck seats and those in the third base lower deck grandstand and left field pavilion between the goal lines). Tax included, of course.

Detroit's league fortunes declined after that and the club see-sawed through World War II. The Lions were winless in 1942, 7–3 in 1945, and 1–10 in 1946, when they averaged just 20,609.

By 1950, Bobby Layne's first year and Coach Bo McMillin's last, attendance was up to 25,267 per game and 1951 marked an historic first — the first crowd in excess of 50,000 to see Detroit

Fans poured in for the Lions' final game at Tiger Stadium, the 1974 Thanksgiving Day game against Denver.

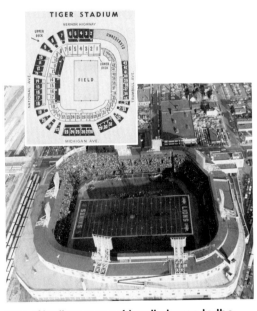

Tiger Stadium was a friendly home to the Lions for 37 seasons and provided many endearing memories for football fans. But, just as the club had outgrown University of Detroit Stadium many years earlier, the team had outgrown Tiger Stadium by 1970 and looked for a new place to call home.

The Lions pushed for the building of a new stadium near Tiger Stadium, on Michigan Avenue or north of the Fisher Freeway. A stadium commission favored a riverfront site (where Joe Louis Arena is currently located), but the Lions felt a facility wedged near Cobo Hall and the Detroit River could not handle the traffic or parking to accommodate an 80,000-seat stadium.

(Above) Lions owner and president William Clay Ford was joined by Harold Cousins, chairman of the Pontiac Stadium Authority, as the first shovels of earth were removed.

(Right) Ford addressed a crowd gathered for the ground-breaking ceremony in Pontiac.

The PonMet, as it was called that first year, was built under budget — less than $55.7 million — and on time (ready for the 1975 season). (Inset) The refined model for the new Pontiac Metropolitan Stadium.

play. A total of 50,567 was on hand October 14 at Briggs Stadium to see the Los Angeles Rams defeat the Lions, 27–21.

The Lions of the 1950s were perhaps the first franchise to generate the kind of interest that is taken for granted today. Television made the team followed all over the state and combined with capacity crowds to turn the players into celebrities.

They weren't mobbed like the athletes of today, but they were accorded deferential and a kind of quiet preferential treatment by the public.

The Lions drew three crowds in excess of 50,000 in 1952 while on their way to a Western Division tie for first with the Los Angeles Rams. A total of 47,645 showed up to see Detroit bump Los Angeles, 31–21, in the playoff.

Pro football had arrived in Detroit, big-time. By the middle of the 1950s, you needed a season ticket, pal, to be sure of watching the Lions in person. It got cold standing out there in line for tickets sold the week of the game.

In 1956, when Detroit reversed a 3–9 season to finish second to Chicago by half a game, all six Lions' home games drew more than 50,000 fans. Another milestone had been reached and it set the tone for two decades.

The Lions drew 56,000 or better for all seven of their home games in 1970,

the first year they qualified for post-season play since their 1962 Runnerup Bowl appearance.

Other franchises were getting newer stadiums, though. They came with lucrative luxury suites, practice facilities, weight rooms, plus office and meeting rooms. The Lions looked at 15 years of near-capacity crowds and realized that the only thing left to get out of Tiger Stadium (as it was now called) was rust.

The football club had been only too glad to hand the baseball club 15 percent of its gross for rent in the early years, with no parking or concessions income to offset it. Now it started viewing the rent as lost revenue.

Coexisting with the Tigers also involved other inconveniences. The Lions could not have their offices in the stadium; there was barely enough room for the Tigers.

And if 25 baseball players felt the club house was cramped, how do you think 45 football players felt when they were crammed into the same amount of space?

Practice at the stadium while the baseball season was in session was strictly out of bounds, and the Lions were generally restricted to just one September game at home.

The team practiced at Cranbrook School, its training camp site, until the Tigers were through at home. This often came with a week or so left in the

On August 23, 1975, a capacity crowd saw Detroit beat Kansas City, 27–24, in a preseason contest. For that first game, the Dome itself was only partially completed, and an earlier rainfall made for a slippery track.

baseball season when the baseball team closed on the road.

The Lions would swoop into Tiger Stadium for practices as soon as the last baseball game was played. In bad weather or when the field was sloppy, Detroit would bus to nearby Wayne State and use the Tartars' field for workouts. Sometimes a local high school field was used.

But over the years the routine and discomfort began to wear thin, especially as pro football's popularity rose. Who likes being made to feel like a benchsitter when they've been promoted to the starting lineup?

It was time to start thinking of moving again. Talking stadium in Detroit has always necessitated the wearing of a faceguard — so you don't get hit in the face by all that pie in the sky.

A 100,000-seat Olympic Stadium at the State Fairgrounds was on the drawing board in 1952 as part of a plan to lure the Olympic Games to Detroit. It took the locals until 1963 to figure out the only Olympics anybody would see in Detroit would be on television.

The next dream was to put a stadium on the Riverfront, about where Joe Louis Arena currently stands. That was deemed impractical in 1967, so it was back to the fairgrounds, this time scaled down to 80,000 seats.

Gov. George Romney promised

Lions' vice president Edwin J. Anderson, heavily involved in new stadium efforts, that he'd back the fairgrounds plan. Romney ran for president, and by May 1969 the fairgrounds plan was scratched.

Next, Gov. William B. Milliken lined up behind Detroit Mayor Jerome P. Cavanagh in favor of a revived riverfront plan. Cavanagh's feeling was a new facility across the street from Tiger Stadium would force relocation of too many (voting) Corktown families.

The Lions finally told the commission if it didn't start thinking in terms of building near Tiger Stadium, on Michigan Avenue or north of the Fisher Freeway, the football team would not participate in the project.

"It's the riverfront or nothing," the commission sniffed to the Lions. The commission quickly discovered that playing poker with someone whose pockets are deeper than yours takes bluffing right out of the game.

Lions owner William Clay Ford didn't think a riverfront site would provide the requisite parking, be able to handle traffic, nor generate sufficient revenue to pay off an 80,000-seat facility.

The Lions immediately began taking part in efforts to find a suburban stadium location. A tentative commitment was signed with Pontiac on March 3, 1970, with Detroit given a courtesy deadline of September 1 to get off the dime.

The more than two years of delays and site audibles went over with Ford like a ding in his Continental. On February 1, 1971, he called the riverfront site the work of "drumbeaters and promoters."

The next day, Ford announced he intended to have a new stadium built in Pontiac.

Pontiac beer distributor Harold Cousins had been named chairman of the Pontiac Stadium Authority in 1968. The next year the Pontiac Stadium Building Authority was formed, because state law says cities cannot

Ford with Cousins on the field prior to the first game in the Detroit-area's newest stadium. Before the facility was opened, Ford saw to it that nearly four thousand bleacher seats were installed on the lower (field) level to ensure that good, economical seats were available to all fans at the Silverdome.

The Silverdome's first regular season contest came in a Monday Night battle (October 6, 1975) against Dallas. Quarterback Greg Landry hands off to Altie Taylor (#42) with Dexter Bussey (#24). The Cowboys won that game, 36–10, before a crowd of 79,784.

Rick Forzano coached the first Lions team to play in the Silverdome.

sell non-tax-backed revenue bonds — but stadium authorities can.

On December 11, 1972, by the margin of 393 votes, residents of the city of Pontiac passed a bond issue to finance construction of a stadium.

The concept as originally revealed showed twin stadiums modeled along the successful side-by-side tandem outside Kansas City, Missouri, the Harry S. Truman complex, one for the baseball Royals and the other for the football Chiefs. In the Pontiac version, a sliding dome was envisioned covering the one in use.

Attendant legal battles over funding and various other aspects of the stadium delayed the opening of construction on what was originally called Pontiac Metropolitan Stadium until September 19, 1973.

The construction manager type of operation was used, allowing the simultaneous hiring of an architect and building manager.

A pit was dug in the middle of 132 acres at the intersection of Opdyke and M-59, with a projected cost of $55.7 million. It came in under budget, and currently an $800,000 annual

subsidy is necessary to make debt payments.

At 80,494 seats, it is the second-largest among NFL stadiums to Los Angeles' Memorial Coliseum, which holds 92,488.

The lowest sideline and end zone seats stand seven feet above field level, which enables fans to see over TV cameras and players on the sidelines. Nearest seats are just 40 feet from the playing field.

Fans get fast food service plus a dining room — the Main Event Sports Bar and Grill — overlooking one end zone. Television sets enable people in the concourses or waiting in line for food to watch game action they might otherwise miss.

On August 23, 1975, the Lions defeated the Kansas City Chiefs, 27–24, in a preseason contest that was the first indoor football game in Michigan. On Monday night, October 6, Detroit lost, 36–10, to the Dallas Cowboys in the Pontiac Silverdome's first regular season game.

The Lions finally had a roof over their heads; a new place to call home. ❖

3

"Everything we do is done in the name of winning. Mr. Ford established that commitment to winning a long time ago — that is our bottom line."

— Chuck Schmidt
Lions executive vice president
and chief operating officer

Russ Thomas, then the director of player personnel, watches as head coach Harry Gilmer barks instructions in the the huddle during the Lions' 1966 training camp.

Behind the Scenes

At times, the action in the front office has been more frantic than the play on the field.

by Chuck Klonke

Operating a professional football team was once a simple matter. The owner and coach took care of most of the day-to-day operations of the team. There were part-time employees in charge of ticket sales and finances, but the large front office staffs that are common among professional sports franchises today were unheard of when G.A. "Dick" Richards bought the Portsmouth Spartans in 1934 and moved them to Detroit where they became the Lions.

The Spartans were nearly bankrupt when Richards, the owner of a chain of radio stations, including WJR, was talked into buying the team and moving it to Detroit. He paid $15,000 for the franchise and agreed to throw in another $8,000 to bail the former owners out of their debt.

Richards inherited Potsy Clark as his coach, but Clark was more than just a coach. He was a quasi-general manager, in charge of player moves, and also served as the team's unofficial scout.

In 1935, the Lions' first championship season, Clark passed up the team's final regular season game with the Chicago Bears so he could scout the New York Giants, Detroit's probable opponent in the league championship game.

Richards was a difficult man to work for. He and Clark had many disagreements. Once in a while, Clark would quit. Other times, Richards would fire him, but they would always get back together.

After the 1936 season, things got so bad between Clark and Richards that they had a mutual parting of the ways and the Lions' star player, Dutch Clark, became coach.

Just like Potsy, Dutch had problems with Richards.

"He was an eccentric," Dutch Clark told author Myron Cope in the book *The Game That Was*. "For example, he liked to bet on the Lions and he would get some of the players to go in with him. Today the ballplayers aren't allowed to bet on their own team, but Richards figured they'd play twice as hard to win 25 bucks or 50 bucks. So he got them going along with him.

"He was a sick man and he was staying home, but every day he'd have his chauffeur run down to my hotel with a handful of notes, telling me how to run the club," Clark continued. "He'd write, 'Dammit Dutch, why don't you send (Ed) Klewicki out there like Green Bay sends out (Don) Hutson and throw to him like they throw to Hutson?' Well, Klewicki was about 5'11" and 218 [pounds]. Hutson could go 50 yards while this boy was going 14. Oh, I was having a horrible time with Richards."

Finally, some of Richards' radio station employees convinced him to move to California for his health, but he still made long-distance phone calls to Clark.

He also hired a young announcer named Harry Wismer, who would later become a club owner himself with the New York Titans of the American Football League. Wismer would watch the Lions practice every day and then report to Richards.

"Richards would then call me and say 'What the hell are you doing that for?'" Clark said.

Before a game against Chicago, Wismer was standing inside the locker room door with a loudspeaker and pretty soon Richards came on to give the team a pep talk.

"When you played the Bears you didn't need a pep talk, but there was Richards cussing and telling us through that box that we should get out there and kick the hell out of the Bears," Clark said. "In one way it was a good thing because the players started laughing so hard they went out loose and beat the Bears."

Dutch Clark finally quit the Lions after the 1938 season because he figured Richards would fire him anyway, and he had a chance to hook on with the Cleveland Rams.

Bill Alfs, who was vice president of the Lions during the Richards regime, advised Clark that "If I were you, I'd take it, because that guy's liable to fire you any day."

Richards hired Gus Henderson to coach the team in 1939, during a era in which the Lions would have five coaching changes in five years.

Richards, who didn't have many friends among the other NFL owners after his efforts to impeach commissioner Joe Carr, got himself in hot water with the club's dealing with Bulldog Turner, an All-American center from Hardin-Simmons. Richards had persuaded Turner to fill out a league questionnaire with the statement "I don't wish to play professional football."

By doing so, Richards figured that other teams would bypass Turner in the college draft, but cagey old George Halas got suspicious. Usually if a player didn't want to turn pro, he'd just ignore the questionnaire.

Because the Lions figured Turner was a lock, they felt they could wait until a later round to select him and took Doyle Nave, who was Southern Cal's hero in the previous Rose Bowl, with the first pick in the draft.

Halas then drafted Turner. Richards was irate and blasted Henderson for his lack of judgment. The league began an investigation and discovered the Lions had paid Turner $100 while he was still playing in college. Detroit was fined $5,000 for tampering, and within a month, Richards sold the team to Fred Mandel, a Chicago department store executive, for $225,000.

In seven years, Richards had made a profit of some $200,000 on the team.

Mandel, who promoted Alfs to president of the club, also made annual coaching changes until he signed the legendary Gus Dorais to a multi-year contract in 1943.

Although the Lions weren't very successful on the field, Mandel gave Dorais a new five-year contract after the 1946 season, but a year later, the owner decided to make a change.

Dorais, however, had a clause in the contract that said Mandel would be obligated to pay off the rest of the pact if he was fired. But there was one loophole for the owner — he would only be responsible for six months' salary if he sold the club.

After much haggling in public and threats by the owner to sell the team, Mandel and Dorais finally reached a settlement in which the former coach would be paid $100,000 for the remaining four years of his contract.

Then a week later, Mandel still sold the team to a group of wealthy Detroit area businessmen headed by D. Lyle Fife, the CEO of an electrical products firm.

The syndicate bought the Lions for $185,000, which meant Mandel lost

(Top) The Lions' first head coach, Potsy Clark (far left), with the team's first club president, George A. Richards (second from left). The gentleman standing third from left is K.T. Keller, president of the Dodge Brothers Corporation and an investor in the new Detroit Lions.

(Middle) One of Edwin J. Anderson's (right) first moves as president of the Lions was to hire Alvin "Bo" McMillin as the club's head coach and general manager.

(Bottom) When owner William Clay Ford hired Joe Schmidt as head coach in 1967, Ford gave the former Lion great responsibility for player trades and drafts.

(Above) Maurie Schubot was the man behind the Lions' ticket windows for 40 years. He began working for the club in 1934, the year the franchise was established in Detroit, and retired as the team's box office treasurer in 1974 when Fred Otto became the youngest ticket manager in the National Football League. Otto (whose father, Norm, was the long-time ticket manager of the Detroit Tigers) currently holds the distinction of being with the same team longer than any ticket manager in the league today.

(Right) There have been a variety of staffers who have worked behind the scenes to help keep the Lions "moving ahead." Chief among them is Roy "Friday" Macklem who served as the club's equipment manager from 1936 to 1981 — a full 45 years. Macklem, at right, distributes equipment to Jerry Neuman, Elmer Hackney and Ernie Rosteck at the Lions' 1943 training camp.

Macklem with assistant Dan Jaroshewich in 1973. Jaroshewich, who took the reins from Macklem in 1980, begins his 21st season on the Detroit staff in 1993.

more than $40,000 on the purchase price alone. He also probably dropped another $500,000 in operating a struggling franchise.

Fife became president of the club and Edwin J. Anderson, the president of the Goebel Brewing Co., was named vice president. A year later, Anderson was elected president of the Lions and held that position until 1961.

One of the first moves of the new regime was to hire Bo McMillin as coach and general manager. McMillin made some wise moves, including a trade for a young quarterback named Bobby Layne. He also brought in rookies like Doak Walker, Lou Creekmur, Leon Hart and Thurman McGraw and picked up Bob Hoernschemeyer in the All-American Football Conference allocation draft.

Those players would become the nucleus for the Lions' three championship teams of the 1950s, but McMillin wouldn't be around to enjoy the fruits of his labors.

Several of the players didn't like the former Indiana coach, who was the owners' second choice when Frank Leahy turned down the job. And many members of the syndicate treated the club like a new toy and were always hanging around the locker room, offering different tidbits of advice.

When some players voiced complaints about McMillin, enough of the owners sided with them and McMillin was replaced by Buddy Parker, assistant coach.

Nick Kerbawy, who had joined the Lions as their publicity director when the new ownership group took over, was elevated to assistant general manager when Anderson replaced Fife as president. Kerbawy then assumed McMillin's GM duties after McMillin was fired.

Kerbawy stayed with the Lions through the championship season of 1957, but was lured away to the Detroit Pistons, who moved from Fort Wayne, Ind., after the 1956–57 season. Anderson then added the general manager's title to his portfolio.

Ironically, Kerbawy was suspended by the Pistons in 1961 when owner Fred Zollner accused him of becoming involved in the Lions' ownership squabble that led to William Clay Ford taking over control of the team.

Anderson was responsible for the day-to-day operations of the Lions until 1967, when he retired and was replaced by Russ Thomas.

Anderson was president of the Lions until January 1961, when he resigned the dual role of president and GM to concentrate on the GM's duties. It was part of a compromise among the

ownership group, several of whom wanted Anderson ousted completely.

Although the team thrived under his direction, Anderson rubbed some of the stockholders the wrong way. They felt he padded the board with his friends, made mistakes in negotiating television contracts and was responsible for the loss of quarterbacks Bobby Layne and Tobin Rote after the two had combined to lead Detroit to the 1957 NFL title.

It was a nasty fight with Anderson on one side and Fife on the other. There were 15 directors and 144 stockholders, and each side campaigned for proxy votes.

The only solution was a compromise, and Anderson asked Ford to become president of the club, with Anderson remaining as general manager.

Order was finally restored and in January 1964, Ford bought out the rest of the stockholders.

He made some changes in the front office. Anderson was relieved of the task of signing players. That job was given to Thomas, who was named director of player personnel.

When Joe Schmidt was hired as head coach in 1967, Thomas was given the title of general manager, although he maintained many of the same duties he had previously. Anderson became a vice president, and former linebacker Carl Brettschneider took over as director of player personnel.

Schmidt was responsible for player trades and drafts, a power his predecessor, Harry Gilmer, didn't have.

There was one more stormy period in the front office. Schmidt and

Brettschneider had lined up together against Thomas, and in 1969, Brettschneider was fired.

Thomas was appointed executive vice president and general manager in 1972 and handled most player personnel matters and the operation of the club. He handed over contract negotiations to Chuck Schmidt, the director of finance, in 1988, and a year later retired.

During his 43-year career with the Lions, Thomas earned the respect of front office people throughout the NFL and was often sought for advice.

"He's been very willing to assist those who have sought his highly-regarded opinions and outstanding experience. He is truly a respected leader in our profession," said George Young, the general manager of the New York Giants.

Chuck Schmidt became executive vice president and chief operating officer of the Lions on December 27, 1989, when he succeeded Thomas as the man in charge of operating the team.

Schmidt has made several moves to improve the day-to-day operation of the Lions, including expanding the player personnel and scouting departments, the construction of a new weight room, and the switch in training camp sites from Oakland University to the Silverdome.

Schmidt also reorganized the front office staff to reflect a new emphasis on marketing, promotions, and community and media relations.

(Above) Ford named Russ Thomas director of player personnel in 1964, Ford's first year as owner. Thomas would later move up the ranks to general manager (1967) and then to executive vice president and general manager (1972).

(Far left) Ford and head coach Darryl Rogers take in a 1985 practice session.

(Middle) Chuck Schmidt, previously the club's vice president of finance, succeeded Thomas as the Lions' top officer, earning the title of executive vice president and chief operating officer after the 1989 season.

The Detroit Football Company Board of Directors Meeting at the Detroit Athletic Club on May 2, 1952. Present at the meeting were L–R: Spike Briggs, second vice president; Joe Monaghan, attorney; Ray M. Whyte, director; William D. Downey, first vice president and secretary; Nick Kerbawy, general manager; D. Lyle Fife, director; Edwin J. Anderson, president; Raymond "Buddy" Parker, head coach; Arthur R. Hoffman, third vice president; George A. Cavanaugh, director; Carl F. Unruh, director; and Ernest Kanzler, director.

(Above) "See Otis" has been the familiar response around the offices of the Detroit Lions for the past 27 years. Otis Canty, pictured with head coach Wayne Fontes, has handled a variety of responsibilities during his tenure with the organization, including his current position as director of player relations and administrative assistant to the head coach.

(Right) Including exhibition and playoff games, head trainer Kent Falb has worked 536 consecutive games for the Lions heading into the club's 60th season. Falb came to Detroit in 1966 as an assistant to head trainer Millard Kelly; he was elevated to his current position the following year.

William Clay Ford Jr. became the Lions' treasurer in 1980.

In 1990, the club established Detroit Lions Charities, a non-profit organization founded to assist charitable and worthwhile causes in Michigan. Currently, the Lions are the only team with two full-time employees — Tim Pendell and Kim French — dedicated to community relations and team charities.

The National Football League has long recognized the Lions as having one of the finest front office staffs in the league. In 1992, the NFL selected three members of the Lions' staff (Fred Otto, Bill Keenist and Mike Murray) to work the Super Bowl and NFC Championship Game — more than any other NFC team.

Ford, who will celebrate his 30th season as owner in 1993, looks ahead to even brighter days as the club aggressively enters the NFL's new era of unrestricted free agency. In the opening weeks of the new marketplace, Detroit dove in head first and signed three proven linemen — Bill Fralic, Dave Richards and David Lutz — who should help revitalize the Lions' offense.

"We are traveling in the unknown," Ford said. "I don't know what the future is going to hold, but we will continue to look for opportunities and take advantage of them. Right after the season we planned on being aggressive in the free agent market, and we were.

"I'd like to see a winner for this team, for the fans. We're going to do whatever you can do, and we're going to do it very forcefully."

Operating a football team is a full-time job and it takes an extensive full-time staff to keep it running. In 1992, the Lions had 64 employees listed in their directory, and Schmidt has since added Michael Huyghue to the staff as vice president for administration and general counsel, and former Lion Larry Lee as director of player programs.

Full-time personnel in coaching, scouting, player personnel, training, equipment, accounting, administration, media relations, community relations, marketing, ticket sales, maintenance — it's a far cry from the handful Dick Richards employed when he bought the Portsmouth Spartans. ❖

Chuck Schmidt with National Football League Commissioner Paul Tagliabue.

4

"How good a football team is the Detroit Lions? That's the jackpot question other teams in the NFL must answer . . . or stand aside and watch Coach Buddy Parker's sturdy crew walk off with the loop championship."

— Wally Wallis
Daily Oklahoman, 1952

Joe Schmidt, Torgy Torgeson and Yale Lary carry head coach Buddy Parker off the Briggs Stadium field after Detroit beat Cleveland, 17–16, to claim the 1953 National Football League Championship, the club's second straight title.

Decade of Dominance

The Lions claimed four divisional titles and three NFL Championships during the celebrated 1950s.

by Larry Paladino

There's no question about it. The Golden Age of the Honolulu Blue and Silver was the 1950s, a time when the Detroit Lions became the dominant team in the National Football League.

Even young people today, if they have the slightest interest in professional football, probably can spew out names of great Lions players of the era — although they might know little else about the franchise that was to bring three NFL titles, an additional Western Conference crown, and two eyelash runnerup finishes to the Motor City in the decade.

There were common names, like Bobby, Jack, Lew, Lou, Leon, Les, Jim, Don, Joe, Carl, Bob, Dick, and Pat.

There were less common ones, like Doak, Cloyce, Harley, Gil, Yale, Darris, Thurman, Dorne, LaVern, Sonny and Jug.

Although there were great players from 1934, the Lions' debut year, through the '40s, and although there were more greats to come in the '60s and beyond, Lions' enthusiasts seem to automatically gravitate to those stars of the '50s: Bobby Layne, Jack Christiansen, Lew Carpenter, Lou Creekmur, Leon Hart, Les Bingaman, Jim Doran, Jim David, Jim Martin, Don Doll, Joe Schmidt, Carl Karilivacz, Bob Smith, Dick Stanfel, Bob Hoernschemeyer, Pat Harder.

And don't forget Doak Walker, Cloyce Box, Harley Sewell, Gil Mains, Thurman McGraw, Yale Lary, Darris McCord, Dorne Dibble, LaVern Torgeson, Sonny Gandee and Jug Girard.

There were others, to be sure, including the coaches who were to bring such greats to the level of champions: Bo McMillan, who was to set things up for Buddy Parker, who in turn was to surprisingly chuck it all in a moment of frustration, leaving George Wilson to perpetuate the glory era.

The single thread that weaved everything together was a brash quarterback from the University of Texas (via the Chicago Bears and New York Bulldogs): Robert "Bobby" Layne.

He was the No. 1 cog in what was to be a precision silver and blue machine most of the decade. Yet for some reason, even in the best of times, fans often booed him.

Perhaps it was because of his less-than-picturesque passes, which often wobbled like wounded ducks. Or perhaps it was his lifestyle, which included an affinity for partying, a disdain for curfews, an occasional

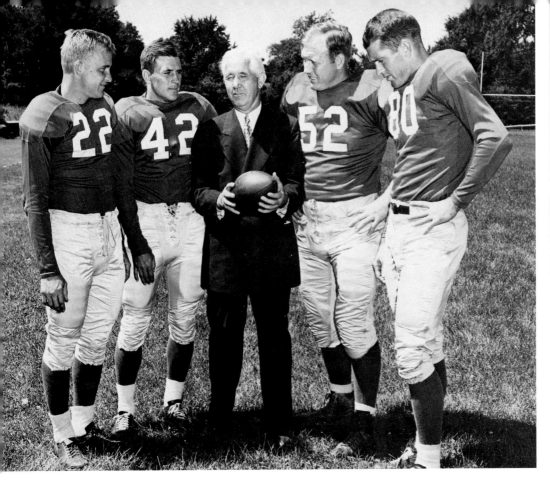

(Left) Head coach and general manager Bo McMillin is credited as an architect for those championship teams of the 1950s. Among the players McMillin brought to Detroit were (L–R) quarterback Bobby Layne, halfback Doak Walker, lineman Joe Watson and end Cloyce Box.

(Top) Detroit's rock-solid backfield from 1951–53 included (L–R) halfback Hunchy Hoernschemeyer, quarterback Bobby Layne, fullback Pat Harder and halfback Doak Walker.

(Above) Dorne Dibble blocked for Layne in Detroit's 24–22 win at Los Angeles in 1951.

run-in with the law, and a candor that enamored him to sports writers looking for a juicy quote.

Regardless, it was the cocky Layne who was to be Detroit's No. 1 Golden Boy of the '50s — and the one who helped guide them all through playoff championship money and the subsequent lucrative individual contracts that titles tend to bring.

Layne simply knew how to win. He could move a team to a touchdown when it seemed all was lost. He had the instincts to call the right play at the right time, knowing his teammates' capabilities and the opponents' culpabilities.

If any moment symbolized Layne, it was in the waning minutes of Detroit's championship game at Briggs Stadium, December 27, 1953, against the Cleveland Browns — the team the Lions had beaten 17–7 a year earlier to claim their second title, but first in 17 years.

Cleveland owned a 16–10 lead in that '53 encounter and Detroit was about to get the kickoff with five minutes left.

On the sidelines, Detroit equipment manager Roy "Friday" Macklem overheard Layne talking, to no one in particular: "Just give me time, boys, and I'll get you into that All-Star game in Chicago."

And, sure enough, the Lions would win the championship and face the College All-Stars in the 1954 All-Star game. A sore-armed Layne saw to it.

With the help of a couple big third-down plays, he drove the team 90 yards in about three minutes, culminating in a 33-yard, picture-perfect, touchdown pass with 2:08 left to Doran. Normally a defensive end, Doran had moved to offense to shore up the passing game. He said he could beat defensive back Warren Lahr, and so the "9-up" play — recommended from the pressbox by assistant coach Aldo Forte — was called, earning Doran his first TD all year.

Karilivacz then thwarted a last-ditch Browns effort by intercepting an Otto Graham pass.

"Gutless guys don't win titles," wrote *Detroit Free Press* columnist Lyall Smith,

This series of photos depicts Layne's touchdown toss to Cloyce Box, a play that keyed Detroit's 24–16 comeback victory over the Rams at Briggs Stadium in 1952.

(Top) Yale Lary tries to elude Cleveland's Ed Sharkey in the '52 title game.

(Above) In a 35–21 win over San Francisco in 1958, Gene Gedman keeps the Lions' offense on the move.

speaking of Layne. "He played almost half the regular season with a passing arm that throbbed when he tried to comb his hair. It throbbed more when he tried to throw a football."

NFL Commissioner Bert Bell called Detroit, "one of the great teams in professional history."

"For balance and poise," said Parker, the Lions were "the best I've ever seen."

Detroit went wild, as it was to do some more in the decade, which produced a 59–48–4 record (55–27–2 from 1951 through 1957).

But how did it develop? The Lions pretty much hit bottom in 1946 with a 1–10 record for Coach Gus Dorais. The seeds of change started to be sown on January 15, 1948, when a syndicate headed by D. Lyle Fife and Edwin J. Anderson bought the club for what today might be the one-game salary of some players, $165,000.

Anderson named Alvin "Bo" McMillin coach and general manager, signing him to a five-year contract.

Those 1948 Lions, though, weren't much better than the '46 version, posting a 2–10 record. Rookie halfback Don Doll was among the newcomers in 1949 when Detroit won four and lost eight. So were Box, Smith, Wally Triplett and John Prchlik, heralding good things for the '50s. Doll was accorded all-league honors, and in

December, Anderson was named president.

McMillin continued to mold a future champion, starting with a trade April 26, 1950, that sent fullback Camp Wilson, the Lions' leading rusher three of four years, to the New York Yanks/Bulldogs for Layne. (Wilson refused to go, though, and the Lions shipped leading receiver Bob Mann to New York instead.)

The 6-foot-1, 198-pound Layne, from Lubbock, Texas (where he operated a sporting goods store), had been a decent quarterback for a poor Bulldogs team. Before that he was with the Bears as a backup to Johnny Lujack and Sid Luckman, after having been drafted by Pittsburgh.

The loss of Mann prompted a move of Box to offense and left Detroit with four quarterbacks. But soon Frank Tripucka would be sent to the Chicago Cardinals. Fred Enke would end up No. 2 behind Layne, who was reunited with another new Lion, Doak Walker, who was a high school teammate of Layne in Dallas — but a college rival.

Layne led Texas to the Southwest Conference title, 12–7, over Walker's Southern Methodist team in 1945. But in 1947, Walker kicked and passed the Mustangs past Layne's Longhorns, 14–13, and the next year won the Heisman Trophy as the nation's best college player.

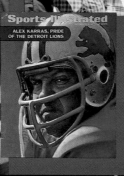

Sports Illustrated

ALEX KARRAS, PRIDE
OF THE DETROIT LIONS

With the Lions trailing 16–10 in the final minutes of the '53 championship game, Layne told his teammates, "Just give me time, boys." Layne made good on his pledge, marching Detroit 80 yards in three minutes, capping the drive with a 33-yard touchdown pass to Jim Doran. Doak Walker's extra point gave the Lions their second consecutive championship.

(Top) Center Vince Banonis walks off the field at Cleveland Stadium carrying the game ball after the Lions won the 1953 NFL championship.

(Above) Running back Tom Tracy is up-ended in Detroit's 20–17 win over the visiting Forty-Niners in 1956.

Meanwhile, Detroit drafted the 1949 Heisman winner, end Leon Hart of Notre Dame. He had good looks, like Walker, and was similarly popular. Before settling in the city, he and his wife, Lois, visited Hollywood, where he was given a screen test by Universal Pictures.

Also new to the Lions in 1950 were guard Creekmur (William and Mary), offensive tackle Gus Cifelli (Notre Dame), halfback Hoernschemeyer (who had played in the All-America Conference, which folded after the 1949 season), and defensive tackle McGraw. McGraw was a heavyweight wrestling champ at Colorado A&M, plus discus and hammer throw champion.

Meanwhile, Dick Rifenburg, University of Michigan star receiver in 1948, left a Detroit sportcaster's job to join the team. He was supposed to play in 1949 with the New York Yanks, but hurt his knee at the All-Star game.

McMillin also added a backfield coach named Raymond "Buddy" Parker, a star of the Lions' 26–7 championship game in 1935 over the New York Giants, and another assistant, George Wilson.

"It'll take about three years to really get rolling. We have a lot of work to do," said McMillin, quoted in a column by Smith (who was later to become the Lions' public relations director).

In August when the Lions gathered for training camp in Ypsilanti, Anderson said the group was, "the best the Lions ever assembled for training — at least it's the best on paper." The captains were Johnny Greene, a Lions end (from Eastern Michigan) since 1944, and offensive lineman Bingaman, who joined the team from the University of Illinois in 1948.

The Lions went to Birmingham, Alabama, for an exhibition game and the *Birmingham News* wrote of McMillin: "Not two teams does he use, not three or four, but seven. He calls his system the 'multi-platoon system.' He used a team to kick off, a different team to receive a punt. Then Bo has his offensive team and defensive team and a very important unit — a point-after-touchdown team."

Detroit won three of its first four games of '50, then fell into a four-game losing skid. The day before that fourth straight setback the *Detroit Times* ran a headline: "Ax Readied for McMillin; Crisler Wanted for Job." Michigan's Fritz Crisler never got the job, but it was clear five days later McMillin would be gone when the board of directors gave him "a unanimous vote of confidence."

The Lions won the next three games: 24–21 over Green Bay, a 49–14 Thanksgiving Day crushing of the Yanks, and 45–21 against Baltimore. Detroit set

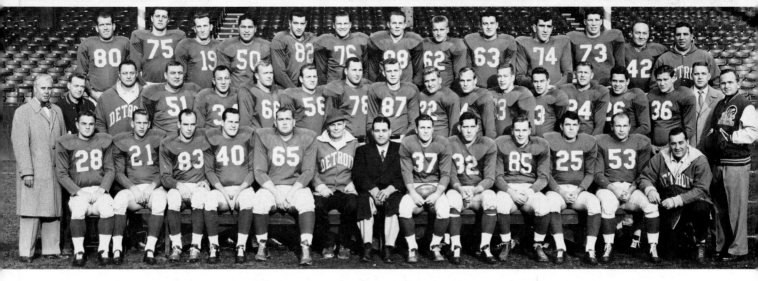

The 1953 Detroit Lions — National Football League Champions

Front Row (L–R): Yale Lary, Carl Karilivacz, Jim Doran, Bob Smith, Les Bingaman, Buddy Parker, Nick Kerbawy, Doak Walker, Lew Carpenter, Sherwin Gandee, Jim David, LaVern Torgeson and George Wilson.

Second Row (L–R): Dr. Richard Thompson, Roy Macklem, Buster Ramsey, Vince Banonis, Pat Harder, Harley Sewell, Joe Schmidt, Oliver Spencer, Dorne Dibble, Bobby Layne, Bob Hoernschemeyer, Ollie Cline, Jug Girard, Jack Christiansen, Gene Gedman, Robert Lee Smith, Bud Erickson and Grant Foster.

Back Row (L–R): Cloyce Box, John Prchlik, Tom Dublinski, Charlie Ane, Leon Hart, Lou Creekmur, Jim Cain, Jim Martin, Dick Stanfel, Bob Miller, Thurman McGraw, Bob Dove and Aldo Forte.

John Henry Johnson, Detroit's top rusher in 1957, blocks for Gene Gedman.

Press credentials for the '57 title contest.

12 records in the New York game and it was the franchise's biggest-ever score. They then dropped the finale to Chicago, 6–3, on two George Blanda field goals, a decision that clinched the conference title for the Bears and finished off the Lions at 6–6. The record apparently wasn't good enough for the impatient investors, still seeking to get out of the red.

McMillin was fired December 19. "The players whom we have been fortunate enough to bring to Detroit give the Lions a nucleus around which to build a championship team," McMillin said. "I am leaving my successor great personnel, the type of which I was not fortunate enough to start with three years ago."

He continued his not-so-subtle zingers: "It has been said and printed that some of my players did not like or respect me. I want you football fans to know that while coaching the Lions I was not conducting a popularity contest. . . . I do not have to apologize for the job I have done for the Detroit Football Club."

The next day Parker, 37, was named his replacement, with a reported one-

year contract paying $12,000. Wilson and Forte remained as assistants and public relations man Nick Kerbawy was promoted to business manager (and eventually to general manager).

The directors voted to pay off the last two years of McMillin's contract ($60,000) to avoid a court fight. A month later McMillin signed a three-year contract with Philadelphia, the Eagles paying $15,000 above Detroit's $30,000 salary.

That summer, 57 Lions reported to training camp (24 holdovers). Newcomers included kicker-lineman Martin (Notre Dame, Browns), end Dibble (Michigan State), center Vince Banonis (U-D, Cardinals), guard Torgeson (Washington State), safety Christiansen (Colorado A&M), fullback Harder (Wisconsin), and Doran (Iowa State). Torgeson came recommended by his coach, former U-M star Forest Evashevski.

Such talent made it a very promising camp. And a shift from the cold cuts of the old regime to a training table of steaks, chops and big breakfasts, made everyone happier.

"All I can say is that maybe we aren't

(Left) Minutes before kickoff at the 1952 NFL Championship game in Cleveland.

(Top) Jim David picked off an Otto Graham pass to stop one Cleveland drive. Said assistant coach Aldo Forte: "With all due credit to our boys, I've never seen Otto Graham pass so poorly . . . Of course, we were great defensively when we had to be. We stopped 'em inside the 30 and that's what won."

(Above) Leon Hart makes a leaping grab for a touchdown in the Lions' 1952 regular season win over the Browns.

In 1956, Howard "Hopalong" Cassady led the Lions in both punt returns and kickoff returns.

champs yet," Banonis said, "but we're sure eating like we are."

Missing, though, was Box. The veteran who was in some of the toughest World War II campaigns, was called back to the Marines and wouldn't return for a year.

The 1951 Detroit team won its first two games, lost, tied, then lost 28–23 to the Bears to fall from first to fourth with a 2–2–1 record. Said ex-Lion Jack Matheson, "In my opinion, they are a year away."

The Lions won the next four, including a 41–28 upset of Chicago. Walker, in his "Doak's Dope" column in the *Free Press*, said, "As we head into the last three weeks of the season it appears we'll have to win them all to take the title."

They beat eventual champion Los Angeles 24–22, but were upset twice by San Francisco, 20–10 at home and 21–17 to close out the season in what Bob McClellan of the *Detroit Times* said would be the Lions' "biggest day in 15 years." Detroit finished 7–4–1, behind the 8–4 of the Rams, who went on to beat Cleveland 24–17 for the championship.

"We'll be back next year to kick the stuffing out of somebody," said Harder with a growl. "It was a good season anyway. We went farther than a lot of people thought we would."

The Lions reported their first profit ever, $65,000, despite paying $30,000 to the departed McMillin. Yet Anderson said the team lost $221,000 the previous three years and, "We're not yet out of the woods." They had spent $2.75 million over four years.

Parker, with a profit-sharing clause, wound up doubling his salary in 1951 and was re-signed to another one-year contract for '52. The team turned down a $250,000 offer from the Dallas Rangers/Texans (the transferred Yanks franchise) for Walker. Dallas would finish 1952 with a 1–11 record and move the franchise to Baltimore.

On March 31, the 57-year-old McMillin died at his home in Bloomington, Indiana, of a heart attack. He had also suffered from stomach cancer. *The Chicago Tribune* ran an eight-column front sports page story, with five photos.

Parker's 1952 slogan was, "The product will be better than ever." And it

(Right) Team Doctor Richard Thompson, co-owner Ray Whyte, general manager Nick Kerbawy and head coach Buddy Parker in the victorious Detroit locker room.

(Top) Defensive center (middle guard) Les Bingaman helps chase down Browns quarterback Otto Graham.

(Above) Layne passed for 2,088 yards on just 125 completions in 1953, an average of almost 17 yards per catch.

In addition to his normal duty as fullback, Pat Harder kicked two extra points and a field goal in helping the Lions win the first of three titles in the '50s.

was, with safety Robert Yale Lary (Texas A&M), kicker-end George "Pat" Summerall (Arkansas), cornerback David (Colorado A&M), guard Stanfel (San Francisco), end Gandee (Ohio State), and quarterback Tom Dublinski (Utah) coming on board. Stanfel had missed the 1951 season due to a knee injury preparing for the All-Star game. Summerall would be traded after a year.

"How good a football team is the Detroit Lions?" asked Wally Wallis of the *Daily Oklahoman* after a September exhibition in Dallas. "That's the jackpot question other teams in the NFL must answer . . . or stand aside and watch Coach Buddy Parker's sturdy crew walk off with the loop championship."

It did just that. With the addition of even more talented young players, the Lions were on the brink. After losing two of the first three, it won eight of the last nine to finish tied in the West with Los Angeles at 9–3. The loss in the stretch was to Chicago, 24–23, on a 2-yard George Blanda-to-Ed Sprinkle TD pass with eight seconds left. One of the victories was 52–17 over the Pack-

ers, their worst loss ever. The Lions faced the Rams in a playoff game at home, snapping the Rams' eight-game winning streak, 31–21, as Harder scored two TDs and kicked a pair of field goals.

A week later, December 28, in Cleveland, the Lions beat the Browns 17–7 for Detroit's first title since 1935. Walker had a 67-yard touchdown run, Layne a 2-yard TD plunge, Harder a 36-yard field goal, and Doll a key tackle on Marion Motley to thwart a threat. It was bedlam at the Michigan Central railroad station as fans greeted their returning warriors that Sunday night. The triumph earned each Lion $2,275 from the largest winner's pool in post-season history: $94,000.

"I've been saying all along that Detroit had the best club in the league," said Cleveland coach Paul Brown. "I guess this proves it."

A headline in the *Times* read: "Youth of Champs Foreshadows More Lion Crowns." How prophetic. In Lincoln, Nebraska, meanwhile, former Lions coach Potsy Clark was saying his '35 team was better.

There weren't many better, though,

than the 1953 Lions. They went 10–2, nosing out San Francisco by a game in the West, then nipping Cleveland at home in a title rematch, 17–16, before 54,577 in the game marked by the Layne-to-Doran heroics.

Free Press columnist Mark Beltaire sat near Parker's wife, Jane, during the game and wrote: "When the wild whooping told her the game was over, Mrs. Parker stood up briefly with a stunned look on her face . . . the kind you see on people in shock. Then she sat down again abruptly, perhaps too drained to trust herself to walk out."

Nearby was director Fife. "Who's excited?" he asked rhetorically. "I don't smoke . . . but I'm smoking."

Beltaire got excited, too. While jumping up to cheer, his right elbow bashed the ear of assistant coach Wilson's mother-in-law. "I never felt it," she said.

It was the culmination of a somewhat turbulent year, featuring especially tough negotiations between Kerbawy and many players. Halfback Smith typified the tactics of many, using a threat to play in Canada as a bargaining ploy, plus a purported job offer to be a disc jockey. He wound up signing for the same $8,000 figure he had inked in 1952. When he walked in Kerbawy's office, the general manager asked for

the contract he was mailed. Smith left it home, but trustingly signed a blank one.

Detroit also signed a guard from Hawaii, Charley Ane, who had 20 credit hours left at Southern California. It created quite a stir.

Also, Kerbawy went to Philadelphia to testify in a U.S. anti-trust suit against the NFL.

Then there was a tough 14–10 Detroit victory in San Francisco before 93,751 at Kezar Stadium in which tempers flared often. David was accused of kneeing quarterback Y.A. Tittle in the back and there were accusations and counter accusations about "dirty play."

Bob Stevens, writing in the *San Francisco Chronicle*, said: "Bobby Layne, whose passing excellence paced the Detroits to victory, roared back at one 49er diehard, using words that would cause an umpire to show a baseball player the shortest distance from one place to the clubhouse. 'Come down here and say that you . . .'"

Another San Francisco columnist wrote of a fight at a fancy restaurant in town, involving Smith, Layne, halfback Hoernschemeyer and two 49er fans. They stepped outside, where "the first guy took a punch at Smith, who flattened him with one swing. Hunchy pushed the other guy over a wall, and that was that."

(Left) As the decade of the '50s ended, Detroit's fortunes were as bright as ever with the emergence of several young players. The 1959 squad featured 10 promising second-year players, including (front row) end Steve Junker, tackle Alex Karras, tackle Bill Glass, linebacker Wayne Walker, tackle John Gordy and end Jim Gibbons, as well as (back row) halfback Ken Webb, halfback Dan Lewis, defensive halfback Dave Whitsell and end Tom Rychlec.

(Top) Lew Carpenter replaced Hoernschemeyer at the right halfback spot in 1955 and led the Lions in rushing that season with 543 yards and six touchdowns.

(Bottom) Jim Doran picks his way through traffic in Detroit's 24–21 win over the Rams in '56. The Lions won their first six games that season, but faltered in three of the final six contests to finish second to the Bears.

(Above) Tom Dublinski often spelled Bobby Layne at quarterback. In the 1954 season-opener against the Bears, Dublinski stepped in for Layne — who started the game with a cold and 102-degree fever — and led the Lions to a 48–23 win.

(Right) Fullback Pat Harder handled many of the Lions' kicking chores in 1952, here connecting on a 30-yard field goal in a narrow 24–23 loss at Chicago. The setback was Detroit's only defeat in its final nine regular season contests.

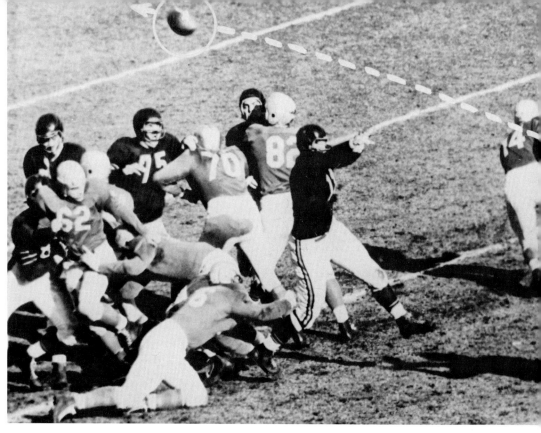

Outstanding players such as linebacker Joe Schmidt helped keep the Lions' defense strong as the 1950s came to a close. Here Schmidt steps in front of Los Angeles' Jim Phillips to grab an interception in 1958.

There were be other tussles over the years, and a few arrests, but there was positive PR, too. Like the time Kerbawy and Anderson were on a plane at the Traverse City airport in the summer of 1953 and the captain asked for a volunteer to get off. A 10-year-old boy needed the seat to fly to Detroit for an appendectomy. The two Lions executives flipped a coin. Kerbawy lost and headed for the door. "Wait a minute," Anderson shouted. "I won, didn't I? I want to get off the plane — for that boy."

Detroit was atop the world in 1954. More good players joined the fold and veterans were constantly in demand. Hart and Creekmur rode camels, while sports writers raced in sulkies pulled by ostriches, at a promotion at Flat Rock Speedway.

Yet there was more of the negative. Hoernschemeyer and Dibble got into it with two men in July at an Ann Arbor restaurant after one of the men made a remark about a woman with the Lions. One man swung at "Hunchy," a report said, who "tried to hit back and accidentally belted a policeman."

In November, Smith was kicked off the team by Parker after shoving assistant coach Buster Ramsey on an airplane in Los Angeles while arguing about diminished playing time.

The team overcame the distractions, clinching the division December 5 with a 13–13 tie against the Eagles. Detroit finished 9–2–1, then got crushed by the Browns in the title match, 56–10, as Otto Graham offset a poor 1953 championship game performance by passing for three touchdowns and running for three more in Cleveland.

"I wish I could explain what happened," Parker said. "We weren't complacent. I still think we have a better team than the Browns. Our luck just ran out. We never had so many things go against us so fast."

Lions stockholders, 125 of them, earned $14 a share — their first dividend in seven years.

It looked like 1955 would bring more success. Parker said an 8–4 record could win the division. Detroit ended up 3–9. In the midst of it, a *Free Press* headline read: "Lions' Collapse Defies Diagnosis."

Walker was honored at halftime of the season finale. It was his last game before retirement.

The following summer, the Lions

(Left) Lavern Torgeson snaps to Bobby Layne as running backs Bob Hoernschemeyer, Bob Smith and Doak Walker go in motion.

(Top) Dorne Dibble zeros in on this Tom Dublinski pass against Chicago.

(Above) Leon Hart picks up yardage after making a reception in the win over the Bears.

Bob Hoernschemeyer ran five times for 29 yards in this 1953 outing against the Rams. His 482 rushing yards paced Detroit that year.

were thwarted in a bid to buy baseball's Detroit Tigers. They needed a "yes" vote by all 10 NFL owners, but didn't get them. They had put in a $250,000 bid to look at the Tigers' books.

Another Heisman winner, halfback Howard "Hopalong" Cassady of Ohio State, was the leading newcomer in 1956, along with halfback Don McElhenny (SMU), fullback John Henry Johnson (the Steelers) and guard Gene Cronin (College of the Pacific). They helped the team to a 9–3 record, but Johnson was nearing the end of his Hall of Fame career.

"The spectacular jump of the Detroit Lions from last place in 1955 to pace setter this season has pro fans in a tizzy," read a report in the *Los Angeles Mirror-News*. "They can't understand how a team can improve so much in a league as well balanced as the NFL."

In an October experiment, the Lions broadcast defensive signals from Ramsey to the helmet of star linebacker Schmidt, who said later, "I caught myself looking around a couple of times to see what he was doing out on the field." Four days later the league banned use of radio helmets.

The '56 season featured the famous late hit by Ed Meadows in the second quarter that knocked Layne out of the last game of the season, a 38–21 loss in Chicago that finished Detroit at 9–3 — a half game behind the Bears. The Lions later said Bears' owner George Halas had issued a "Get Layne" order. That was later dismissed as inaccurate and Parker apologized.

The year 1957 was to be a strangely triumphant one, with Parker under a new two-year, $70,000 contract. In August he stunned a downtown Detroit banquet audience by quitting, saying, "I've been in football a long time. I know the situations. I don't want to get in the middle of another losing season."

As reported by Dave Diles, then with The Associated Press, Parker said, "There's been no life . . . No go . . . It's a completely dead team."

The departure came soon after Graham, the principal speaker, said, supposedly tongue-in-cheek: "Paul Brown had a standard $50 fine for a player violating curfew. If that held on the Detroit club, some players would be bankrupt. I won't talk any longer. The players are anxious to be checked in on the bus, so they can hurry out again. Let's get the bed check over so we can start the parties."

After toastmaster Bob Reynolds introduced Parker, the coach said: "I've got a situation here I can't handle anymore. These ballplayers have gotten too big for me or something. I'm getting out."

Wilson was given control of the team and Parker accepted a five-year contract to coach Pittsburgh. A year later he was

(Above) Head coach Buddy Parker, flanked by assistant coaches George Wilson and Buster Ramsey, led the Lions to titles in 1952 and '53. Wilson stepped in when Parker abruptly quit before the '57 season and guided the team to another NFL championship.

(Top right) The 1957 Lions offense included (front) Jim Doran, Darris McCord, Stan Campbell, Charley Ane, Harley Sewell, Lou Creekmur and Dorne Dibble, and backfield stars Gene Gedman, John Henry Johnson, Bobby Layne and Howard Cassady.

(Bottom right) Bobby Layne's 25-yard field goal in the final seconds of the first half gave the Lions a 10–7 win over the Rams at Briggs Stadium in 1957.

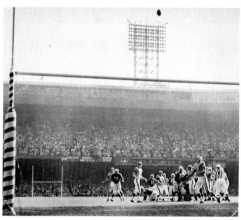

The lines were long when tickets for the 1957 NFL Championship game went on sale at the Lions' offices.

to say, "there were too many quarterbacks on the board of directors" of the Lions. But in 1959 he told Watson Spoelstra of *The Detroit News:* "Every man is entitled to one mistake in a lifetime. I made mine when I left the Lions."

Wilson guided the team to an 8–4 record and first-place tie with the 49ers. Detroit won the playoff in San Francisco, 31–27, behind substitute quarterback Tobin Rote after trailing 27–7 in the third quarter. Rote, a former Packer, had replaced Layne, who broke an ankle a few weeks earlier. The next week at home, Rote threw four TD passes and the Lions clobbered perennial title rival Cleveland, 59–14, for Detroit's fourth overall championship and third of the '50s.

For the fourth straight year the Lions turned a profit, $151,052. Wilson was named AP Coach of the Year. And a few months later, Kerbawy quit to accept a reported $1 million offer from basketball's Detroit Pistons. Anderson became the Lions' GM.

The Lions, as they were a decade earlier, were in transition. They fell to a 4–7–1 record in 1958, then to 3–8–1 in 1959. That year the team sold 41,629 season tickets — the first time in nine years they did not set a sales record.

Young standouts like defensive tackle Alex Karras (Iowa), halfback Terry Barr (Michigan), quarterback Earl Morrall (Michigan State), guard John Gordy (Tennessee), defensive end Bill Glass (Baylor), fullback Nick Pietrosante (Notre Dame), end Steve Junker (Xavier), halfback Danny Lewis (Wisconsin), and others dotted the lineup as the '50s came to an end.

With some still-solid veterans mixed in, there would be more good seasons in the immediate years ahead. But the "Golden Age" faded into history with nary a single newspaper analysis in December 1959, about that glorious Lions decade.

It can't return. But who's to say whether or not there's another golden age on the horizon? ❖

Layne accepts the Lions' 1954 Most Valuable Player award from team president Edwin Anderson and coach Buddy Parker.

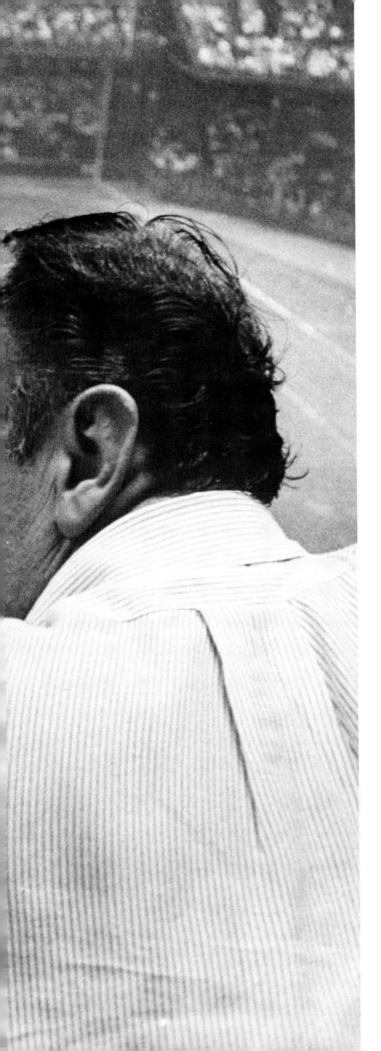

5

"*It's spotted, it's booted, it's up, and IT'S GOOD!*"
— Van Patrick

Van coined many phrases that are still heard today,
such as "cliffhanger," "home run ball" and "fearsome
foursome."

They Told the Story

Hall of Fame announcer Van Patrick heads the list of broadcast greats who have called the action in Detroit.

by Walter Dell

There were many great announcers who called the action in the early years of the Detroit Lions. Graham McNamee, Bill Stern and Ted Husing are just a few of the pioneers who became sports broadcast legends in these parts.

But the man I call "The Late Great Van Patrick" was the man who set the standard. Van was a proud man, a man of great confidence, and a man with a flamboyant personality. Most of all, he was a courageous man who battled cancer to the very end.

Van was on the air in Buffalo in 1945 when Bill Veeck, who had just purchased the Cleveland Indians, hired Van to broadcast Indians games, and in 1949, he was on the first World Series telecast. He began broadcasting University of Michigan football games in 1948 and Lions games in 1950. He was the Detroit Tigers' play-by-play man from 1952 to 1959. He did the Lions game on radio or television every week for 24 years.

As time passed, Van became the announcer for Notre Dame football, but he also grew closer and closer to the Lions. He loved the Detroit Lions. He was not a homer, but the Lions were his team.

Van kept the busiest schedule in all of sports broadcasting. On Saturdays, Van would cover the Notre Dame football games, on Sunday he'd broadcast the Lions games, and the next day he'd do the radio play-by-play for the NFL's Monday Night game. All the while, he'd do daily radio reports that were broadcast nationally and sports reporting for WJBK-TV in Detroit. It was a busy schedule — he logged more than 150,000 miles most years on an airplane — but Van loved it.

Some say that his calls from the booth were sometimes predictable, but that was part of the man's style and charm. When the Lions lined up for an extra point, that familiar, honey-toned voice would describe: "It's spotted, it's booted, it's up, and *it's good!*"

Van also coined many sports phrases that are still heard today, phrases like *cliffhanger, home run ball* and *fearsome foursome.*

Life in the radio booth was always an adventure with Van. He loved to go to Baltimore when the Colts played at Memorial Stadium, even though the broadcast facilities were not the best (they were located low in the lower deck). The baseball infield was never sodded. If Johnny

Unitas was sacked or Alan Ameche was brought down after a hard run, Van liked to say "another one hits the dust." He also loved the Maryland crab cakes served in the press box.

Van's favorite place to broadcast was at the Los Angeles Coliseum where the Rams played when the franchise was moved from Cleveland. The Coliseum had fine broadcast booths. It was a mammoth structure which was built for the 1932 Olympics. From the press box you were a long way from the playing field. Field glasses, or extra good eyes, were essential, but it was a nice facility for comfort with arm rests and casters on the chairs.

Van knew many Hollywood celebrities, many of them on a first name basis. He would get them press box passes when the Lions came to town. He would also tell them to stop by the broadcast booth and say hello. Most of them did, and Van was delighted to mention their names over the air.

Things weren't nearly so nice in Chicago when the Bears played their home games at Wrigley Field. The visiting broadcast booth was a rickety affair built in the stands. When it rained, a leaky downspout would spray water on the broadcast crew. The listening audience would hear about this frequently. The booth was cramped for space as well — because Van was a big man.

But that wasn't the worst part. At Wrigley Field, the press box reporters had to march through our broadcast booth to get to the rest room, which was a portable toilet. Van would mention privately that many of the reporters would stop to listen to him so they could learn what was going on.

Of course, we also had to contend with the odor. One time, during a commercial break, a man passing through yelled out "Where's the toilet?" Van responded: "You're standing in it!"

During those broadcasts in Chicago, Van would constantly rant and rave about how the officials allowed George Halas to move out onto the field to berate them. The officials would take the abuse from Halas, but only would ask him to "please stay behind the sidelines." Van would frequently mention that, because Halas was one of the founding fathers of the National Football League, he could get away with anything — and he usually did.

Van was a man who commanded a great deal of respect. One year the

(Above) Van Patrick with Lions owner William Clay Ford at the Indianapolis Motor Speedway in 1968.

(Right) The Old Announcer interviewing head coach George Wilson. That's Alex "I'll walk back to Detroit" Karras behind Wilson.

Lions played the Patriots in a pre-season game in Montreal. The game was played at Jarry Park, which was the baseball park for the Expos before Olympic Stadium was built. The team arrived two days before the night game so there could be some sight-seeing. The day before the game, we visited the stadium. The baseball press box was behind home plate, which was in one end zone of the football field.

When Van saw this, he went into a rage. He told them in no uncertain terms that he would not do a game from such a horrible spot. He was told nothing could be done, but Van instructed them to get some lumber and build a scaffolding in the bleachers on the sidelines. It was completed by game time the following evening. Yes, indeed, Van did have clout.

The Old Announcer also had a great rapport with the players. After the merger of the American Football League and the NFL, the big talk was who would be the first NFL team to lose to the AFL. It was felt it would be a distinct disgrace to be the first NFL team to lose to an AFL team. When the Lions traveled to Denver to play the Broncos in a pre-season game, no NFL team had

lost. The Broncos bragged that they would defeat the Lions. Alex Karras vowed, if the Lions lost to Denver, he would walk back to Detroit.

Well, the Lions were beaten. And when Alex boarded the bus for the airport, Van yelled out, "To start walking to Detroit, you go that way!" Alex just glared at Van.

Van always had a running feud with Howard Cosell. They strongly disliked each other, to put it mildly. In 1972, Detroit traveled to Dallas to play a Monday Night game. The local Chamber of Commerce sponsored a dinner that Monday afternoon, and Van and Howard were seated side-by-side.

Howard said, "You know, Van, there are only three or four really great sports broadcasters in this country."

Van replied, "Howard, there is one less than you think."

Howard's reply cannot be repeated.

At the age of 58, Van passed away in a South Bend hospital on a Sunday afternoon when the Lions were playing the Green Bay Packers in Milwaukee's County Stadium. When the news reached the broadcast booth, silence immediately prevailed. Bob Reynolds, his long-time broadcast partner, broke

(Above) Bob Reynolds, Patrick's long-time broadcast partner, took over for Van in the radio booth.

(Left) Frank Beckmann (right) succeeded Reynolds as play-by-play announcer, and at one time was joined behind the mic by Dale Conquest and Charlie Sanders.

into tears. The Detroit Lions had lost a good friend, and America had lost a great man.

Since that dark day in 1974, Detroit has had the good fortune to have some of the finest announcers in pro football. Bob had been Van Patrick's analyst for many years, then succeeded Van behind the play-by-play mike. Bob was a true professional; he did his homework well — he always believed in good preparation.

Bob maintained it was tougher to be a color man than to do play-by-play. In fact, Bob was sometimes too wrapped up in doing his own job. One time during a broadcast, Van said, "How about that, Bob?"

Bob paused. "I don't know, Van," he said. "I didn't hear you." The long-time sports director of WJR, Bob also loved his Lions. In his many years covering the Lions, he missed only one game when he was hospitalized in Chicago after a Bears game. Bob is a great gentleman and a fine friend.

Lions football was described as vividly as ever when Frank Beckmann took over for Bob Reynolds in the 1980s. Frank was on cloud nine when he became the No. 1 man on Lions'

broadcasts. He loved pro football and loved being around the players. A fun-loving man, he enjoyed life on the road in the NFL, and Frank was always well-prepared when the game started.

Unfortunately, Frank did not like air travel. During the 1983 playoff loss at San Francisco, it was Frank's voice that expressed the agony and disappointment when Eddie Murray's late-second field goal missed the mark. When the charter took off after the game, it developed some mechanical trouble and had to circle San Francisco Bay to drop off fuel so it could land. After the charter landed and repairs had been made, coach Monte Clark stepped off the plane to go to the East-West college game — and that's when Frank decided to go back to Detroit on AMTRAK.

Holiday travelers had filled the trains, so big Frank reluctantly took a flight back to Detroit the following day.

Whereas Frank Beckmann had been a fixture on the Detroit sports scene for many years, Mark Champion came to town in 1989 as a relative unknown. Mark had been the play-by-play man for Tampa Bay for 10 years when he headed north to take over as Lions announcer when WWJ was awarded the rights to the

was his game — the Detroit Lions were his team. From his first broadcast in the Detroit booth, he was comfortable and in command.

Like the play-by-play announcers, Lions fans have been treated to some tremendously talented analysts over the years. Some of the fine color men include Russ Thomas, J.P. McCarthy, Bruce Martyn, Ray Lane, Dave Diles, Mike Lucci, Charlie Sanders, Steve Garagiola and Dale Conquest.

Jim Brandstatter is the current analyst in the booth, serving as an excellent complement to Mark Champion. Jim's background as a former college player at Michigan is most valuable, but his greatest strength is his ability to explain the game in layman's terms.

These men in the radio booth have helped bring the drama and excitement of Detroit Lions football to three generations of fans. The legacy left by the immortal broadcasters such as the Late Great Van Patrick has been enormous, and with any luck at all, the very best and brightest will treat us to more cliffhangers and home run balls during the next 60 years.

ABOUT THE AUTHOR

Detroit's 60th Anniversary season will mark Walter Dell's 32nd year in the Lions' radio broadcast booth. Dell began his work as a statistician in 1962, and has since worked with every Detroit announce team.

Says Dell: "One of my most memorable games was in my first year with the Lions in 1962. It was the Thanksgiving Day game with the Packers, the start of the Lombardi era. It was one of those rare games of perfect execution. Bart Starr spent most of the afternoon on the Tiger Stadium turf.

"The Detroit Lions have always been my team — and I am proud to have been a small part of them." ❖

(Top) WWJ's Mark Champion (right) and Jim Brandstatter (left), pictured here with Detroit head coach Wayne Fontes, are in their fifth year together in the Lions' broadcast booth.

(Bottom) Author and statistician Walter Dell has spent 31 years in the Lions radio booth.

broadcasts. Being a new name in town, he knew it would be tough, but it did not take him long to adjust to the Lions.

He worked especially hard that first year getting to know the coaches, the players, and the plays. He attended every day of training camp. Pro football

Van Patrick was the play-by-play voice of the Lions every week for 24 years.

6

"I have never seen anything like this in my life, and I hope to God I never see it again."

— Dr. Edwin Guise
Team physician, October 24, 1971

On November 1, 1971, in Milwaukee, the Lions and the Green Bay fans observe a moment of silence in memory of Chuck Hughes.

Forever Lions

A haunting legacy
of tragedy and
heartbreak has taken
some special people
from the Lions.

by Richard L. Shook

They were warriors and conducted themselves accordingly. There was, they knew, a price to be exacted for going out onto the field of battle.

Precisely what that price would be they could not know. Most likely it would be pain, mental anguish, or some sort of wound that could hobble them long past the glory days.

To succeed in professional football, whether as a player or a coach, you understand that sacrifices must be made to compete, to challenge, to win.

The trick lies in acknowledging the risk, looking at it, then putting it in a box marked "Do Not Open" within the mind. You respect its contents, but do not fear it. One cannot compete, at any level or in any profession, with the box open and fear of consequences governing behavior.

Love can keep the cover on the box. And when you love, truly love, the cost is never a question. When the time comes, you pay it.

Thus it was for Eric Andolsek, Len Fontes, Chuck Hughes, Don McCafferty and Lucien Reeberg — warriors doing battle on a field they loved. They gave the final years of their lives in service to a sport and team they cherished; they are "Forever Lions."

Also always to remain a Lion is Mike Utley, whose warrior spirit lifted his team even as he himself was lifted in paralysis off the field of battle. His fighting attitude from a wheelchair continues to inspire people around the world.

Utley vows to walk unaided again one day — and who can doubt it? He has progressed to walking short distances on crutches.

Do people of Utley's bent make football, or does it make them? Whatever, football is filled with Mike Utleys.

"I was on top of the world," he said. "Only 27 other people were doing what I was doing — playing right guard in the National Football League. Then I break my neck and hit what I thought was rock bottom. How do you break a 22-inch neck?

"But I have no regrets about football. Sure, football put me in this chair. But it also got me to stand up because I was able to use the same physical and mental toughness I learned in football to attack this one step at a time.

"I plan to walk. Like a normal person? I hope so. But if not, I'll still be walking."

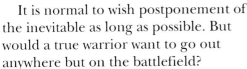

It is normal to wish postponement of the inevitable as long as possible. But would a true warrior want to go out anywhere but on the battlefield?

Only one man has done so in pro football, Lions' wide receiver Hughes. He died on the field October 24, 1971, after suffering a heart attack with 62 seconds remaining in a game against the Chicago Bears. He ran a routine pass route and was returning to the huddle following an incompletion to tight end Charlie Sanders when he collapsed.

Reeberg, a talented young giant of an offensive tackle who became a starter early in his only season, died of heart failure January 31, 1964, due to uremic poisoning as he was preparing to undergo tests. One moment he was joking and laughing with others in a room, the next he was gone.

McCafferty, the so-called "Easy Rider" of a coach who led the Baltimore Colts to the 1970 Super Bowl championship, died of a heart attack on July 28, 1974, a Sunday afternoon at home as he was preparing for another day in his second Lions' training camp. He had succeeded Joe Schmidt the season before.

Tragedy struck the Lions three times in an eight-month period of 1991–92. Right guard Utley suffered his spinal cord injury in a game against the Los Angeles Rams November 17, 1991.

But the "thumbs up" sign he gave to his teammates as he was carried off the field on a stretcher helped rally them to a 21–10 victory and the start of a stretch run to one of their most memorable seasons.

On May 8, 1992, defensive backs coach Fontes, older brother to head coach Wayne Fontes, suffered a fatal heart attack and died at home in the early pre-dawn hours.

The third blow came on June 23. Andolsek, the left guard in a line that only a year earlier was poised to rival famed Detroit lines of the '50s and '60s, was struck and killed by a runaway truck while cutting weeds in the yard of his Thibodaux, Louisiana, home.

Andolsek was struck by the cab part of a lumber truck whose driver, police said, fell asleep at the wheel. Andolsek was using a weed trimmer to neaten up the area around a telephone pole in his front yard when the cab felled him, continuing another 400 feet before coming to a stop.

The 25-year-old had become a starter in 1989, played in 50 straight games, and was potentially a perennial Pro-Bowl player at the time of his death. He had just been named to his first All-NFL team.

Andolsek was Detroit's fifth-round draft pick out of Louisiana State University in 1988. Nearly cut by Coach Darryl

(Top) Andolsek earned a spot on the *USA Today*'s 1991 All-Pro Team.

(Middle) At 6-feet-6 and nearly 300 pounds, Utley was a force on the Lions' front line.

(Bottom) Dr. Keith Burch, trainer Kent Falb, assistant trainer Joe Recknagel and coach Wayne Fontes attend to Utley on the field.

(Left) In his final game — the Lions' NFC title contest at Washington — Andolsek made his 50th consecutive start at left guard.

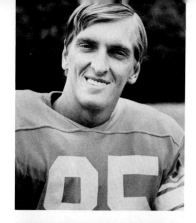

Chuck Hughes played two seasons with the Lions after a three-year stint with the Philadelphia Eagles.

Hughes made his first catch of the 1971 season just minutes before he collapsed on the Tiger Stadium field, a 32-yarder from Greg Landry.

Dr. Guise leaned over and began giving oral aid. Dr. Thompson began pounding Hughes' chest. It was a grim scene.

The crowd watched in silence.

Rogers, the 6-foot-2, 280-pounder was retained because of his tenacity. He didn't start, but played in every game of his rookie season.

Andolsek's nickname was "Table." His teammates said it was because you could play cards on his back and shoulders when he assumed his business position.

Chris Spielman knew Andolsek's mindset. The Lions linebacker and former Ohio State great learned they were of a similar bent when the Buckeyes played LSU and the two team-captains fought — during the coin toss. They quickly became friends and roommates in training camp.

"He set standards," said Spielman, who delivered the eulogy at Andolsek's funeral. "He played with everything: his heart, his soul. Everything."

Utley has involved himself heavily in advancing the Mike Utley Foundation (5050 North 40th Street · Suite 200, Phoenix, Arizona 85018), which he formed to assist patients with spinal cord injuries, research and education.

Also 25 at the time, Utley was hurt on the first play of the fourth quarter when Rams' tackle David Rocker jumped up to deflect what wound up being a touchdown pass. As Rocker and Utley separated, the Lions' 6-foot-6 guard lost his balance and fell awkwardly, and Utley's head snapped back when the force of his 300-pound frame hit the turf.

He suffered a fracture of the sixth cervical vertebra, plus damage to the soft tissue and ligaments surrounding it. The sixth and seventh vertebra were eventually fused.

Utley prefers to be termed "an

injured athlete" rather than crippled or handicapped. "I'm an athlete, and an athlete always comes back from his injuries."

His weight, once down in the low 200s, is back in the 250 range. He has regained much use of his arms, can walk short distances with crutches, drives a car, swims — and is proud he can open a twist-top beer bottle by himself.

Utley's thumbs up gesture galvanized a Detroit team that continually surprised the experts in 1991, routing Dallas in the playoffs before getting bounced by Super Bowl winner Washington in the conference championship game.

"When I did that," Utley explains his gesture, "I wanted the guys to just go like hell. Shoot, when one guy goes down, you can't stop. I wanted people to know that there's always a goal, and you do everything you can toward it.

"I didn't want people to quit because I'm in a chair. I still do as much as I did before — it just takes a little longer to do it."

"I think the main reason for our success (in '91) was him," said Chuck Schmidt, Lions' executive vice president. "Going down to visit someone who is paralyzed, laying there with a 'halo' (a neck brace to prevent head movement) on his head is not something people want to do.

"But I think people who went down to see him, including myself, came away feeling better than when we went in. The reason was Mike.

"That really became a catalyst for the attitude on our football team. People genuinely cared for him. He's a rarity."

Athletes felled by injury on the field of battle are fairly commonplace. Disabling injuries of various degrees are an acknowledged professional hazard.

Which is why no one was prepared for what happened to Hughes. No one before or since has died during action on a football field.

The well-liked native Texan's nickname was "Coyote." He was a native of Abilene who had gone to Texas-El Paso

86

(Top) Lucien Reeberg defied the odds, earning a starting assignment as a rookie after being drafted in the 19th round of the 1963 draft.

(Bottom) Will Robinson's scouting report described the Hampton Institute star as "amazingly quick and agile" for his size.

(Left) Reeberg (#61) joined John Gordy (#75), Bob Whitlow (#51), John Gonzaga (#79) and Daryl Sanders (not pictured) on the '63 offensive line; Earl Morrall (#14) is the quarterback.

for his schooling and to play football. He loved golf and was a good friend of Lee Trevino.

The Chicago Bears were slightly more than a minute away from completing a 28–23 victory over Detroit the day Hughes slumped to the Tiger Stadium grass on his way back to the huddle.

The alert in the pressbox quickly discerned this wasn't just a knee injury, pulled leg muscle or a simple case of a guy having the wind knocked out of him. Middle linebacker Dick Butkus of the Bears saw it even quicker — and frantically motioned to the sideline for medical help.

You could see doctors kneeling close to Hughes' face, trying mouth-to-mouth resuscitation and the most ominous sign of all came when one of them began pounding on the 28-year-old's chest. Reporters knew then he had not just swallowed his tongue, and witnesses with binoculars said they could see Hughes' ominous blue pallor.

"I felt his pulse and there was none," said Lions team physician Dr. Edwin Guise. "So we began cardiac massage."

He never regained consciousness and was pronounced dead at Henry Ford Hospital about an hour later, although doctors treating him at the time feel he was dead shortly after he hit the grass. They were only able to detect an occasional flickering of a heartbeat, they said, and were unsure about that.

An autopsy disclosed Hughes died from an acute heart seizure stemming from a heart artery clogged by blood clots.

"He had a hardening of the main artery supplying blood to the heart," explained Dr. Richard A. Thompson, Lions' team physician. "A clot had formed in this artery, shutting off the flow of blood."

Hughes had complained of severe abdominal pains after getting hurt in a game September 4, but was tested and nothing abnormal was found.

When he continued to complain of feeling poorly, though, another batch of tests was performed including an EKG, blood studies, plus an arteriogram (injecting dye into the arteries). Again, the results were negative.

Hughes, a seldom-used wide receiver, had entered his final game when Larry Walton re-injured a leg muscle early in the second half. Hughes had caught his first pass of the season moments earlier, a 32-yarder from Greg Landry, and was crunched between two defenders.

"He came back to the huddle," Landry said, "and seemed okay. Nobody thought anything of it."

Three plays later, Hughes slumped face-down onto the grass near the 25-yard line as he was trotting back to the huddle, his life over.

Utley returned to the Silverdome as an honorary captain for the Lions' 1992 Thanksgiving Day contest against Houston.

Jackie Simpson never had an opportunity to coach in a game for the Detroit Lions. On February 11, 1983, Monte Clark hired Simpson, 46, to be the Lions' defensive coordinator; But just four months later, on June 2, Simpson suffered a fatal heart attack in his Bloomfield Township hotel room.

In 1964, the Lions lost a promising offensive lineman with the death of Reeberg, who didn't play football as a senior at Hampton Institute (Va.) because he had been dropped from the team for fighting.

He was a discovery of part-time scout Will Robinson. (Yes, *the* Will Robinson of Detroit Miller and Pershing high schools, Illinois State and the Detroit Pistons. In the 1950s and '60s, when Robinson wasn't teaching the Spencer Haywoods and Ralph Sampsons, he spent football Saturdays scouting for the Lions, mostly at predominately black schools.)

Reeberg's quickness and size caught Robinson's eye during his junior season and he turned in a pretty good scouting report on the 6-foot-4, 300-pound giant.

Detroit drafted the popular and fun-loving Bronx native in the 19th round, in part because it felt nobody else knew about him. He checked into training camp at 317 pounds but eventually was down to 282.

Coach George Wilson tried Reeberg at defensive tackle during the exhibition season but also played him on the other side of the line.

Then, as he became disenchanted with the work of veteran right tackle

Bob Scholtz, Reeberg was inserted into the starting lineup for the fourth game and played beside guard John Gordy the rest of the way.

"Toward the end of the season," Gordy said, "I thought he had as much potential as anyone I've played with on the line."

It wasn't just his size which let you spot Reeberg on the field. About two plays into a game his too-short shirt tail would start flapping in the breeze.

Reeberg also had trouble keeping track of the down, often leaving the field following a play only to have to hustle back at the frantic urging of his teammates because fourth down was coming up.

Offensive linemen who have size, quick feet, and play well as rookie starters were about as common then as they are now. The Lions felt by getting Reeberg on a program to trim his weight to 265 pounds he would become even better.

He was hospitalized January 22, 1964, for being overweight and because he'd been having kidney problems.

Reeberg, 20 days shy of his 22nd birthday, was being tested for the cause of hematuria (blood in the urine). He also had a history of high blood pressure, which was not evident during his 1963 seasonal physical exam.

He had played some basketball January 31 and was laughing, joking around with people in the room as he was being prepared for kidney tests. Suddenly, his heart just stopped beating and Reeberg was dead.

An autopsy showed he died of heart failure due to uremic poisoning. The death of McCafferty was a shocker, too. Detroit had gone 6–7–1 in his only season. That was good for second in the NFC Central Division but it was a season behind Minnesota, 5½ games.

There was a caveat: The Lions started that season of adjustment 1–4–1 but finished well under their imposing physical specimen of a coach.

Some said the players took advantage of his easy-going manner (he wasn't

Len Fontes — pronounce that "fon-TEZ" — owned a championship ring as a member of the New York Giants' Super Bowl XXI staff.

Len (right) with brothers John and Wayne before the 1991 NFC Championship Game. "Our dream was whoever got a head coaching job, we'd work together. That was our dream," Wayne said.

called "Easy Rider" because he was a whip-cracker). A few of his friends hinted he was looking at a condominium in Baltimore and intended to retire following the 1974 season.

Regardless, Detroit seemed to be warming to the professional style of the 6-foot-5, 250-pound former player. It could have been McCafferty was just getting a grip on the Detroit player situation and would have pulled the weeds from that garden over the next season or two.

His was an intellectual approach to coaching, indicated by the way he always put a new wrinkle or two into a game plan, and judging by the reaction to his death, he seemed to have won most of his players over to his style. Remember, this was a man who had coached a Super Bowl winner.

He played end/linebacker for Ohio State in 1941 and on Coach Paul Brown's national champions of 1942. There followed three years on an Army team at Fort Bragg, then a short stint as an end with the New York Giants.

McCafferty went into coaching as an assistant at Kent State for 10 seasons,

moving to Baltimore as receivers coach when Weeb Ewbank asked him in 1959. He stayed with the team until succeeding Don Shula in 1970.

The Colts went 11–2–1 that year and won the Super Bowl title over Dallas (remember Jim O'Brien's last-minute field goal?). He guided Baltimore to a 10–4 mark in 1971, losing to Shula's Miami team in the AFC title game.

New club ownership fired McCafferty in 1972 after Baltimore got off to a 1–4 start. Incoming GM Joe Thomas ordered McCafferty to go with young players, but McCafferty had no intention of being referred to in Colts' history books as the guy who benched legendary Johnny Unitas — even if that great quarterback was fading at 39. Maybe "Easy Rider" was the wrong nickname.

When Joe Schmidt resigned on January 26, 1973, Lions' owner William Clay Ford wanted a name coach, someone with a proven ability to win, to succeed him. McCafferty fit the bill.

NFL veterans were on strike the summer of 1974, but a rookies' workout was scheduled for the afternoon McCafferty collapsed. He had come

(Above) Don McCafferty coached just one season in Detroit, posting a 6–7–1 record in 1973. Players responded to his easy-going manner; he led Baltimore to a 16–13 win over Dallas in Super Bowl V.

(Right) William Clay Ford wanted a proven winner to succeed Joe Schmidt as head coach of the Lions, and he found one in Don McCafferty.

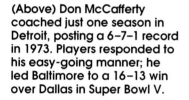

Eric Andolsek (above) and Mike Utley (opposite page) were emerging as two of the top young linemen in the NFL when their careers were tragically cut short.

(Right) "Thumbs Up!" The Lions rallied behind Mike Utley's injury to advance to the 1991 NFC Championship game.

indoors complaining of chest pains after finishing lawn work at his Orchard Lake home.

Dr. Joseph Kessler, a neighbor, applied cardiac massage within a minute but "Mac" was pronounced dead upon arrival at a hospital. He was 53.

Detroit Coach Wayne Fontes felt the ache of personal loss when his brother died in 1992.

Len Fontes once said he was spending the happiest years of his life working for his more boisterous, outgoing, limelight-loving brother. Len, like most of his family, pronounced his last name "Fon-TEZ"; Wayne felt "Fonts" rolled off the tongue better and was more masculine.

Len, a four-sport prep star at Wareham, Massachetts, had a baseball tryout with the Boston Red Sox before going to Ohio State to play safety for Woody Hayes. He played on Hayes' 1957 national championship team.

The family moved to Canton, Ohio, where the up-and-coming Wayne could benefit from the stiffer athletic competition. Wayne wound up at Michigan State.

"Our dream was whoever got a head coaching job, we'd work together," Wayne said. "That was our dream. Len

wasn't only my brother, he was a great coach."

Len joined the Lions in 1990, prior to which he had spent 1983–88 as defensive backs coach of the New York Giants, winners of the Super Bowl in 1986.

"Len got the best out of players," said Detroit Director of Player Personnel Ron Hughes. "We all knew Bennie (Blades) had the talent to be a Pro-Bowl player. Well, Len got him to play like one."

Len and Wayne were deep into making out a game plan for 1992 when Len woke up one night, gasping for breath sometime before 4 a.m. that spring morning.

Wife Mimi's first call went to Wayne and the coach beat paramedics to the scene. Wayne performed unsuccessful CPR on his brother, who was pronounced dead at a local hospital at the age of 54.

Wayne returned to his family to fill Len's position with the team, tapping younger brother John to coach Detroit's defensive backs.

Eric Andolsek, Len Fontes, Chuck Hughes, Don McCafferty, Lucien Reeberg. And Mike Utley.

The Lions honor them, because they honored the Lions. ❖

(Top) Lew Carpenter helped lead the Lions to a 28–24 win in 1954.

(Middle) Leon Hart spurts from the pack in a 24–20 loss to Green Bay in 1956.

(Bottom) In 1958, Gene Gedman carries the ball in a 24–14 win over the Packers.

(Right) In one of the most heralded wins in club history, Detroit's defense jolted the 1962 Packers, 26–14.

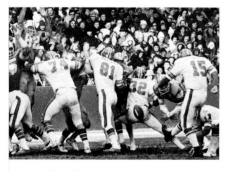

The Lions lost a heart-breaker in the final game at Tiger Stadium, 31–27 to Denver in 1974.

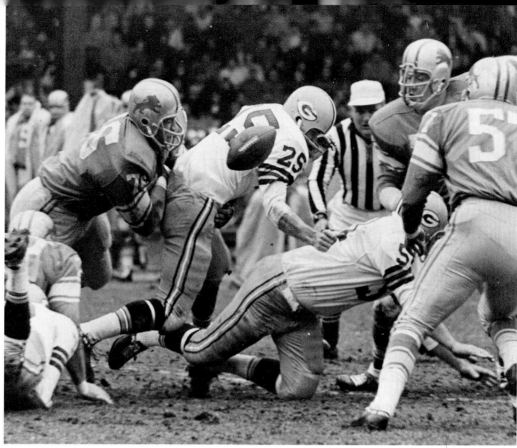

Anticipation was building so much that Richards saw an opportunity to take advantage of the still-young medium of radio. He was a close friend of Deke Aylesworth, president of the National Broadcasting Company, who agreed to carry the game over 94 stations, including Richards' own station in Detroit, WJR.

Graham McNamee would handle the play-by-play and Don Wilson (Jack Benny's old sidekick) the color commentary.

The day before the game, though, a circuit court judge, Arthur Webster, ruled that station WXYZ in Detroit also could broadcast the game. WXYZ had sought a restraining order against WJR, which would not allow another station to carry the contest.

Regardless of radio, people wanted to be there in the stands that memorable day. More than 26,000 jammed into the stadium, taking up every seat and any decent standing sightlines. Thousands were turned away — up to 50,000, according to one report.

A tradition had begun. And the quality of the game that day would cement it into the psyche of Detroiters.

The Lions lost 19–16 in what Leo Macdonell of the *Times* called "a thrill-saturated pigskin tussle — a tussle the like of which has been rare, if equalled, on the gridirons of a football-minded nation."

Detroit lost in the waning minutes when Nagurski threw a 2-yard pass to Bill Hewitt just two plays after Joe Zeller had intercepted a Glenn Presnell pass and returned it to the Detroit 4-yard line. Chuck Bernard blocked the extra point try, but the damage was done.

It had seemed like Detroit — which played without injured back Frank Christensen — would surely win. Fullback Ace Gutowsky played like a demon, rushing for 85 yards, scoring two touchdowns, making interceptions and many tackles in a 60-minute performance. He gave Detroit an early lead in the first quarter by scoring on a 2-yard run after a 27-yard interception return by Buster Mitchell. Dutch Clark kicked the extra point.

Chicago came back with a TD in the second quarter on a 14-yard Keith Molesworth-to-Eugene Ronzani pass, with Nagurski booting the point after.

The Lions countered with nine points in the quarter, six on a one-yard Gutowsky plunge (Hewitt blocked the kick) and three on a 34-yard Presnell field goal.

The Bears pulled within three points at 16–13 in the third quarter when Jack Manders kicked field goals of 15 and 42 yards. Perhaps frustrated by the lack of second-half points, Presnell took to the air in the final quarter, only to have the outcome crash down with the Hewitt interception.

Macdonell called it a "storybook game (that) challenges the word picture talent of a Damon Runyon."

"It was a heartbreaker for the Lions and their followers," Macdonell wrote, "and with heavy heart today they feast over the crumbs of a game that put the Detroit team out of the running for the championship honors."

Times sports editor Bud Shaver had this to say: "Many Thanksgiving Days will roll into eternity before 26,000 Detroiters will forget that one in which the Chicago Bears knocked the Detroit Lions out of a chance for the National Football League championship at U-D Stadium.

"It was a grand day and as stirring a contest as you will encounter in a lifetime. Everything was perfect except for the final score. The Bears won 19–16. . . . The 26,000 fans filled every inch of space in the Titans' stadium and they came prepared to see Bronko Nagurski behind a giant line rip that

Greg Landry and Detroit struggled in the mud against the 1968 Eagles, 12–0.

(Bottom) O.J. Simpson won the battle — he rushed for an NFL-record 273 yards — but Detroit won the war, 27–14, in the 1976 game.

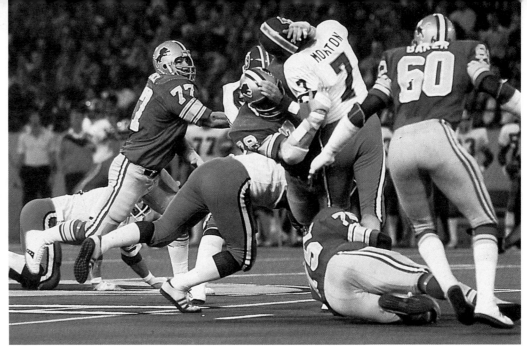

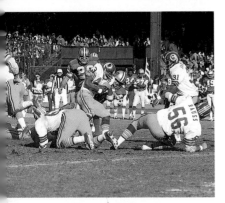

(Top) Bill Munson fought the snow and a strong Viking defense in a 27–0 loss in 1969.

(Middle) Altie Taylor and the Lions ran away from Oakland, 28–14, in 1970.

(Bottom) Larry Hand had a solid performance in 1973's 20–0 loss to Washington.

(Right) The Silver Rush gave Denver the orange crush, 17–14, in 1978.

smaller wall of blue and silver to shreds. Instead they saw the valiant Lions halt the human catapult and force the Bears to take to the air with passes and Jack Manders' placekicks to beat them.

"Bronko Nagurski is supposed to be a great line bucker, and he is all that they say he is. He came down only when two or three Lions were hanging on his legs and shoulders and he didn't stop driving until his face was pressed deep in the sod. But Nagurski, with all of his 230 pounds of driving bone and sinew, wasn't half the line bucker that Ace Gutowsky was yesterday."

The Lions, Shaver was to write more than a week later, "collected not only the customers money, but their whole-hearted loyalty as well. Until the Lions put up their game stand against the Bears, professional football was still just a new big enterprise which had most of Detroit's best wishes, but little else. In their last home game the Lions won them over. They became Detroit's own team . . ."

Detroit lost the season finale in Chicago, 10–7, then the Bears went on to lose the overall championship to the New York Giants, 30–13 — the same team the Lions beat 9–0 September 23 in their first game ever in the Motor City.

With such a memorable first Thanksgiving effort, it would seem difficult for the Lions to match it. But there would be many more such big games over the next six decades. Yet even in mediocre seasons, Thanksgiving in Detroit just wasn't a holiday without a Lions game.

It wasn't uncommon for folks to take their kids to the big Hudson's Parade downtown, then hustle over to Tiger Stadium for the Lions game.

"I feel the Lions' Thanksgiving Day series had a lot to do with the overall popularity of professional football through the years," said the late Russ Thomas in 1985.

"It literally has been a way of life for people in Detroit," added Thomas, the long-time executive vice president and general manager of the team.

Detroit's tradition started becoming a national tradition because of radio. But in 1956, it really kicked in when Green Bay dashed the Lions' title hopes with a 24–20 victory on a late touchdown pass by Tobin Rote in the first nationally televised Thanksgiving Day NFL game.

Because of that and the other Thanksgiving TV games to follow, "The Lions of the '50s became the favorite pro team of fans around the country who had no loyalties to a home pro team," wrote Bruno Kearns, sports editor of the *Pontiac Press,* in a 1980 Lions game program "Pro."

One person with a great perspective of the games is Roy "Friday" Macklem, former Lions equipment manager, who joined the team as an equipment man in 1936 for $25 a week. He had worked at Eastern High School as an equipment aid — the same Eastern High that regularly played on Thanksgiving Day.

"When I started with the Lions I was somewhat used to Thursday football," Macklem said in a 1979 edition of "Pro," discussing what at the time was about to be his 38th Lions Thanksgiving Day game.

"I'm always so busy on game days that I never have had time for the big dinner and all," he said. "I don't really like turkey, anyway.

"Everyone seems to be up for Thanksgiving. I don't know. It's probably the national exposure and the thinking that most of the other teams are watching. I always look forward to it just because the players do."

One of his most memorable Turkey Day games was the so-called "Mud Bowl" in 1968 when Philadelphia's Sam Baker kicked four field goals in a 12–0 Eagles victory at Tiger Stadium. It was the lowest scoring Thanksgiving Day game ever.

One of the ballboys asked Macklem during the game, "Why is it that every time the Eagles kick, they throw in a dry ball from the bench?"

"I said, 'Why didn't you tell me earlier, they're not supposed to do that. Only the home team can supply game balls.' So they (the Lions) were using wet balls the whole game. Philadelphia kicked dry ones."

Wayne Walker, one of the Lions' all-time great linebackers who went on to become a TV sportscaster with the CBS affiliate in San Francisco, also cited that game as his most memorable on Thanksgiving. He played in a Detroit-record 200 games, from 1958 through 1972.

"The mud was ankle deep even before the game started," Walker said, "and Sam Baker made sure the ball was covered with mud before the opening kickoff." That, of course, made it tough on the Lions' return men.

Entering their 60th season the Lions had played 53 Thanksgiving Day games,

(Top) The line gave Rick Kane all the room he needed in Detroit's 1979 blanking over Chicago, 20–0.

(Middle) Doug English was relentless in a 27–10 victory over Kansas City in 1981.

(Bottom) Garry Cobb and the defense put up a good fight against the Giants in 1982, but New York prevailed, 13–6.

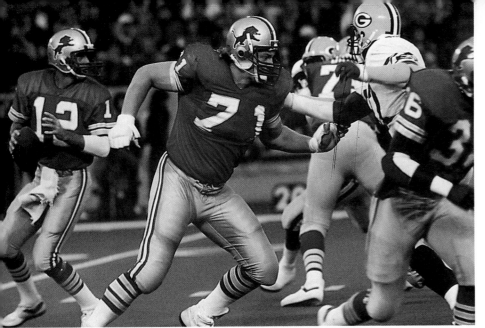

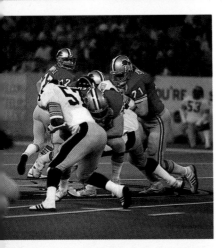

(Top) Joe Ferguson, Rich Strenger, and the rest of the Detroit offense was in high gear against the 1986 Packers — but it wasn't enough, 44-40.

(Middle) The Lions used a combination of power and finesse to throttle Pittsburgh in 1983, 45-3.

(Bottom) James Jones had no room to run against Minnesota in 1988, 23-0.

winning 26, losing 25, and tying two. They've appeared before 2,747,723 spectators — an average of 51,844. They've outscored opponents 1,086 to 1,049. There have been 13 games decided by six points or fewer, with seven by three or fewer. Detroit is 5-6-2 in the close games.

Their first five games were at U-D, then they moved to Briggs (now Tiger) Stadium. In 1975, the Lions made their Pontiac Silverdome debut. Tiger Stadium could hold close to 58,000 for football. Silverdome capacity is 80,494.

So today the game can be enjoyed by so many more spectators. The 24-21 loss to Houston in 1992, for instance, drew 73,711. The poorest turnout in the series was for a game against the Boston Yanks at Briggs Stadium in 1946, the year Detroit had a 1-10 record. Only 13,010 showed up for that contest.

Houston's visit was the Oilers' first to Detroit on Thanksgiving Day. The Oilers were the Lions' 21st opponent in the series. The Packers lead with 15 games and the Bears have played in 12, with No. 13 coming during Detroit's 60th season.

Vince Lombardi, legendary coach of the Packers during their championship years in the '60s, did not like to have his team go up against Detroit on Thanksgiving Day.

"He said it was an unfair advantage to the Lions," recalled former star Detroit end Ron Kramer, who had played with Green Bay. "The Packers would lose a day traveling and hardly have any time to prepare for the game. There were only three days anyway, but the Lions were the home team and always had more time."

Here's a rundown of some of the other significant games in the Thanksgiving Day series, which was suspended from 1939 through 1944 due to World War II:

1935 Lions get revenge over 19-16 loss of first Thanksgiving Day game a year earlier by clinching the division title with a 14-2 victory over Chicago. Detroit goes on to beat the New York Giants 26-7 for its first championship.

1945 Bob Waterfield passes for 329 yards, 303 of them to Jim Benton, to guide the Cleveland/Los Angeles Rams to a 28-21 triumph.

1947 Sid Luckman passes for 383 yards in the snow to lead the Bears over Detroit 34-14 before 29,446.

1948 The Chicago Cardinals use their 28-14 decision to help send them to a 11-1 season and a West championship ahead of their inter-city rival Bears, who finish 10-2.

1949 The Bears win 28-7, but Bob Smith scores the lone Lions TD with a 102-yard interception return, which remains a Detroit record.

1950 Detroit gets the New York Giants and New York Yanks to swap home dates, preserving the Thankgiving Day game, won by the Lions over the Yanks, 49-14.

1951 Jack Christiansen returns punts 89 and 72 yards for touchdowns and Bobby Layne throws three TD passes in 52-35 Lions victory in the first of 13 consecutive Thanksgiving Day games against Green Bay. It is the highest scoring game in the series.

1952 The Lions take over first place in the conference for good with a 48-24 decision over the Packers. Detroit wins the title over the Cleveland Browns 17–7 after a 31–21 divisional playoff victory over Los Angeles.

1953 Enroute to its second successive NFL championship, Detroit overcomes a 15–7 Green Bay halftime lead to win 34–15, keyed by a 97-yard Layne to Cloyce Box touchdown pass.

1954 The Lions again beat the Packers, 28–24, before 55,532. Layne, though, throws his 100th and 101st career TD passes and Christiansen had two TD returns: An interception for 30 yards and a punt for 61 yards.

1956 Tobin Rote erases Detroit's title hopes by passing the Packers to a 24–20 victory in the first Thanksgiving Day game on national television. Detroit would become "America's Team" long before the Dallas Cowboys would appropriate that tag.

1957 Although the Lions lose to San Francisco 24–10, they wind up tied with the 49ers for the division lead and defeat them in a playoff game 31–27, then go on to crush the Browns 59–14 in the title matchup.

1962 This is the famed "grudge match" in which the Lions defeat Green Bay 26–14 as the "Fearsome Foursome" of Darris McCord, Alex Karras, Roger Brown and Sam Williams thrill the crowd of 57,598 — and 32 million television viewers — by sacking Bart Starr 11 times, snapping the Packers' 10-game winning streak. It avenges a 9–7 loss at Green Bay earlier in the season which came on Paul Hornung's field goal with 27 seconds left.

1963 The Lions' 13–13 tie with Green Bay proves to be the game that knocks the Packers out of the West title by a half game behind Chicago.

1970 Detroit scores 14 fourth-quarter points to knock off the Oakland Raiders 28–14.

1975 In the first Thanksgiving Day game in the Silverdome, Detroit is blanked by the Rams 20–0.

1976 Buffalo's O.J. Simpson sets an NFL rushing record with 273 yards, but the Lions come out 27–14 winners over the Bills.

1977 The Bears win 31–14 as Walter Payton runs for 137 yards, totals 107 yards in receptions and scores two TDs.

1978 Doug English sacks Denver's Craig Morton four times in a 17–14 victory over the defending American Conference champion Broncos.

1979 Detroit hands the Bears their only loss in eight weeks with a 20–0 decision, the Lions' first (and only) shutout in the Thanksgiving Day series. Opponents have shut out Detroit seven times.

1980 Vince Evans scores on the last play of regulation for Chicago, then Dave Williams returns the overtime-opening kickoff 95 yards for a touchdown as the Bears win 23–17. It is the only overtime game in the holiday series and the shortest overtime game in NFL history — 21 seconds.

(Top) The Chiefs upended Pete Mandley and the Lions in 1987, 27–20.

(Above) Jerry Ball and Detroit stopped Cleveland in 1989, 13–10.

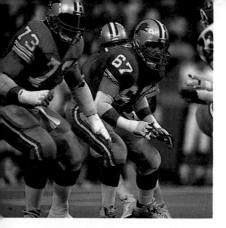

(Top) Harvey Salem and Ken Dallafior helped pave the way for a 40–27 win over the Broncos in 1990.

(Right) Barry and buddies burned the Bears, 16–6, in the 1991 contest.

1982 Billy Sims rushes for more than 100 yards, but a 97-yard interception return by linebacker Lawrence Taylor for a TD leads the Giants to a 13–6 victory.

1983 The Lions crush Pittsburgh 45–3 as Dexter Bussey passes the 5,000-yard career rushing mark for a briefly-held Lions record. Robbie Martin has an 81-yard punt return for a TD against his old team. It is the series' most lopsided victory.

1984 Green Bay, in its first Thanksgiving Day game since 1963, loses for the only time in its final eight games, 31–28, as Gary Danielson brings the Lions from behind with a 305-yard, three-TD passing day, including two to tight end David Lewis.

1985 Eric Hipple throws four touchdown passes (three to Leonard Thompson) to lead the Lions past the playoff-bound New York Jets 31–20. Ken O'Brien of the Jets is sacked seven times.

1986 Walter Stanley returns a punt 85 yards for a TD with 41 seconds remaining to give the Packers a 44–40 triumph.

1989 Rookie Barry Sanders rushes for 145 yards in a 13–10 upset of heavily-favored Cleveland in the 50th Thanksgiving game.

1992 Sanders, only in his fourth season, gets his 50th career touchdown, but the Lions lose to Houston 24–21 before 73,711.

What lies ahead in the series? Undoubtedly there will be more big games and historic moments. With Thanksgiving coming when it does, seasons often can be made or broken at that time of year.

"I think a lot of guys looked forward to those games just so they could have the days off," Macklem said. "But we always had a lot of fun, except when I had to stay behind and dig mud out of everybody's shoes."

With the Silverdome home, though, that's not a problem anymore. The biggest problem, for fans and players alike, probably is the same one that's been around for 60 years: planning a Thanksgiving dinner that won't get underway until it's dark outside and stomachs are growl'n'. ❖

Milt Plum led the Lions against the Colts in 1965.

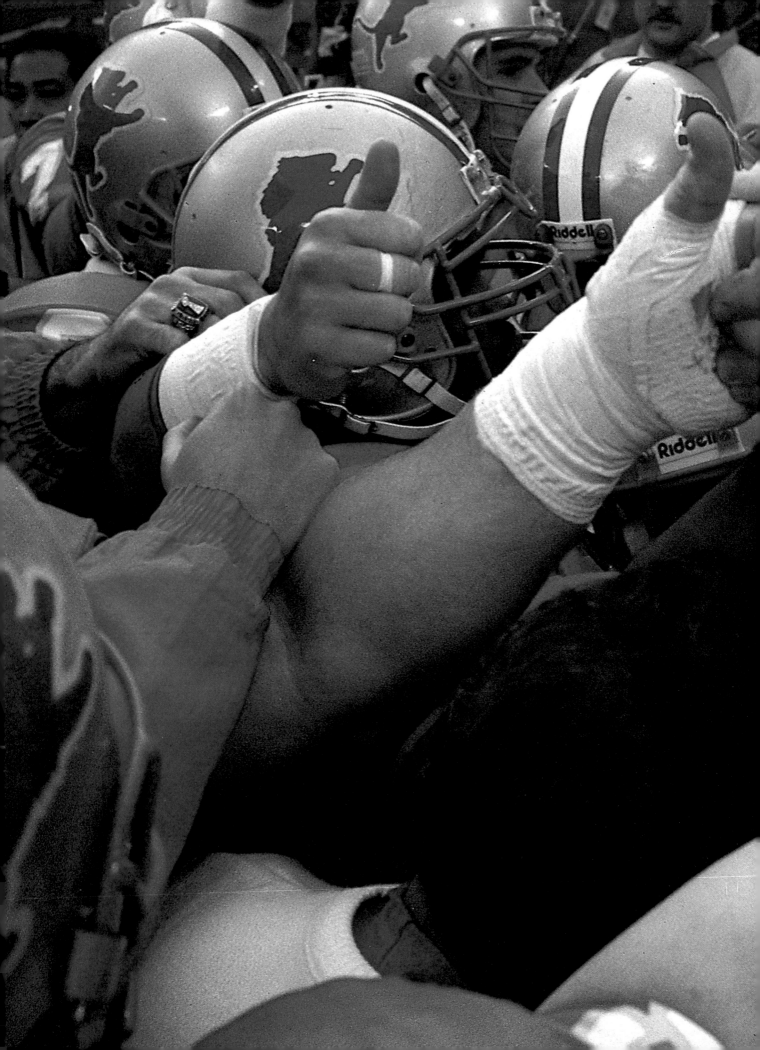

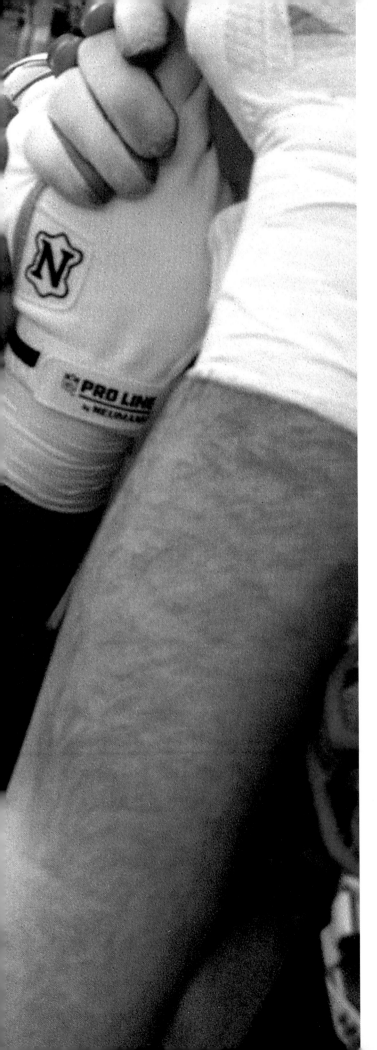

8

"You either get sick of losing or you get used to it. We got sick of it."

— Barry Sanders
Running Back, 1991

The Lions rallied behind their "Thumbs Up" battle cry to post a club-record 12 regular season wins in 1991.

Roar Restored

The Lions claimed the 1991 Central Division crown and advanced to the NFC title game for the first time in club history.

by Chuck Klonke

It didn't start out like the Lions' most memorable season in more than three decades.

In fact, the 1991 NFL season began like a nightmare for Detroit with a 45–0 thrashing by the Washington Redskins, but by the time it ended — with another loss to Washington in the NFC championship game — the roar had been restored.

"If you want to label it something, you would have to label it a Cinderella year," said Wayne Fontes, who guided the Lions to a 12–4 regular-season record, the NFC Central Division championship and an impressive 38–6 playoff victory over the Dallas Cowboys before a packed house at the Silverdome.

"It was a year in which the underdog won. It was a year where everything seemed to go well for us. We got the right bounces. We had a tremendous amount of adversity, but we seemed to flourish through the adversity.

"It was a year filled with tremendous ups and downs," Fontes continued, "nothing more catastrophic than losing a guy like Mike Utley. Through his injury this team grew; it became a closer team. We became an unselfish team. This team drew strength from Mike's tremendous courage."

Utley, who was developing into one of the finest young offensive linemen in the NFL, suffered a career-ending spinal injury when he fell awkwardly on his head during the second half of the Lions' 21–10 victory over the Los Angeles Rams on November 17. The injury came on an 11-yard touchdown pass from Erik Kramer to Robert Clark which turned out to be the winning score.

Detroit held on to its lead and went on to win the final six games of the regular season, spurred on by the "thumbs up" signal Utley gave his teammates as he was wheeled off the field on a stretcher.

The Lions' streak continued in their first playoff game since 1983. Dallas and Detroit were both up-and-coming young clubs. The Cowboys had improved from a 1–15 record two years earlier. The Lions had finished 6–10 in 1990, but there was no question which was the better team on January 5, 1992.

Dallas Coach Jimmy Johnson came into the game with a plan to

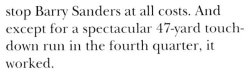

stop Barry Sanders at all costs. And except for a spectacular 47-yard touchdown run in the fourth quarter, it worked.

The net result of the strategy, however, proved fatal for the Cowboys.

While concentrating their efforts on Sanders, the Cowboys' defense ignored receivers Willie Green and Herman Moore and quarterback Kramer, who engineered the Lions to victories in those last six regular season games as the replacement for the injured Rodney Peete.

Kramer completed 29 of 38 passes for 341 yards and three touchdowns. He opened the scoring with a 31-yard scoring strike to Green, then hit Green for a nine-yarder and Moore for a seven-yard touchdown in the third quarter.

Detroit's other touchdown came on a 41-yard interception return by cornerback Melvin Jenkins. All Dallas could

muster was a pair of field goals by Ken Willis.

The performance was especially satisfying for Kramer, who had taken verbal abuse from some of the Cowboys during the week preceding the game.

"They just didn't give us any respect, but that isn't something you worry about," Kramer said. "You have to just let it roll off your back.

"This is the way the Run 'n' Shoot is supposed to work," he continued. "The rush was never there and there were (passing) lanes open on every play."

Sanders might have summed up the Lions' dream season the best.

"You either get sick of losing or you get used to it. We got sick of it," he said.

Some of the magic wore off the following week on the return visit to Washington, but the Redskins, who would beat Buffalo in the Super Bowl a week later, had a lot to do with it. Washington made Kramer hurry nearly

(Top) Quarterback Erik Kramer embodied the Lions' 1991 season, rising from relative obscurity to national prominence.

(Bottom) Brett Perriman led the Lions with 62 catches for 668 yards in '91. He had five receptions in the title game.

(Left) Dan Owens sends a message to Dallas quarterback Troy Aikman: "Not this year."

(Top) Melvin Jenkins' 41-yard interception return for a touchdown broke open a close game against Dallas.

(Bottom) Washington's veteran defense kept Kramer on the run as the Redskins registered five sacks. Still, Kramer completed 21 of 33 passes for 249 yards.

(Right) Bennie Blades helped keep Washington's offense in check for the first half, but the 'Skins exploded for 24 points after intermission to advance to Super Bowl XXVI.

Mike Utley's "Thumbs Up" became the rally cry for the 1991 Lions.

all his throws and the Redskins' first two scores were gifts from the defense.

The fans had barely settled in their seats when Charles Mann sacked Kramer and forced a fumble that Fred Stokes recovered at the Lions' 11. Two plays later, Gerald Riggs went in from the two.

The next time Detroit had the football, linebacker Kurt Gouveia intercepted Kramer's pass and returned it 38 yards to set up a field goal by Chip Lohmiller that gave Washington a 10–0 lead.

Detroit made some adjustments to give Kramer more time to throw and during one stretch in the second quarter he completed 10 straight passes, including an 18-yard scoring strike to Green.

Riggs scored on another short burst to give Washington a 17–7 lead, but Eddie Murray's 30-yard field goal late in the half closed the gap to 17–10 at halftime.

The second half belonged to the Redskins. Lohmiller kicked a 28-yard field goal early in the third quarter and

quarterback Mark Rypien, who completed 12 of 17 passes for 228 yards, fired a 45-yard touchdown pass to Gary Clark. Rypien also hit Art Monk for a 21-yard touchdown in the fourth quarter and cornerback Darrell Green capped the scoring with a 32-yard interception return.

Although they were disappointed that their season came to an end, the Lions gave credit where it was due.

"They're a great team," said linebacker Chris Spielman. "They were the better team this year. It's hard for me to face that, but they were."

The young Lions had come a long way since that early September night when Washington built a 21–0 first-quarter lead and coasted to a 45–0 victory. Detroit didn't have Barry Sanders that night, so the Lions managed only nine first downs and 154 total yards.

Sanders was back in action the next week when Detroit returned to the Silverdome to face the Green Bay Packers and it didn't take long for him

to make his presence felt. On the Lions' first possession of the game they put together a 16-play, 83-yard drive that took more than 10 minutes. Sanders scored on a four-yard run, capping the longest drive in more than 15 years for the Lions.

Peete completed a career-high 25 passes in 38 attempts for 271 yards. Ten of those fell into the hands of Clark, who gained 143 yards despite one broken finger, another dislocated one and ligament damage to several other digits.

The Lions were on their way.

A goal-line stand with less than five minutes remaining when Miami had a first down at the Detroit three, assured the Lions of a 17–13 victory over Dolphins in Week 3.

Sanders carried the ball a career-high 32 times for 143 yards and nine of those rushes went for first downs. Peete passed 26 yards to Green for one

touchdown and ran six yards for the second.

Week 4 brought the Lions their third straight victory as Sanders rushed for 179 yards and two touchdowns and Indianapolis had a franchise-low four net yards as Detroit posted a 33–24 victory over the Colts.

Tampa Bay was the streaking Lions' next victim. Sanders had 160 yards and three touchdowns in a 31–3 rout of the Buccaneers in Week 5. Detroit's defense forced four turnovers and the Lions didn't allow a touchdown for the first time in 45 games.

The Lions boosted their record to 5–1 in Week 6 with one of the greatest comebacks in club history. Trailing Minnesota 20–3 with less than seven minutes left, Detroit scored three touchdowns in 6:14 to win 24–20. The winning touchdown was a twisting, darting 15-yard dash by Sanders with 36 seconds left in the game.

(Above) The Lions were Dome-inating in 1991 as the only team in the NFL to finish a perfect 8–0 at home.

(Top) In the victorious Detroit locker room, Wayne Fontes presents the game ball to owner and president William Clay Ford.

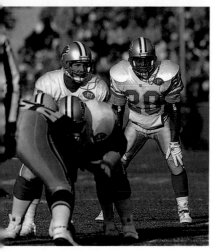

(Top) Chris Spielman and William White sacked quarterback Steve Young, but the Niners walked away with an easy 35–3 win.

(Bottom) The Packers keyed on Kramer and Sanders, holding Detroit to just 14 first downs at Lambeau Field, but the Lions made enough big plays to win.

(Right) The Lions' defense couldn't stop Tampa's Reggie Cobb, who ran for a career-best 139 yards and three touchdowns. Detroit slipped to 6–4, but the loss would be the team's last of the regular season.

"The fourth quarter by this football team is the finest football I've ever been associated with in my life," Fontes said. "When you ask me someday what I remember, I'll remember this comeback. It was a thing of beauty to see on the sidelines. It touched all our hearts."

Owner William Clay Ford was as excited as his coaches and players.

"I didn't think about giving up, but I wouldn't have given too great of odds," Ford said.

The Lions were on a roll, but the new NFL schedule forced them to take the next week off and it didn't look like the same team when they traveled to San Francisco and lost 35–3 to the 49ers. Sanders was held to 26 yards in seven carries and Detroit controlled the ball for less than 15 minutes.

In some ways, that defeat was harder to swallow than the opening game loss to Washington.

"That one wasn't this bad. We're a better team right now," Fontes said. "We didn't have the same fire we had in previous games. We just got an old-fashioned butt-kicking."

The players were confident they could bounce back.

"If we respond like we did after the Washington game, we'll be all right," said nose tackle Jerry Ball.

They were just fine the next week when the Dallas Cowboys visited the Silverdome. For the first time since 1971, the Lions' offense, defense and special teams each scored a touchdown as Detroit rolled to a 34–10 victory.

The triumph was a costly one, however, as Peete suffered a ruptured Achilles' tendon and was lost for the season. Kramer, a free agent pickup who spent the entire 1990 season on the injured list, stepped in and completed nine of 16 passes for 108 yards, including touchdown passes of 26 yards to Green and 10 yards to Sanders.

"That takes away from a great win," Fontes said of the injury to Peete. "Rodney has been doing a great job."

Kramer and Peete had become close friends during their competition for the starting job and now that Kramer was No. 1 for the rest of the season, he wasn't especially happy.

"It's not even a mixed feeling," he said. "I feel bad all the way around, but I also feel a sense of responsibility; that I've got to keep my end of the bargain."

The Lions had heard rumblings that during their winning streak they had beaten some of the weaker teams in the league. The win over the Cowboys silenced some of the critics.

"That stuff about beating weak teams

is a crock," said defensive end Marc Spindler, who blocked a 47-yard field goal attempt that William White returned 55 yards for a touchdown and recovered quarterback Troy Aikman's fumble to set up Murray's second field goal of the game.

Fontes bristled when someone suggested that the Cowboys had played poorly.

"You make your own turnovers," he said. "They didn't just drop the ball on the ground. They were hit. They didn't give us the interceptions. We made them."

The Lions stumbled a bit the next two weeks while they were adjusting to their new quarterback. Chicago won the battle for first place in the NFC Central, 20–10, on a frigid afternoon at Soldier Field.

The next week Tampa Bay's Reggie Cobb ran for a career-high 139 yards and a club-record three touchdowns as

the Buccaneers beat the Lions, 30–21. Sanders had his fifth 100-yard rushing game of the season and receiver Brett Perriman, obtained in a trade with New Orleans shortly before the season opened, had the first 100-yard receiving game of his pro career with six catches for 127 yards.

The Lions needed a return home, where they were unbeaten, and got it in the tragedy-marred victory over Los Angeles.

During the next week, the players and coaches made a silent pact that they "would get the job done," for Utley, who had been such an inspiration to his teammates.

Sanders exploded for a team-record 220 yards rushing and four touchdowns in a 34–14 romp over the Vikings in Minnesota.

"We wanted to win this game for Mike Utley," Fontes said after Detroit had boosted its record to 8–4.

(Above) Rodney Peete engineered one of the greatest comebacks in club history against Minnesota. Trailing 20–3 in the fourth quarter, the Lions scored three touchdowns in the final seven minutes to claim a 24–20 win.

(Top) The Lions congratulate Barry Sanders after one of his team-record four rushing touchdowns — coming on a record 220 yards — at Minnesota.

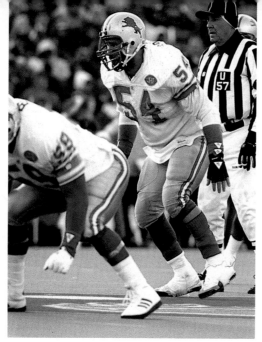

(Left) Willie Green was the "Touchdown Machine" for the 1991 Lions, catching seven TD passes during the season and another three in the playoffs.

(Bottom left) Center Kevin Glover and guard Eric Andolsek were among the Lions who helped Detroit out-muscle Chicago, 16–6, on Thanksgiving Day.

(Middle) Chris Spielman recorded a career-high 18 tackles in Detroit's 17–14 overtime win at Buffalo. That victory, combined with Chicago's loss at San Francisco the following night, secured the NFC Central Division crown and a first-round bye in the playoffs.

(Right) Mel Gray's 78-yard punt return for a touchdown provided the winning points at Green Bay. The win over the Packers clinched Detroit's first playoff berth since 1983.

The quest continued on Thanksgiving Day as the Lions beat Chicago 16–6 and moved into a tie with the Bears for first place in the division. Murray kicked three field goals and Kramer hit Clark with a nine-yard pass for the only touchdown of the game.

It marked the first time since 1970, when the Lions closed out the season with five straight victories to finish 10–4, that the team had a 9–4 record.

On December 8, Detroit completed its first undefeated home season since 1962 with a 34–20 victory over the New York Jets that featured two touchdowns by Sanders and five turnovers by the Jets. The Lions broke a 14–14 tie with a 73-yard touchdown pass from Kramer to Green in the second quarter.

Detroit clinched its first playoff berth since 1983 on an icy Lambeau Field in Green Bay with a 21–17 victory over the Packers. The Lions took the lead early in the fourth quarter on a three-yard touchdown pass to Clark and Mel Gray clinched the victory when he returned a punt 78 yards for a touchdown.

It took overtime on the final weekend of the regular season for Detroit to snap Buffalo's 17-game home winning streak with a 17–14 win over the Bills. The winning points came on a 23-yard field goal by Murray 4:23 into the extra period.

The Lions watched with glee the following night as San Francisco crushed the Bears 52–14 to assure Detroit of the NFC Central title.

The quest to "get the job done" was complete. The combination of Fontes' hugging, back-patting and cheerleading and the closeness that came from Utley's injury provided the emotional lift the team needed.

"I've never seen a team like this that could rally around and care so much for one guy," said cornerback Ray Crockett. "You can't imagine or begin to explain the way a team can come together and unite into one group of people."

Punter Jim Arnold, who dropped 27 of his punts inside the 20-yard line, summed up the season by comparing it to a popular television series.

"We kind of Star Trekked this one," he said. "We went where nobody thought we could go. It's been a heckuva ride." ❖

(Right) Barry Sanders received the Maxwell Football Club's Pro Player of the Year Award.

(Inset) Wayne Fontes won universal praise as the NFL's Coach of the Year. 7B

9

Sixty-seasons worth of interesting and semi-interesting Notes, Quotes, Facts and Figures . . . all from the Lions' Den.

Jimmy Allen (right) was assisted by James Hunter (left) and tight end David Hill in the Lions' version of "Another One Bites the Dust."

Lion Tales

Notes, clips and quips
from six Lion decades.

by Dan Arthur

Graham T. Overgard's
"Gridiron Heroes."

Forty-five players reported to the Lions' first training camp in Detroit. Head Coach Potsy Clark trimmed the roster to the league limit of 25 players three weeks later, before the first regular season game. In 1993, NFL teams will be permitted to carry 53 players on their active roster.

• Question: Where were the first offices of the Detroit Lions located? Answer: Shortly after the club's move from Portsmouth to Detroit, Lions owner G.A. Richards — who also owned radio station WJR — set up head coach George "Potsy" Clark with a temporary office in room 2107 of the Fisher Building. WJR's offices are on the 21st floor, where today Potsy's first place of business is part of a bigger conference area.

• According to the August 19, 1934, edition of the *Detroit Times*, Detroit obtained a new player from the Detroit Zoo. The headline read "Tired of Sissy Games, Jo Mendi Joins Lions." The famous Chimpanzee was dressed in a Lions' uniform — jersey No. 0 — and given a football. (No, he never made it past training camp . . .)

• Detroit's mascots for their inaugural season were two Lion cubs named "Grid" and "Iron"; They were donated by the Detroit Zoo.

• Detroit's first head coach, Potsy Clark, praised quarterback Dutch Clark (no relation) for his great leadership abilities. "They (the players) never question any play he calls; they regard him as infallible," Potsy once said. "This confidence is not misplaced. I have never known Dutch to criticize any player. Anytime a play goes wrong he takes the entire blame, regardless of who is responsible."

Potsy Clark said Dutch Clark once played outfield on a baseball team with Hall of Fame pitcher Grover Cleveland Alexander, who told Clark where to play a hitter during one crucial part of a game. Clark didn't make the adjustment, and a scratch double was hit to that spot to win the game for the opponent.

Clark apologized to Alexander, who, Potsy Clark related, said to Dutch: "'Naw, it was my fault. I pitched him the wrong ball.'"

"I could always understand why teams played a lot harder behind Alexander than they played behind other pitchers," Potsy said, "and it's the same with quarterbacks."

• The Lions were instrumental in Detroit earning the label "City of Champions" in 1935–36. The Lions won the NFL Championship; the Detroit Red Wings won the National League title and the Stanley Cup; the Detroit Olympics won the International League championship and the Teddy Oke Trophy; and the Detroit Tigers won the 1935 World Series. In addition, Joe Louis, the world heavyweight champion, and Gar Wood, the undisputed "King of Speed" on water, were just two of several local athletes who excelled individually in 1935–36.

• Head Coach George "Potsy" Clark urged his players to run barefoot prior to the start of training camp, hoping the players' feet would become tough enough to absorb the pain caused by new shoes.

• In a letter sent to his players before the start of the 1937 training camp, Head Coach Earl "Dutch" Clark urged his players to get as much sun as possible, but to stay out of the water. "Every player will be expected to report with a good coat of tan over his whole body," wrote Clark. "Swimming is not a good conditioning exercise."

• As the new pro football franchise took root in Detroit, owner G.A. Richards called for an original fight song to be written for the Lions. In the late 1930s, Wayne State University director of bands Graham T. Overgard, who was also the Lions' director of entertainment, penned the lyrics and music for "Gridiron Heroes — The Victory Song of the Detroit Lions." The big marching band sound of "Gridiron Heroes" has become one of the NFL's oldest and most popular fight songs; today, it is still played after each Lions' score at the Silverdome.

"Gridiron Heroes"

(Verse) Hail the colors Blue and Silver let them wave. Sing their song and cheer the Gridiron Heroes brave, Fighting for fame, winning the game, Dashing to victory as they go.

(Chorus) Forward down the field, A charging team that will not yield. And when the Blue and Silver wave, Stand and cheer the brave, Rah, Rah, Rah! Go hard win the game. With honor you will keep your fame. Down the field and gain, A Lion victory!

You probably know them best as the Lion, Lion Cub, and "Huddles" on the Detroit sideline, but the team's mascots have a true family tradition which dates back many years. Dan Baker (far right) has served as the Lion mascot for 20 years, roaming the sidelines in 1960 and '61 and every season since 1975. It is a job previously held by both his father, William (1934–59), and brother, Bill (1962–74). Currently (at least while they still fit the uniform), his sons Brian and K.C. alternate as the Lion Cub on the sidelines. Relative newcomer Jeff Melinat (far left) becomes his alter-ego "Huddles" on football Sundays at the Silverdome.

(Above) Running mates? President Nixon with Lions quarterback Greg Landry.

(Right) A photo from the 1963 training camp. That season, these six Detroit Lions totaled 66 years of NFL experience with Jim Martin (#47) heading the list with 13, Dick "Night Train" Lane (#81) with 12, Harley Sewell (#66) with 11, Joe Schmidt (#56) with 11, Yale Lary (#28) with 10, and Darris McCord (#78) with 9.

Normally, you'd only see this combination standing together once in a . . .

Direct from the archives of the Detroit Lions . . . a photo of the 1943 team with special notations indicating those players who were called to military service before the '44 season.

• Prior to the 1941 season, the Lions devised a numbering system for the players so fans would have an easier time of identifying the players. The following number classifications were used:

Wingbacks	10 – 19
Blocking backs	20 – 29
Fullbacks	30 – 39
Tailbacks	40 – 49
Centers	50 – 59
Guards	60 – 69
Tackles	70 – 79
Ends	80 – 89

Following Detroit's lead, a similar numbering system was later put into use on a league-wide basis by the NFL.

• During the 1930s and 1940s, it was common for an injured player to stumble to his feet and then stagger to the sidelines and collapse. The players believed they were displaying their courage. Dr. C.L. Tomsu, the Lions' team doctor in 1941, thought other-wise. After Lloyd Cardwell ran off the field with a fractured fibula, Tomsu ordered the ritual to end. "Players hurt will be carried or helped from the field," Tomsu said. "We have stretchers on hand and we'll see they reach the dressing room safely and there determine the extent of their injuries."

• Owners moved the annual college draft from December to April in 1942. At this time, the owners would have a better idea of which players would be available to the NFL. The league was losing many players at this time to active service in the military.

• During the early days of professional football, the sport was unstable and its future was uncertain, at best. It wasn't always known where the money was going to come from, and players insisted on being paid before they played. Former Detroit coach Alvin "Bo" McMillin liked to tell the story of the day he played in Milwaukee and was upset by a hard tackle.

"The boys looked down at me and figured I'd broken my leg," said McMillin. "There was a big bulge on my leg and it looked like the bone was sticking right out. It wasn't, though. I'd been paid with 100 one-dollar bills. I was afraid to leave it in the clubhouse, so I stuck it down in my stocking."

An annual occurrence at training camp was the "Photo Day" session when special publicity pictures were taken. Here is a photo of tackle Roger Brown flying through the air at the Lions' 1966 camp at Cranbrook, and a look behind the scenes to see how the photo was staged.

(Below) 20–20 Vision? These officials had the Lions seeing double.

Lifelong friend Bobby Layne (right) was on hand to celebrate Doak Walker's induction into the Pro Football Hall of Fame in 1986.

• Detroit star players Bobby Layne and Doak Walker began their friendship long before they played for the Lions. Layne and Walker grew up only a few blocks apart in Dallas, Texas, and were friends as children. They both started in the backfield at Highland Park High School in 1943. After stints in the military during World War II, Layne went to Texas University while Walker played for rival Southern Methodist University. Layne and Walker joined the Lions in 1950 as the two friends were reunited.

• Bobby Layne was master of the setup. He might run two plays to set up one. Or several series just to sucker the defense for a particular pattern. An example:

Championship game, 1953. Cleveland leading, 16–10. Four minutes to go. Detroit ball, Lions' 20.

"Awright fellers," Layne says in the huddle, "y'all block and ol' Bobby'll pass you raht to the championship. Ol' Bobby'll get you six big ones."

Layne completes four of six passes including surprising strikes to Jim Doran, a defensive specialist whom Layne knows is always open when he spells big Leon Hart at end.

Doran, playing defense, had two key sacks on Cleveland quarterback Otto Graham in the 1952 game. Now, Hart is hurt and Doran comes in to replace him.

Layne hits Doran three times in the drive, the last time for 33 yards and the winning touchdown.

• Money meant little to legendary QB Bobby Layne, who was always buying dinner, drinks or helping friends and teammates in trouble.

"In 1954 we had just finished training camp," said Lions' tackle Gil "The Hoss" Mains. "Bobby and I were standing outside (the team hotel) waiting for a cab.

"Bobby always had several $100 bills. He was sorting his money and found a $1 bill. 'How the hell did this $1 bill get in there?' he said, and threw it down on the street. I ran over and picked it up. I had $2 in my pocket."

Cab drivers and waiters used to hover around Layne, who had no moths in his wallet.

"I used to say that I want to come back in another life as Bobby's cab driver," his wife, Carol, said, "because he tips so well. I used to say that. And Don Meredith stole it."

• Dick "Night Train" Lane played in the All-Star game following the 1961 season

"Paper Lion" was a hit with Detroit fans. Alan Alda, as George Plimpton, finds his new helmet is a tight squeeze. The real Plimpton reads excerpts from his best-selling book to the Lions during a break at training camp.

Separated at birth? It's easy to see why sports fans in the 1960s may have confused Lions linebacker Wayne Walker and New York Rangers captain Bob Nevin. Walker is the man on the right . . . I think.

despite suffering appendicitis. He played through the pain, scoring the first touchdown for the Western All-Stars on a 42-yard interception return. He underwent an appendectomy two days later.

• Former Lion quarterbacks Fred Enke and Karl Sweetan have an interesting connection. Both were drafted by Detroit and both eventually started at quarterback for the Lions; Enke was drafted and started in 1949, and Sweetan was drafted in '64 and started in 1966. Amazingly, in the 16 years separating the two quarterbacks, the Lions never started a quarterback they had drafted. Detroit starters from 1950–65 — Bobby Layne, Tobin Rote, Earl Morrall, Jim Ninowski, Milt Plum and George Izo — were all acquired by the Lions through trades or as free agents. In fact, the Lions drafted few quarterbacks in the era. Jack Kemp and Warren Rabb were cut while Pete Beathard, John Hadl and Eddie Wilson were lost to the American Football League. Sweetan and Tommy Myers, a 1965 pick, were with the team in 1966.

• Filming of the George Plimpton book, "Paper Lion," began in early 1968. Alan Alda starred as Plimpton, the *Sports Illustrated* feature writer who masqueraded as a quarterback with the Lions during training camp. The world premier was held Thursday, October 3, 1968, at the Adams Theater. The film introduced Lauren Hutton to the silver screen, and featured actual members of the Detroit Lions, including coach Joe Schmidt, Alex Karras, John Gordy, Mike Lucci, Pat Studstill, and Roger Brown. To this day, current Lions head trainer Kent Falb still receives an annual residuals check for his extensive role ("Next!") in the United Artists' motion picture.

• Detroit rookie tight end Charlie Sanders checked into his first training camp with the Lions at 230 pounds, 28 pounds heavier than his sophomore season at Minnesota. The Gophers wanted to switch Sanders from flanker to defensive end his junior season. He responded by lifting weights and consuming an extra 4,000 calories a day in malted milks, bulking up to 232 pounds. Sanders, still athletic despite the extra weight, shifted back to tight end his senior season and led the team with 276 yards and two touchdowns on 21 receptions.

• Greg Landry impressed President Richard Nixon while Landry led the Lions on their playoff march in 1970. Nixon called Landry a "great quarterback" and remembered him as "big, good looking and personable" from a meeting three years earlier when Nixon was running for President and Landry was a campus leader at the University of Massachusetts.

• After 40 years, Blanche Verhougstraete retired as the Lions' mascot in 1977. The 4′5″ typesetter with a Detroit firm began her duties as the Lions' mascot in 1938 at 10 years of age.

• Mike Lucci's Hollywood career didn't end with "Paper Lion." The Detroit linebacker played a gang member in the 1973 film "Motown 9000." In the movie, Lucci is shot and killed by a police sharpshooter.

• Head Coach Monte Clark wanted to surround himself with rough, mean players, and he believed Al "Bubba" Baker fit the mold.

"Floyd Peters, my defensive line coach, saw Al Baker on a bridge feeding the fish," Clark once said. "Floyd said, 'Oh, gee, what kind of defensive lineman did we draft? Some kind of softie?'

"Then all of a sudden, Al reaches into the water, pulls out a plum of a fish, and tries to kill it. Floyd said, 'Then I knew we had a good one.'"

• On May 26, 1979, the Lions conducted their version of the "Gong Show." The team held a one-shot workout for players that were not drafted. Of the 93 participants, only wide receiver John Arnold was signed. He played for the team from 1979–80.

• In 1980, Jimmy "Spiderman" Allen and James "Hound Dog" Hunter recorded a remake of Queen's popular hit, "Another One Bites the Dust," and the song topped the charts in the Detroit area as the Lions raced out to a 5–1 start. Unfortunately, the club lost

six of their next eight contests and finished second to Minnesota in the NFC Central with a 9–7 mark.

• If you were to create a "Detroit Lions Years of Service" chart, you'd have to write Roy "Friday" Macklem's name at the top of the list. Macklem joined the Lions' staff as equipment manager in 1936, and retired in 1981 after 45 years with the club. The Lions' man Friday worked 40 Thanksgiving Day games. "Just about every Thanksgiving game had its share of miserable weather," Macklem once said of the many Turkey Day battles at Briggs (Tiger) Stadium. "One game, during the early years, was played in a temperature about 5 below zero. It was always cold. You know, the

Lions executive vice president Chuck Schmidt and NFL commissioner Paul Tagliabue reached new heights in 1991.

(Above) Billy Sims (left) was the first to congratulate Barry Sanders when the Lions' rookie rushing record was set . . . and broken.

(Right) Opponents in the 1970s didn't drive the lane very often when playing the Detroit Lions basketball team.

(Top) In 1975, the Lions named their new practice field at the Silverdome in honor of senior vice president Edwin J. Anderson. A commemorative plaque was presented to Anderson in appreciation for his 27 years of service to the club.

(Bottom) The Lions have had many colorful players over the years, just ask Stan and Curtis. The 1992 team, in fact, featured a Brown (Lomas), Green (Willie), White (William) and Gray (Mel).

players used to use linament to keep warm. This was before the electric heaters. But the guys would rub linament on all exposed areas and it would keep them warm. I don't know why they couldn't use it now, even. Those electric heaters can't go out on the field with you."

• If you thought the similarities between Presidents Lincoln and Kennedy were eerie, then you should find the Sims-Sanders connection downright frightening. Billy Sims (initials B.S.) and Barry Sanders (also B.S.) each made a phenomenal instant impact on the Lions. Sims, the 1978 Heisman Trophy winner from Oklahoma, was the Lions' number one draft pick and broke the club's rookie rushing record enroute to becoming Detroit's all-time leading runner. Sanders, the 1988 Heisman Trophy winner from Oklahoma State, was the Lions' number one draft pick and broke the club's rookie rushing record enroute to becoming Detroit's all-time leading runner. Each wore jersey No. 20. Each captured the imagination of Lions fans everywhere.

• In 1991, the Lions unveiled their one-of-a-kind hot air balloon. Prior to Detroit's Thanksgiving Day contest with Chicago that season, Chuck Schmidt, executive vice president, took NFL Commissioner Paul Tagliabue for a lift in the Silverdome.

• The Lions have had a long history of community involvement, and in 1991, the club expanded those efforts in establishing Detroit Lions Charities (DLC), a non-profit organization founded to assist a wide variety of activities and programs that benefit education, civic affairs, and health and human services in Michigan. Funding for DLC comes from several sources including proceeds from the Detroit Lions Invitational, an annual golf outing, and through "Lions Live," a sports memorabilia and autograph fun-fair held yearly in the Silverdome. ❖

This 1976 photo depicts three sideline veterans in Detroit. For many years, Eddie Howland (left) was the leader of the "chain gang" which works along with the NFL game officials. Howland joined the crew in 1940, just two years after Blanche Verhougstraete began what was to be a 40-year reign as the Lion Cub mascot. She began prowling the sidelines at age 10 in 1938, and retired after the 1977 season. On the far right is equipment manager Roy "Friday" Macklem, the team's resident philosopher, humorist and seer for 45 seasons; he began working for the Lions in 1936.

10

"And when it was done, there were the Lions, shouting, jumping, screaming, on top of a miracle victory to surpass anything ever seen on a gridiron."

— George Puscas
Detroit Free Press, December 5, 1960

Billy Sims joins Barry Sanders as unanimous selections to the media's Modern Era All-Time Lions squad.

The Envelope, Please

The Lions' Golden Era and Modern Era teams and the five greatest games in club history as selected by the Detroit media in a special anniversary poll.

As a part of the Lions' celebration of 60 years of pro football, a media poll was conducted to select two all-time teams — a Golden Era Team (first 30 years, 1934–63) and a Modern Era Team (second 30 years, 1964–93).

Local sports reporters and broadcasters were asked to select the top two players per position for each era. The media were also asked to choose Offensive and Defensive MVPs, Most Outstanding Coaches, and a variety of other categories, including the Greatest Game in Lions History.

The results of the all-time team poll are on the next few pages. Following those lists, the top five games in Lions history are profiled with excerpts from previously published stories. Four of the recaps include the actual newspaper accounts as they appeared in the Detroit papers the day following each game; those stories were written by famed sports journalists Joe Falls, George Puscas and Lyall Smith. The fifth story was excerpted from the book *NFL Top 40: The Greatest Pro Football Games of All Times* by the late *Detroit News* sports columnist, Shelby Strother.

(Opposite Page) Joe Schmidt
Golden Era Defensive MVP

DETROIT MEDIA
ALL-GOLDEN ERA TEAM
First 30 Seasons, 1934-63

Bobby Layne
Golden Era
Offensive MVP

	FIRST TEAM	
Offense		
End	Cloyce Box	1949–50, 52–54
Tackle	Lou Creekmur	1950–59
Guard	Harley Sewell	1953–62
Center	Alex Wojciechowicz	1938–46
Guard	Dick Stanfel	1952–55
Tackle	Charley Ane	1953–59
End	Gail Cogdill	1960–68
Fullback	Pat Harder	1951–53
Halfback	Doak Walker	1950–55
Halfback	tie: Whizzer White	1940–41
	Bob Hoernschemeyer	1950–55
Quarterback	Bobby Layne	1950–58
Defense		
Lineman	Darris McCord	1955–67
Lineman	Thurman McGraw	1950–54
Lineman	Les Bingaman	1948–54
Lineman	Roger Brown	1960–66
Linebacker	Wayne Walker	1958–72
Linebacker	Joe Schmidt	1953–65
Linebacker	LaVern Torgeson	1951–54
Halfback	Jim David	1952–59
Halfback	Dick Lane	1960–65
Safety	Jack Christiansen	1951–58
Safety	Yale Lary	1952–53, 56–64
Specialists		
Placekicker	Jim Martin	1951–61
Punter	Yale Lary	1952–53, 56–64
KO Returner	Doak Walker	1950–55
Punt Returner	Jack Christiansen	1951–58

	SECOND TEAM	
Offense		
End	Leon Hart	1950–57
Tackle	George Christensen	1934–38
Guard	John Gordy	1957, 59–67
Center	Vince Banonis	1951–53
Guard	John Gonzaga	1961–65
Tackle	Oliver Spencer	1953, 56, 59–61
End	Jim Doran	1951–59
Fullback	John Henry Johnson	1957–59
Halfback	Bill Dudley	1947–49
Halfback	Ernie Caddel	1934–38
Quarterback	Dutch Clark	1934–38
Defense		
Lineman	Alex Karras	1958–62, 64–70
Lineman	Gil Mains	1952–61
Lineman	Bill Glass	1958–61
Lineman	John Prchlik	1949–53
Linebacker	Jim Martin	1951–61
Linebacker	Carl Brettschneider	1960–63
Linebacker	Alex Wojciechowicz	1938–46
Halfback	Dick LeBeau	1959–72
Halfback	Bob Smith	1949–54
Safety	Don Doll	1949–52
Safety	Gary Lowe	1957–64
Specialists		
Placekicker	Doak Walker	1950–55
Punter	Bob Smith	1949–54
KO Returner	Jack Christiansen	1951–58
Punt Returner	Bill Dudley	1947–49

GOLDEN ERA MVP HONORS

Offensive MVP	Bobby Layne
Defensive MVP	Joe Schmidt
Outstanding Coach	Buddy Parker

DETROIT MEDIA
ALL-MODERN ERA TEAM
Second 30 Seasons, 1964–93

**Barry Sanders
Modern Era
Offensive MVP**

FIRST TEAM

Offense

Receiver	Leonard Thompson	1975–86
Tackle	Keith Dorney	1979–87
Guard	Bob Kowalkowski	1966–76
Center	Ed Flanagan	1965–74
Guard	John Gordy	1959–67
Tackle	Lomas Brown	1985–Present
Tight End	Charlie Sanders	1968–77
Receiver	Fred Scott	1978–83
Running Back	Barry Sanders	1989–Present
Running Back	Billy Sims	1980–84
Quarterback	Greg Landry	1968–78

Defense

Lineman	Doug English	1975–79, 81–85
Lineman	Al Baker	1978–82
Lineman	Larry Hand	1964–77
Lineman	Alex Karras	1958–62, 64–70
Linebacker	Wayne Walker	1958–72
Linebacker	Mike Lucci	1965–73
Linebacker	Chris Spielman	1988–Present
Cornerback	Lem Barney	1967–77
Cornerback	Dick LeBeau	1959–72
Safety	Mike Weger	1967–75
Safety	Bennie Blades	1988–Present

Specialists

Placekicker	Eddie Murray	1980–91
Punter	Jim Arnold	1986–Present
KO Returner	Mel Gray	1989–Present
Punt Returner	Lem Barney	1967–77

SECOND TEAM

Offense

Receiver	Gail Cogdill	1960–68
Tackle	Rockne Freitas	1968–77
Guard	Russ Bolinger	1976–82
Center	Kevin Glover	1985–Present
Guard	Chuck Walton	1967–74
Tackle	Daryl Sanders	1963–66
Tight End	David Hill	1976–82
Receiver	Pat Studstill	1961–67
Running Back	Dexter Bussey	1974–84
Running Back	Mel Farr	1967–73
Quarterback	Gary Danielson	1976–84

Defense

Lineman	Roger Brown	1960–66
Lineman	Jerry Ball	1987–92
Lineman	William Gay	1978–87
Linebacker	Charlie Weaver	1971–81
Linebacker	Paul Naumoff	1967–78
Linebacker	Michael Cofer	1983–Present
Linebacker	Ken Fantetti	1979–85
Cornerback	James Hunter	1976–82
Cornerback	Ray Crockett	1989–Present
Safety	Dick Jauron	1973–77
Safety	Tom Vaughn	1965–71

Specialists

Placekicker	Errol Mann	1969–76
Punter	Herman Weaver	1970–76
KO Returner	Alvin Hall	1980–85, 87
Punt Returner	Mel Gray	1989–Present

**Lem Barney
Modern Era
Defensive MVP**

MODERN ERA MVP HONORS

Offensive MVP	Barry Sanders
Defensive MVP	Lem Barney
Outstanding Coach	Joe Schmidt

SPECIAL RECOGNITION

Mr. Detroit Lion	Joe Schmidt
Mr. Consistency	tie: Doak Walker, Joe Schmidt and Ed Murray
Most Underrated Player	Dexter Bussey
Most Dedicated Player	tie: Charlie Sanders and Chris Spielman
Most Colorful Player	Bobby Layne

The Greatest Games

5th

John Henry Johnson helped lead the charge over the Colts.

BALTIMORE AT DETROIT
OCTOBER 20, 1957

	1	2	3	4	T
Colts	7	14	6	0	27
Lions	0	3	7	21	31

by Joe Falls · *The Detroit Times*

When, on that gray Sunday afternoon in 1953, Bobby Layne hit Jim Doran with a dramatic touchdown pass in the final three minutes of play to clinch the National Football League championship, the ardent followers of the Detroit Lions thought they had seen it all.

And they had — until yesterday.

Then, before their disbelieving eyes, they witnessed a comeback which was even greater than the one accomplished in the gloom of Briggs Stadium four years ago.

They saw the irrepressible Layne lead the Lions, not to another title-winning victory, but to a victory of equal, and perhaps more, importance: for it was a victory which saved the pride and the prestige of a tottering football team which insists it still has a claim to greatness.

Simply, the Lions proved that they're still the "old pros" of the game, that they still have that insatiable desire to win.

If you doubted it, you should have been in the Detroit dressing room following the fantastic 31–27 victory over the Baltimore Colts.

You would have seen old men acting like schoolboys after winning one for Old Central High.

You would have seen Coach George Wilson grinning happily, almost foolishly, as if trying to figure out exactly what had happened, but not really caring, just so long as it happened.

Layne shrugged it off as another day's work.

"Shucks," he drawled in his deepest Texas accent, "We've played some close ones before."

It was a comeback in the tradition of Detroit's championship years of 1952– 53–54. Only greater.

Actually, the Lions had every right to fold up their footballs and go home. The Colts all but ran them out of the park, zooming into a 27–3 lead as Johnny Unitas connected on four touchdown passes.

Tobin Rote got the Lions started, pitching what appeared to be a meaningless, face-saving touchdown pass to rookie end Steve Junker late in the third quarter.

It made the score 27–10 but, actually, it was the opening the Lions needed, got, and exploited.

Wilson switched to Layne in the final session and what happened will never be forgotten by the howling, hysterical crowd of 55,764.

Displaying all the emotions of a cigar store Indian, Layne, with a tremendous assist from Howard Cassady, directed the Lions to three touchdowns in the final eight minutes — the last two coming with 89 seconds to play.

It was a magnificent example of comeback football and when Layne hit Cassady with the winning pass with 46 seconds remaining, the fans erupted into a standing, full-throated ovation which would have done proud to Milwaukee.

The Lions, having pulled close on the deadly Layne-to-Cassady combination, needed a break in the final minute and they got it by forcing the Colts into a costly fumble.

Trying to run out the clock deep in their territory, the Colts took a calculated gamble by sending Lennie Moore wide on a modified statue-of-liberty play. He appeared to be headed for a decisive first down when he was jarred by Carl Karilivacs. The ball squirted from his grasp like an overripe peach and Yale Lary pounced on it.

With the ball resting on the Colt's 29, the Lions lined up quickly — almost before the Baltimore defense was ready — and Layne hit Cassady as he streaked down the sidelines. He caught the ball near the goal line and he went across untouched.

(Reprinted with author's permission from the *Detroit Times,* Oct. 21, 1957)

Lions Silence Critics, Claim Second Straight Title

1953 NFL Championship Game

CLEVELAND AT DETROIT
DECEMBER 27, 1953

	1	2	3	4	T
Browns	0	3	7	6	16
Lions	7	3	0	7	17

by Lyall Smith · *Free Press* sports editor

There were those who said it was just plain luck when the Lions pulled game after game out of the fire during the regular season.

"Just luck," said the critics. "Wait'll they bump into the Cleveland Browns. Just wait . . ."

In the pressbox before the battle, those voices could still be heard. A consensus of the scores of writers in from all over everywhere to record this title game picked the Browns to grab the crown of world champions off Lion heads.

But when it was ended those same nonbelievers were shaking their heads. Not in bewilderment. Just in plain unashamed admiration of a team that refused to be beaten by a team that had been favored to do just that.

The Lions won it like the champions they are. They beat a team they had defeated a year ago. They beat a team that had forged ahead on three field goals by Lou Groza, its incomparable kicker.

They beat a team that had come from behind a 10–3 halftime deficit to tie the score on its only touchdown of the game. They beat a team that led them as the final seconds ticked off the clock.

"Just plain luck?"

Just plain guts, I'd say. Who can say otherwise.

It was a battle of breaks . . . until the fat was in the fire for the Lions. Every point until the heated final-quarter fireworks was racked up as the aftermath of a recovered fumble or an intercepted pass.

The Lion making the biggest catches? Jim Doran, that's who.

He caught his first touchdown pass of the year on the dramatic 33-yard heave from the cool arm of a cool Texan named Layne. That catch capped an 80-yard Detroit drive.

It was a drive in which Doran personally accounted for 68 yards on three catches to give him a day's total of 95 yards on four receptions.

And that was exactly 20 yards, plus one touchdown, *more* than he had gained during the entire season.

Amazing? Sure it was. But remember last year in the title game against Cleveland.

The big touchdown in that one was scored by halfback Doak Walker — a player who . . . like Doran this time — had failed to score a single touchdown during the regular campaign.

The pressbox was jammed with 141 football writers from all sections of the pro circuit except the Pacific Coast. But that section was represented by Jack Kramer, the tennis champ.

"I flew in from Los Angeles just for the game," Kramer said. "I really go for pro football."

Another pressbox occupant was Harvey Kuenn, brilliant young shortstop of the Tigers. Like Kramer, he flew in for the title battle . . . from his home in Milwaukee. Harvey is working as a public relations good will ambassador for a bank in West Allis, Wis.

Thurman McGraw didn't have much of a chance to get in a relaxed mood for the big game. His wife presented him a belated Christmas gift Sunday morning. It was a spanking new baby boy . . . second one for the McGraws.

When Yale Lary boomed off his 73-yard punt in the second quarter, it was the second-longest punt in the 21-year history of the playoff game.

(Reprinted with permission from the *Detroit Free Press*, Dec. 28, 1953)

Jim Doran made this key third down reception, good for 18 yards, on the Lions' winning drive.

The Greatest Games

3rd

	1	2	3	4	T
Lions	3	0	0	17	20
Colts	2	6	0	7	15

BALTIMORE AT DETROIT
DECEMBER 4, 1960

by George Puscas · *Detroit Free Press*

Somebody say that it really happened. Assure us that it's true.

In a simply incredible game — fantastic, unbelievable, it was — the Detroit Lions Sunday whipped the Baltimore Colts, 20–15, before 57,808 thundering and appalled fans in jammed Memorial Stadium.

It couldn't happen. But it did.

With 15 seconds to play, the Lions led, 13–8.

With 14 seconds left, Baltimore led, 15–13.

And when it was done, there were the Lions, shouting, jumping, screaming, on top of a miracle victory to surpass anything ever seen on a gridiron.

Football games just don't end the way this one did — not even that original "miracle" game between these same two teams in 1957 could stand with this.

It left proud Baltimore stunned and uncomprehending. For long minutes after Jim Gibbons had taken a 65-yard pass from Earl Morrall to win the game on the last play, thousands stood on the gridiron, looking about, saying little or nothing, refusing to leave and accept the Colt defeat.

These were the same Colts who bare seconds earlier had completed a dramatic race against the clock covering some 80 yards in less than one minute, to score a sensational touchdown and apparently secure victory over the Lions.

They had managed it on one of the decade's great pass catches, a diving, sprawling, rolling snare by Lennie Moore on a 37-yard pass from John Unitas.

Whoever would have thought the Lions could come back from that?

No one did. Thousands were on the field within a flash after Moore's catch had lifted Baltimore to its 15–13 lead.

It would not have been so extraordinary for officials to call the game there, believing that it was all over and order impossible to restore.

But the field was cleared, the kickoff came. And on the second play, Morrall, the forgotten quarterback, stepped back, threw a pass down the right sideline.

Gibbons, having crossed over from his left end position, took the ball in stride, outlegged pursuing Colts to the end zone.

When Jim Martin kicked the 20th point, the game and football's most incredible finish of the ages was done.

Name your own hero.

It could be Gibbons. It could be Howard (Hopalong) Cassady, and how could you ignore an astonishing Detroit defense?

But you can't forget Morrall. The quarterback, who everyone agreed cannot pass in pro style, pitched two touchdown passes that brought the Lions to the .500 mark at 5–5 for the first time since they won the world title in 1957.

He had come off the bench at the start of the fourth period, when the manhandling Jim Ninowski had received from Colt rushers had upset him and left Detroit helpless.

With eight minutes to go, Morrall stepped back for his first pass from the Baltimore 40, spotted his roommate, Cassady, all alone down the middle of the field.

The ball floated into Cassady's arms at the goal line and the little halfback crashed into the goal posts with Detroit's first touchdown and a 10–8 lead.

It followed then Martin to supply added points. He kicked what seemed merely an "insurance" field goal from 47 yards out with two minutes remaining.

That proved enough time for Unitas, and he brought the Colts upfield to pitch his great pass to Moore and set up the astounding sequence which finished the game.

(Reprinted with permission from the *Detroit Free Press,* Dec. 5, 1960)

The Colts-Lions series has produced many incredible finishes.

20-Minute Spree Crushes Packers

Thanksgiving Day

GREEN BAY AT DETROIT
NOVEMBER 22, 1962

	1	2	3	4	T
Packers	0	0	0	14	14
Lions	7	16	3	0	26

by George Puscas · *Detroit Free Press*

Remember it as the 20 minutes which rocked the football world . . . 20 minutes which frowned on gridiron history . . . 20 minutes in which the Detroit Lions thrust themselves among the great teams of gridiron lore.

On this chill, windy Thanksgiving Day, as tough and as brutal a team as ever strode on a gridiron smashed, wrecked and left in ruin the pride of a team which had come to be known as the greatest of all time.

Detroit 26, Green Bay 14. The Packers are human after all.

From the opening kickoff through the first few minutes of the second period . . . that was all the Lions required to deal these Packers their first defeat in 19 games, break their run toward a second straight world championship, and bring the Lions themselves closer to their title dreams.

For sheer force and emotion, not many games compare with this one.

A roaring crowd of 57,598 fans, second largest football gathering ever crammed into Tiger Stadium, sat enthralled, then driven to near hysteria by the overwhelming might and dominance of the vengeful Lions.

Millions more across the nation watched via television the destruction of a Packer winning record unmatched by any team since 1942.

No one Lion emerged as the conquering hero in this one, but there were two who stood clearly above the rest. They were Gail Cogdill, surely one of the great pass catchers of recent times, and ponderous Roger Brown, 303-pound defensive tackle.

Launching the route of the Packers, Cogdill snared two touchdown passes of 34 and 27 yards from quarterback Milt Plum for the first scores of the game.

Brown led a vicious, unstoppable Lion rush which completely overpowered, then brought to frustration and collapse a Packer offense which stood as the very best in pro football.

How great was the rush? It produced nine points which rocketed Detroit to a 23–0 lead after just 18 minutes and 16 seconds of play.

Sam Williams ran six yards with a fumble for a touchdown, and Brown tackled Packer quarterback Bart Starr in the end zone for a safety.

How great, really, was the Lion rush?

Starr, attempting to pass, 10 times failed to get the ball away, was thrown for 110 yards in losses. Seven other times Packer runners were tossed for losses.

The Packers were never in it. Detroit's lead went to 26–0 early in the third period. In the final period the Packers got down as close as the Lions' 37-yard line for only the second time in the game.

Green Bay's touchdowns followed then, both of them tainted by Lion errors.

Earl Morrall played most of the final period at quarterback for the Lions, but this was no knock against Plum. Milt hit eight of 16 passes and manipulated the Lion attack flawlessly.

This defeat was the first in 19 games, over all, for the Packers, dating back to the second last game of the 1961 season. They had won 11 straight league games, a record unequaled by any other team since the Bears of 1942 won 12 in a row.

With their hardest, most valued game of the year behind them, the Lions now take a rest.

They will be idle Sunday, returning to Tiger Stadium the following week to meet Baltimore.

(Reprinted with permission from the *Detroit Free Press,* Nov. 23, 1962)

2nd

Alex Karras and Jerry Kramer look on as Sam Williams hauls down Jim Taylor for another Packer loss.

1st

1957 NFL Playoff Game

DETROIT AT SAN FRANCISCO
DECEMBER 22, 1957

by Shelby Strother · *Detroit News*

	1	2	3	4	T
Lions	0	7	14	10	31
49ers	14	10	3	0	27

When you're playing on the road and getting your head handed to you and your championship hopes are evaporating like cheap perfume, the exasperation will come out.

"What the hell is happening to us?" yelled George Wilson, head coach of the Detroit Lions. He was running out of brimstone and fiery oratory. He'd given speeches at visitors' locker rooms everywhere and already had made several such impassioned pleas at friendly Briggs Stadium in Detroit.

Fans in Kezar Stadium in San Francisco were frolicking. The scoreboard at halftime read: 49ers 24, Lions 7.

"You guys are quitters," Wilson said. "We've totally given up out there."

Chins drooped. The coach's words had the sting of truth. They seemed to coincide with the ugly numbers on the scoreboard.

"How in the world did we get in this position?" moaned all-pro safety Jack Christiansen.

A dozen heads shook. Others just stared at the cement floor, numb with disbelief. The San Francisco 49ers were in the next room, gloating. At halftime of the playoff game to determine who would represent the Western Conference against the Cleveland Browns the following week, the Lions were getting embarrassed.

Quarterback Y.A. Tittle already had thrown three touchdown passes for San Francisco. He had completed 12 of 19 passes, humbling the famed Detroit secondary known as Chris's Crew, and had made it look as though his team could score whenever the mood struck. The Lions' offense also had been a no-show. And Detroit was unable to lick its halftime wounds in solitude because of the thin walls of the Kezar Stadium dressing rooms and the loud, obnoxious, already-celebrating 49ers.

"Oh, they were really jawing and talking about what kind of cars they were going to buy with their money," remembered Jim

David, the Lions' cornerback whose sprained ankle had worsened despite several shots of Novocain. David couldn't help his team anymore this game. But as he changed into street clothes his anger remained.

"We sat there, all steamed and getting madder and madder with everything they were saying," he said.

Middle linebacker Joe Schmidt roared, "Listen to those SOBs! Listen to them!"

Listen they did. For a minute, the Lions' locker room was quiet. But the constant chatter in the other room brought more eruptions of temper.

Somebody threw a helmet against the wall. Christiansen lamented once more, "How did we get in this position?"

Wilson decided he didn't need to say anything.

The Detroit Lions had swum in dire straits before. All season — beginning before it ever began when head coach Buddy Parker had shocked everyone by abruptly resigning three days before the first preseason game — the Lions constantly seemed to be playing catch-up.

Halfway through the regular season, they had a 3–3 record. On one game, against Baltimore, the Lions trailed 27–10 with eight minutes left, then scored three touchdowns, the last one coming with 39 seconds remaining, to win 31–27. They fell behind Cleveland and its impressive rookie running back, Jim Brown, then, against Chicago, saw their leader, Bobby Layne, carried off the field with a broken ankle, but scrambled back to win both games.

On the final day of the regular season, with the Lions needing a victory to force a playoff with the 49ers, the Chicago Bears jumped on top quickly, led 10–0 at halftime, and were primed to be spoilers for their old rivals from Michigan. But, with Wilson, who was given the coaching job when Parker bolted, delivering a halftime tirade that assaulted their sense of pride, the Lions rallied and pulled out the victory.

Jack Christiansen (#24) jars the ball loose from San Francisco's R.C. Owens as Jim David reaches for the ball.

Christiansen wanted to know how they'd gotten in that position, trailing the 49ers 24–7 at the half, and yet the journey surely must have seemed familiar. The question was where was the escape route? And could the Lions find their way once more?

In a corner of the room, Layne leaned forward on his crutches and said, "It ain't over yet. We know what to do."

There was no rousing bedlam. The Lions quietly filed back out to the field, where the P.A. announcer was declaring that tickets to the championship game now were on sale at the box office.

On the first play from scrimmage, San Francisco's great halfback Hugh McElhenny swept right end, cut back to the left, and meandered through Detroit traffic on the way to the goal line and another touchdown. But the Lions were able to force McElhenny out of bounds at the Detroit 9.

"Hell of a way to start a comeback, huh?" David said later. "When you hold them to a seventy-one-yard gain on the first play, how are you supposed to feel good about things?"

Yet it was that play — the inability of McElhenny to get into the end zone — that started one of the great turnarounds in NFL history.

The 49ers could move only six yards in three plays against the Lions' defense, with Schmidt screaming constant reminders of the halftime eavesdropping. San Francisco's Gordy Soltau kicked a 10-yard field goal.

"That was a minor victory in itself," Wilson said. "It was 27–7 and that didn't look good at all. But because we'd finally shown some spirit, I thought things were getting better. We just needed someone to make a big play."

The Lions took the ball and sputtered once more. Tittle and the 49ers' offense headed back onto the field, ready to resume the carnage. But the veteran quarterback was slammed from his blind side and fumbled. Detroit linebacker Bob Long recovered at the San Francisco 27.

"Normally, we'd give it to one of our running backs and just pound it down their throats," Wilson said. "But we really didn't have a healthy one . . . other than Tom Tracy, that is."

Tracy (nicknamed The Bomb) was a squat man who was neither a power runner nor a breakaway threat. He had not carried the ball for the Lions in any of the previous four games. Now, with Howard (Hopalong) Cassady and John Henry Johnson both banged up, Tracy became an obvious choice.

Nine plays later, behind the stubborn running of Tracy, and aided by a pass-interference penalty against the 49ers, the Lions had a touchdown.

"That little one-yard run by Tracy really lit a fire," Layne said.

Layne's absence had thrown a big load on Tobin Rote, the backup who had been obtained from Green Bay in the previous offseason. A fellow Texan, Rote was bigger, stronger, and threw a tighter spiral than Layne. But nobody considered him the leader Layne was.

After Tracy's touchdown, he got another one. The Lions' defense stopped the 49ers when three passes by Tittle fell incomplete. After the punt, Rote handed the ball to Tracy, who headed into the line, veered suddenly to the right, and broke open for a 58-yard touchdown run. Now it was 27–21.

"We got 'em, we got 'em," Rote yelled as he came to the sideline, where the Lions' frenzied defense was ready to go back.

"When one unit revs up, the other usually will, too," Wilson said. "For the rest of the third quarter, it was a question of which was more dominating — our offense or our defense."

Again, the Lions stopped the 49ers, forced a punt, and moved to a third touchdown within a span of four minutes and 29 seconds.

The 49ers now were keying on Tracy, and Rote noticed it. A fake to Tracy froze the San Francisco secondary, and Rote then dropped back and threw a 36-yard pass to end Steve Junker. Tracy got around the corner for 10 more yards. Five plays later, on the second play of the fourth quarter, halfback Gene Gedman scored from the 2. The game was tied, but after Jim Martin kicked the extra point, the Lions had a 28–27 lead.

But there still was a lot of time — more than 14 minutes — left to play.

"Don't forget what Tittle did to you in the first half," Wilson urged.

The swagger had switched sides of the field.

As Gene Gedman tumbles into the end zone, two officials signal the touchdown that pulled the Lions into a 27–27 tie with the 49ers.

"Kick the hell out of them now," David yelled.

Schmidt slapped teammates' helmets, individually reminding them what was at stake. The seventh-round draft pick out of Pittsburgh had become perhaps the finest linebacker in the game. As the Lions lined up for the kickoff, Schmidt noticed how subdued the stadium had become.

The 49ers got the ball four more times in the game. Each time a different Lions defensive player claimed a turnover.

"You can't really say one was more important than the others," Wilson said. "We needed them all. But I would have to say Joe Schmidt's interception was fitting and appropriate."

Defensive end Gil Mains had recovered a fumble by Joe Perry. Carl Karilivacz had intercepted a pass by Tittle and so had defensive tackle Roger Zatkoff, his coming in the game's final minute.

But Schmidt's was the most special.

"Here's this guy who simply wouldn't let us lose," said Lions safety Yale Lary. "When he got his interception, I was hoping he'd take it all the way in. Because he deserved to have something special like that, the way he led us on defense that day."

As it was, the high-stepping Schmidt was run out of bounds at the 2.

"The thing a lot of people don't remember," David said, "is that we should have blown the game wide open. We fumbled once on their three and couldn't get it in after Joe's interception with three tries from the two. It could have been a blowout."

Instead, the Lions got a field goal from Martin that made the 31–27 final score somehow deceiving.

Rote and Tracy were surrounded by reporters afterward. Ken Russell, the rookie tackle, was able to dress almost unnoticed. Only his teammates would appreciate the job he did filling in for injured Charlie Ane.

Lions end Dave Middleton was headed for Tennessee. In a few days, the Detroit Lions would play for the championship of pro football. But before that, the medical school of the University of Tennessee had about 14 hours of exams for the third-year student.

Middleton made it back in time for the championship game with Cleveland. Tobin Rote threw four touchdown passes and scored another as the Lions routed the Browns 59–14. It was Detroit's third NFL championship in six years.

Afterward, Browns head coach Paul Brown blamed at least part of the loss on himself.

"I was personally scouting our opponent by watching the playoff game on TV. I had a clipboard and tried to pick out strengths and weaknesses that might help us.

"But I scouted the wrong team for a good part of the game."

(Reprinted with permission from NFL Properties, Inc.; excerpted from *NFL Top 40: The Greatest Pro Football Games of All Times* by Shelby Strother, published by Viking-Penguin)

San Francisco's Marv Matuszak (#54) tries to chase Lions end Steve Junker.

11

The Canton Lions

Eleven of the greatest players in Detroit Lions history have been inducted into the Professional Football Hall of Fame, located in Canton, Ohio.

by Richard L. Shook

In 1992, Lem Barney became the 11th Lion enshrined in the Hall of Fame.

Lem Barney

LEM BARNEY

Defensive Back · Enshrined 1992

"It ain't braggin'," renowned pitcher Dizzy Dean once said, "if you can do it."

And Lemuel Joseph Barney, the famed "Supernatural" of the Detroit Lions, could flat-out do it.

Barney inherited the left cornerback spot patrolled in unparalleled fashion for Detroit by Dick Lane — and became the "Spiritual Son of Night Train."

He intercepted 10 passes his first season, returning three for touchdowns to set an NFL rookie record, totaled 56 interceptions in a career that went from 1967 through 1977 and ran back seven for touchdowns (tied for second in that NFL career listing).

Barney punted on occasion (averaging 42.3 yards as the regular in 1969), and ran back both punts and kickoffs with that special Barney elan.

And sometimes he didn't run back punts, which says more about his ability than his courage. Punting so Barney could run the ball back made about as much sense as turning the ball over on downs on your own 2-yard line.

Therefore many punters sacrificed distance for height so their coverage teams could get to Barney before the ball did. Barney is tied for the NFL record of seven fair catches in one game, which he did in 1976 against Chicago.

The Barney playing legend began with his very first scrimmage. He stepped in front of Gail Cogdill and deflected the first pass of the workout. On the next throw, he leaped over Cogdill to make a one-handed interception.

"Interference," yelled Cogdill, a former All-Pro split end, with a glare at the bold newcomer.

"Offensive or defensive?" brash Barney responded. "If there was ever anybody better than Lem," Jim David, Barney's former coach, said in 1992, when Barney was inducted into the NFL Hall of Fame, "I never saw or heard of

him. Nobody before or since measured up to him."

The legend grew with his first regular season game. Starting at left corner against defending Super Bowl champion Green Bay, Barney picked off the first pass Bart Starr threw in his direction.

Starr sent Boyd Dowler in Barney's direction with Elijah Pitts as a trailer. The ball was intended for Pitts but Barney made a diving interception, somer-saulted and got up for a 24-yard prance into the end zone.

"Man," Barney recalled saying to himself at the time, "this game is going to be easy." He acknowledged later "it wasn't that easy."

In the last game of his rookie season, against Minnesota, Barney picked off three passes in one quarter and ran one of them back for a touchdown. He allowed just one touchdown all season and was named NFL Defensive Rookie of the Year. Teammate Mel Farr was offensive rookie of the year, the only time both honorees have come from the same squad.

He played 140 games, missing just 14, but after his first four seasons was apparently declared off-limits by quarterbacks. Only 14 of his interceptions came in his last seven seasons.

Kickoffs were run back an average 25.5 yards (with one touchdown) by Barney and his average for 143 career punt returns was 9.2 yards (with two TDs). His 21.2 punt return average for 1969 just misses the top three all-time.

He played in seven Pro Bowls, was named All-Pro three times and was voted on the All-60s teams on the strength of just three seasons.

Barney's 1,051 return yards with his 56 interceptions is the Lions' standard by more than 250 yards.

JACK CHRISTIANSEN

Defensive Back · Enshrined 1970

Even giants have giants. Such a man was Jack Christiansen. He came into the NFL as a sixth-round draft choice out of Colorado A&M (now Colorado State) in 1951. By the time he retired as a player in 1958, pro football was forever changed.

Christiansen, who died of cancer at 57 on June 29, 1986, was honorary chief of the first defensive backfield, "Chris' Crew," celebrated for its collective prowess.

Their skill and fame helped change the way football put defensive units together. No longer would running back rejects be shunted to the other side of the line. With the rise of Chris' Crew, teams looked for players adept at coverage, hitting and intercepting.

Less remembered is Christiansen's punt return ability. He was so good running back punts, teams redesigned coverage to stop him.

He was All-NFL defensive back six straight years, played in five Pro Bowls (opening the 1956 game with a 103-yard kickoff return), was the league's leading interceptor twice. Christiansen intercepted 46 career passes and made 85 punt returns for 1,084 yards with eight touchdowns. He was an NFL Hall of Fame inductee in 1970.

His career average of 12.75 yards per punt return ranks No. 2 on the all-time NFL list to George McAfee's 12.78 for the Chicago Bears. His 21.47 average for the 1952 season (15-for-322) is second all-time to Herb Rich's 1950 mark of 23.0 yards for Baltimore.

Twice Christiansen returned two punts for touchdowns in a game, an NFL record since equalled by four others. But he did it in the same season, 1951, a standard tied just by Rick Upchurch of Denver in 1976 (but never by another rookie). His eight career touchdowns on punt returns is also a record he shares with Upchurch.

Christiansen's 11 career return touchdowns are the most in Lions' history, one better than Lem Barney's total.

Ever try to pick a strand of fresh cooked spaghetti off the stove? That's what Christiansen was like on punt returns. He was slippery as motor oil and had more speed changes than a mountain bike.

In those days teams massed defenses on punt returns. Guys who ran them back must have been chosen for their expendability. Or else they weren't overly imaginative.

But it changed with Christiansen, who made the punt return a genuine weapon instead of mere change of possession. He was so dominant as a return man other teams had to utilize a spread formation on punts to contain him, which kept him from duplicating his fantastic first season. He still has two of Detroit's top-four punt return yardage figures for a game.

Christiansen, Yale Lary and Jimmy David were the constants during Detroit's 1952–57 glory years. Several right halfbacks (as cornerbacks were known in those days) played the side opposite David during Chris' Crew's heyday.

"Jack wasn't a real screamer," former teammate and fellow Hall of Fame member Joe Schmidt said. "You never saw Jack rattled about anything. He was always in control of the situation and in control of himself."

He was an impact defensive player, and in an era of great change in football, Christiansen was a dominant figure. So dominant was he that in 1972 Football Digest selected him as one of the top 25 players ever to perform in the NFL.

Jack Christiansen

Dutch Clark

EARL "DUTCH" CLARK

Quarterback · Enshrined 1963

He never bettered 10 seconds in the 100-yard dash, didn't have the size to run over people and wasn't a terrific passer, yet when the NFL established its Hall of Fame in 1963, one of the first 17 players was an original Detroit Lion named Earl Harry "Dutch" Clark.

"He's like a rabbit in a brush heap," said Coach George "Potsy" Clark (no relation), succeeded by Dutch as coach of the Lions. "No back ever followed interference better.

"But in the secondary, he's a dervish. Just about the time you expect to see him smothered, he's free and gone."

Clark, who wore No. 7, is designated a quarterback because he threw passes but he really was a single wing tailback. In those days, signals were called by the blocking back, but such was Clark's feel for the game he was put in charge of calling Coach Potsy Clark's plays.

Dutch was also the last of the great dropkickers, an art which died out toward the end of his career because the league slimmed the football. Quarterbacks could grip and throw the sleeker model better, which pumped up offenses.

The Clarks led the Lions to their first championship in only their second season in Detroit, 1935, and the club was fortunate Dutch was with it. It was the middle of the depression, and Clark had "retired" after spending the 1931 and 1932 seasons with the Portsmouth Spartans. He could earn more as athletic director and coach at Colorado School of Mines.

Dutch earned his nickname because an older brother was called "Big Dutch," though the family was Irish, due to an inability to speak plainly as a child. Earl was soon called "Little Dutch," then just "Dutch" as he got bigger.

Offered a contract for 1931, Dutch quickly signed to see if he could prove Associated Press sports editor Alan

Gould correct. Gould had irritated the Eastern establishment after the 1928 season by picking Clark over the more celebrated East Coast quarterbacks for the top spot on his All-America team.

"Every time I had some success," Clark said, "Gould took great pleasure in reminding people who'd first noticed me. That was my greatest thrill — vindicating Gould. A lot of people thought he was crazy.

"I agreed with them. I felt I was a newspaper champion. The greatest satisfaction I got in professional football was proving myself. To myself. That was the reason I went to play professionally."

For the magnificent sum of $144 per game, Clark became a pro smash. He was Rookie of the Year and All-Pro, completing more than half his passes at a time when 35–45 percent was the norm.

Dutch gained fame despite being a quiet person. The 6-footer, whose playing weight went from 175 to 185 as he aged, came between the eras of Bronko Nagurski and Sammy Baugh. Still, Clark gained notoriety.

In 1936, the year after the Lions won the championship, Clark paced a powerful ground attack to 2,855 yards, a record that stood for 36 seasons until the Miami Dolphins took advantage of a lengthened schedule to break it in 1972.

Clark gained 628 yards, third best in the league that season, completed 53.6 percent of his passes (league average: 36.5), and was the NFL's leading scorer.

He took over the reins as player/coach for the Lions in 1937 and '38 before becoming disenchanted with the owner.

Clark quit when the Cleveland Rams offered him a job as their coach for 1939. He coached them for four seasons before quitting to join the Army in World War II.

Detroit Lions
in the Pro Football
Hall of Fame

Lem Barney

Gary Thomas

Jack Christiansen

Earl "Dutch" Clark

John Henry Johnson

Cory Thomas

Joe Schmidt

In addition to these 11 players, there are three
other Hall of Famers who spent part of their
careers with Detroit. Those players are Frank
Gatski (played with Lions 1957, enshrined 1985);
Ollie Matson (with Lions 1963, enshrined 1972);
and Hugh McElhenny (with Lions 1964,
enshrined 1970).

Frank Gatski

Ollie Matson

Hugh McElhenny

Bill Dudley

BILL DUDLEY

Halfback · Enshrined 1966

In a time when professional football could barely guarantee its own future, the Detroit Lions figured "Bullet" Bill Dudley was a sure thing.

Dudley was a 5-foot-10, 176-pound halfback/defensive back, smallish for a target of attention even in those days of pre-bulked up players and one-platoon football.

William McGarvey Dudley, who wore No. 35 with the Lions, was called Bullet Bill more for his explosive scoring habits than his speed. His running style suggested he should be called "Ricochet" Bill for the way he bounced off tacklers and feinted his way around.

Dudley wrapped his credentials around World War II. He had a sensational rookie pro season with Pittsburgh in 1942 and was service football's No. 1 player in 1944 while serving as a flight instructor at Randolph Field, Texas.

He became Pittsburgh's top draft choice, helping the Steelers go from last in 1941 to second in the Eastern Division when he joined them.

Returning from Army duty late in 1945, the blond, grey-eyed athlete immediately sparked the heretofore winless Steelers to a victory. Dudley, who led the NFL in rushing with 696 yards his rookie season, led the league in rushing (604 yards) and punt returns to earn MVP honors in 1946. He also led the league with 10 interceptions, showing he was not the slouch on defense many offensive backs were.

In the last game of that season, Dudley tore a knee ligament when one of his blockers fell on his leg. That's it, Dudley said, "I'm too small for this game." He said he was going to retire.

What the outgoing, wryly humorous Dudley could not say until much later was he didn't get along with icy, sarcastic, humorless Jock Sutherland, who had become the Pittsburgh coach in 1945.

Steelers owner Art Rooney offered to tear up his contract and give the star a raise to $20,000 a year, but Dudley declined. He was going to get married and return to his alma mater as assistant football coach.

The game could hardly afford to let one of its brightest stars get away. Enter into the picture Lions' owner Fred Mandel Jr., whose team had slumped to 1–10 in 1946 after going 7–3 the year before.

Mandel first offered Dudley $1,000 a game, which apparently included exhibitions. Then came the clincher: the sum would be guaranteed as a cold Detroit winter. Two weeks later, after a trade with Pittsburgh, he signed for $25,000 — the most money in professional football at the time.

Dudley's attitude of approaching each season as if he were an untried rookie quickly won over his new teammates and he was elected captain of the Lions — getting every secret ballot vote but his own.

He was more of a receiver with the Lions than he had been with the Steelers, ranking 13th in 1947 with 27 catches for 375 yards and seven TDs. In 1949 he was 17th with 27 catches for 190 yards and two scores. In between, he caught 20 passes for 210 yards and six TDs.

He continued his outstanding return ability. Overall he had three seasons where his punting average exceeded 40 yards plus one at 39. He was ranked in the top 10 in punt returns five times. Dudley ended his career returning 124 punts for 1,515 yards (12.21 average), three for touchdowns.

His kickoff return average was an unbelievable 30.05 — 58 for 1,743 yards and a touchdown — which would put him second all-time to Gale Sayers except for failure to meet the 75-return minimum.

JOHN HENRY JOHNSON

Fullback · Enshrined 1987

His namesake was a steel drivin' man, but John Henry Johnson was a yardage drivin' man.

Johnson counted three years with Detroit among his 13 professional seasons but one was crucial — helping the Lions to the 1957 NFL championship.

He was the fullback on that title team, although it sometimes gets lost in the history books because Tom "The Bomb" Tracy took the injured Johnson's spot in Detroit's famous 31–27 come-from-behind victory over the San Francisco Forty Niners in the Western Division playoff.

John Henry, who wore No. 35, was big for his time and he'd be no Tiny Tim today. Johnson stood 6-foot-2, started his career around 215 and ended it at 230 pounds.

He was a hard-driving runner but it was his blocking that earned Johnson his fame. That was the reason the Lions acquired him in a trade with San Francisco for back Bill Stits and a draft choice.

Bobby Layne was losing a step or two and the Lions needed someone to help keep defenders off his belly.

"I knew I was a good blocker," Johnson said, "'cause I never got the back of my uniform dirty. Sometimes I didn't get the front of it too dirty, either."

"Ol' John Henry's got the meanest elbows in football," Layne said. "Guys come at me and he puts an elbow in their throat, and they don't come so fast anymore."

Johnson's 1957 total of 621 yards was fourth-best in the league and, at the time, was the fourth-highest figure in Lions' history. He averaged 4.8 yards per carry and also caught 20 passes for 141 yards.

Detroit traded Layne to Pittsburgh the next year and Johnson was utilized even more as a blocker. In 1959, Nick Pietrosante supplanted him and the

Lions, feeling the need to rejuvenate after two sub-.500 seasons, reunited Johnson with Layne in 1960 by trading him to the Steelers for draft choices in 1961 and 1962.

Johnson twice gained 1,000 yards for the Steelers, in 1962 and at the age of 35 in 1964. He finished his career with Houston of the AFL in 1966.

Johnson, whose nickname was "Mumbles," ("for the way I talk when I'm excited") went to Arizona State but played for last-place Calgary of the CFL after getting out of school. He made All-Canada — at five positions.

Coach Frankie Albert of San Francisco, who signed him for the Forty Niners in 1954, called Johnson "the best defensive back I've ever seen."

So naturally he put Johnson in as the fullback for runners Hugh McElhenny and Joe Perry plus quarterback Y.A. Tittle to form one of the league's most famous backfields.

As a rookie, Johnson finished second in the league in rushing with 681 yards (and a 5.3 average).

For his career, Johnson, who joined the Hall of Fame in 1987, gained 6,803 yards on 1,571 carries and scored 48 touchdowns. He also caught 186 passes for 1,478 yards and seven TDs.

And was responsible for who knows how many sore Adams apples, crunched ribs, bruised shoulders, arm knots and tender tailbones. John Henry was a bonedrivin' man.

John Henry Johnson

Dick Lane

DICK LANE

Defensive Back · Enshrined 1974

The "Night Train" ran on Sunday afternoons. That's "Night Train" as in Dick Lane. It is legend how The Train stepped off the Beverly Boulevard bus in 1952 and into the record books. No. 81 in your program, arguably the No. 1 cornerback in NFL history.

Lane finished his stellar career with the Detroit Lions in 1960–65, playing in half his six Pro Bowls and earning four of his five All-NFL designations. He was inducted into the NFL Hall of Fame in 1974.

Quarterbacks are known for picking on rookies, but the QBs of his first season either didn't read the papers or weren't bright enough to light up a room.

Night Train intercepted 14 passes his 12-game rookie season, still an NFL record even though they now play 16 games. His 298 interception return yards that year are No. 2 in league history.

His college experience consisted of one semester — the football semester — at Scottsbluff Junior College (now Western Nebraska CC) in 1947. The native of Austin, Texas, then joined the Army for four years, where his athletic skills caught him an invitation to accept a scholarship at Loyola (L.A.) University when he got out plus an off-hand invite to "drop by" the Los Angeles Rams.

Loyola dropped football before Lane could drop in. "Because I got married, I immediately had to get a job," he said, "and I worked at an aircraft factory filing metal for F-84 planes."

One day, scrapbook in hand, he stepped off the Beverly Boulevard bus after noticing the Hollywood offices of the Rams. He talked his way past officious secretaries to take Coach Joe Stydahar up on his year-old offer to "stop by any time."

Stydahar looked at the would-be

player's scrapbook — and immediately signed him (for $4,500) plus five other players for the upcoming 1952 season.

"I was a small, very wiry kid so therefore nobody gave me a ghost of a chance of making it. But I had a big heart."

As a rookie, Lane "went both ways, played both offense and defense, and blocked a lot of field goals and extra points."

The 6-foot-2, 210-pound Lane quickly settled in at left corner. After two seasons with the Rams, he was traded to the Chicago Cardinals and following the 1959 season he was dealt to the Lions.

Train led the league in interceptions twice with L.A. and once with Chicago. His career interception return yards of 1,207 are still No. 2 in league history.

He injured his left knee in 1964 and missed most of the season, underwent surgery but was still bothered his final year. He was activated for the last half of 1965, then retired. The Train was headed for the musuem.

He was tagged Night Train due to his liking of Buddy Morrow's hit record of the same name, which came out in 1952 and went nonstop around Lane's turntable right after he heard it.

To get tips on how to play offensive end, Lane was continually going to Tom Fears' room for advice. "Here comes Night Train," another rookie would yell every time Lane knocked on Fears' door. The nickname stuck.

It first appeared in print after Lane tackled Washington's Charlie Justice on the 5-yard line and broke his collarbone in Los Angeles' first exhibition game.

"Rookie Dick 'Night Train' Lane derails Charlie 'Choo Choo' Justice," it read. "I thought it was pretty good to be mentioned in a big paper like that so I decided to keep the nickname."

YALE LARY

Defensive Back/Punter · Enshrined 1979

When Robert Yale Lary was at his best, his foot was as big a weapon for the Lions as quarterbacks, running backs and wide receivers.

He helped changed the face of pro football as a member of "Chris' Crew," the defensive backfield which spotlighted how pass defenders who weren't offensive rejects could make a significant contribution to victory.

Lary also showed how a skilled practitioner of the punter's art could be responsible for points without crossing the goal line.

The native Texan was a superlative defensive back from 1956–64, with time out for a tour of Army duty in 1954–55. He became one of the best punters in the game's history upon his return from the service.

Lary played right safety alongside Jack Christiansen in Chris' Crew, then stabilized Detroit defenses in the early 1960s when the Lions were the best pro football team not based in Green Bay. The position he played is known today as free safety, the center fielder of the defensive backfield.

There was definitely a period of adaptation for Lary after he was done playing halfback and safety for Texas A&M in 1955. He was the the Lions' top selection though but a third-round choice since Coach Buddy Parker had traded away the first two rounders.

In his last game as a collegian, Lary had sparked A&M to a 23–21 upset of Texas with touchdowns on a 67-yard run and a 20-yard pass reception.

So when the Fort Worth native signed a $6,500 contract and was given No. 28, Parker tried him first on offense. The move went over like sand in ice cream.

"Leon Hart (6-foot-4, 250) was playing defensive end in a scrimmage," Lary later recalled, "and I was supposed to block him. After making a fool of myself a couple of times, Buddy Parker suggested I give defense a try."

The 5-foot-11, 189-pound Lary had also punted for Texas A&M, so Parker tested his proficiency there, too.

Lary learned to punt in the same Texas winds that later taught Lee Trevino to outwit, not out-muscle, them. Lary would line-drive punts to maximize his distance when the wind was blowing in his face.

Unlike Trevino, though, the technique did not bring Lary success outside the Lone Star state. Parker took one look at Lary's liners and told him, "You do that up here and somebody's gonna run it down your throat."

Lary's parents were not raising a dummy. He made the adaptation to full-time defensive whiz and honed his punting skills through non-game practice with the Lions and in the service.

He made 50 career interceptions and only recently, with expanded schedules allowing for more opportunities per season, has Lary been shoved off the list of top 20 all-time interceptors. He remains third on the Lions' list and his 787 career return yards are No. 2 in Detroit history to Lem Barney.

Lary won punting titles in 1959, 1961 and 1963, missing in 1962 by just 3.6 inches. A year he didn't win, 1960, Detroit opponents averaged less than one yard per return on his punts.

From the end zone, Lary could consistently punt past midfield with enough hang time to let coverage get down and do its work. Once, Lary had a string of six games and 32 punts with no return and he had just four blocked out of 503 in his career.

Lary was named All-NFL four times and played in nine Pro Bowls.

Yale Lary

Bobby Layne

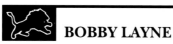

BOBBY LAYNE

Quarterback · Enshrined 1967

Other quarterbacks can wear Robert Lawrence Layne's shoes, but they can't fill 'em.

"Bobby Layne was the chief and the rest of us were Indians," said fellow Hall of Fame member Yale Lary, a teammate during the Layne-led glory years of the 1950s.

Layne quarterbacked Detroit from 1950 into the 1958 season, when he was traded to the Pittsburgh Steelers and reunited with Coach Buddy Parker. He retired in 1962.

He and Philadelphia Eagle Chuck Bednarik, the last of the two-way players, were the first players voted into the NFL Hall of Fame immediately following the minimum five-year waiting period. Layne disdained use of a face mask throughout his career and was the last player in the league without one.

Blond and blue-eyed, Layne was the archetypical gun-slinger to the rescue at his position. He led his team to championships, did it with bravado and did it with a flair uniquely his own.

Layne sparked Detroit to three NFL championships, four Western Division titles and a pair of second-place finishes. He kicked field goals for a time and was the 1956 league scoring champion.

For his career, Layne completed 1,814 passes for 26,768 yards and 196 touchdowns. He may have had a lead belly, but he had light feet. His 411 rushing yards in 1952 ranked him No. 9 in the league — and only 12 backs had more than his 94 carries.

He ran for 2,451 yards in a career that accumulated 372 points. During Layne's eight-plus seasons with the Lions he ran 432 times for 1,793 yards (4.2 average). Thirteen of those runs wound up in the end zone.

Layne cast a larger-than-life shadow because he was larger than life. The lasting contribution he made to the strategy of football can be seen today — the last two minutes of every close game. He turned the two-minute drill into an art form.

The Detroit players loved their 6-foot-1, 198-pound quarterback, and Layne was a great believer in team unity. Maybe he thought of the Lions as an extension of college football; graduate school for players. Virtually everyone who played on those teams recalls how close-knit they were.

Much of that stemmed from Layne's Monday after-practice habit of taking over a bar across the street from Tiger Stadium. Players would come in for treatment of injuries, to get loose, or just to be together. Even non-drinker Doak Walker attended.

"He divided people into 'leavers' and 'stayers,'" Lary said. "I was a 'stayer.' We were all pretty close . . . close in a way you don't see too much of any more."

"Bobby had a little more money than the rest of us," said Jack Christiansen, yet another Hall of Fame teammate. "And he spent it on the team. If we went out to have a few beers, he'd pay for the whole thing. Not only by his ball playing did he get the loyalty from the other players, but also from the other things he did as well."

Layne still holds Detroit records for career pass attempts (2,193), completions (1,074), yardage gained (15,710), TD passes (118), touchdown passes in a season (26) and the top two spots in yards gained through passing in one game (374 and 364). Someone may break them, but it is doubtful such feats will be accomplished quite so colorfully.

JOE SCHMIDT

Linebacker · Enshrined 1973

Middle linebacker was like a teenager's bicep when Joe Schmidt entered pro football in 1952. It just needed definition.

"He was something new and different in pro football," said Aldo Forte, Detroit line coach under Buddy Parker, "and there's never been anyone like him. He was the first of the great middle linebackers."

Linebacking was a nebulous thing before Schmidt became the Lions' seventh-round draft choice in 1952. Some teams used four while others had none because they utilized a seven-man line.

Most clubs in the early 1950s employed a 5–2 alignment which featured a burly man-mountain line-clogger like 300-plus pound Les Bingaman in the middle at guard.

Then some teams began dropping off their defensive ends and moving the middle guard back a step or two. And when offenses began replacing their tight end with a slot receiver, defenses were forced to change to accommodate the extra pass catcher.

The less mobile hulk in the middle was forced out, in favor of a quick but hard-hitting middle linebacker as the backbone of the 4–3. Detroit couldn't make the switch until the incredible bulk Bingaman retired at the end of the 1954 season.

Some teams dipped their toes in the water. Detroit dove off the high board. "By 1955," Forte said, "we had made the swing all the way to the new defense.

I guess we were one of the first teams to go all the way with it, and Joe was moved into the middle linebacking spot.

"He took to it like a duck to water. We became a great defensive team, but it was mostly his doing. You might say that Joe's performance as a middle linebacker caused a complete change in the thinking of football coaches about defense."

Schmidt called the defensive signals . . . run, pass, which direction, etc. He had to know the yard line, which hash mark the ball was on, the down and how far to a first down, personnel changes, the quarter, the score, opponent tendencies, the coverages available and then make sure everyone knew the call. All this in less than 30 seconds.

The braininess Schmidt brought to the position, his "clean but mean' tackling style, all helped to glamorize defenses.

"He was the best at his position," Parker said. "He had an instinct for defense that few players ever acquire. He wasn't big, as defensive players go, but he was one of the surest and hardest tacklers you'll ever see."

Joseph Paul Schmidt wore No. 56 for Detroit from 1953 through 1965 — also coaching the club from 1967–72 — and did it with such distinction he was selected to the Hall of Fame in 1973.

The 6-foot, 222-pounder was All-Pro in eight of his 13 seasons and played in 10 Pro Bowl games. He served as captain of the Lions for nine seasons and made 24 career interceptions.

Shoulder injures in 1962 and 1964 hastened the end of his playing career. He continued on the field in 1965 then, still only 33, finished out the last year of his contract as a linebacker coach under Harry Gilmer.

In January 1967, a week before his 35th birthday and one bare season from the playing field, Schmidt was named head coach of the Lions.

He lasted six seasons before a variety of non-coaching reasons induced him to announce his resignation January 12, 1973. One day later he was voted into the Hall of Fame. For Lions fans, he'd already been there for a long time.

Joe Schmidt

Doak Walker

DOAK WALKER

Halfback · Enshrined 1986

How many times have we heard athletes say they want to retire at the top of their game?

Every year — and often by the same people. Right up until they are politely asked to take their eroded skills into the coaching or broadcasting booth.

Not Doak Walker. He walked away from the glamour, glory and good times of professional football after just six seasons, still in his prime and with his services still in demand.

He freely admits he left for the same reason today's athletes hang on by their greedy fingernails — for money — but leaving a lifetime full of the lifestyle could not have been easy. Even in 1955, at age 29.

"I'd been on three division champions, two world champions, I'd been to five Pro Bowls, I'd been All-Pro four times," he told the *Detroit News'* Jerry Green in 1986. "What else was there to do?"

The most money Ewell Doak Walker II ever took from a season was $35,000, big-time bucks in those days. But his sense of business, good looks, personality and popularity in his native Texas (and later, Colorado) let him walk away with no regrets.

The Lions retired his No. 37 in a ceremony held Dec. 11, 1955, as he closed out a six-year career with a game against the New York Giants. And a marvelous career it was.

The 5-foot-11, 173-pound Texan was the first junior to win the Heisman Trophy, which he did in 1948 while at Southern Methodist. He had won the Maxwell Trophy as a sophomore.

It took Walker a career to gain what Barry Sanders gets in a season — 1,520 yards rushing. But remember, he was playing for "T" formation teams which used quarterback Bobby Layne, no ox as a runner, behind center with three backs crossing the "T" right in back of him.

With limited work, Walker averaged 4.9 and the most he ever rushed for in a season was 386 yards (on 83 attempts) his rookie year. But in three of his six seasons he was above 500 yards receiving and two others were above 400.

He caught 152 passes for 2,539 yards, averaged 39.1 yards as a sometimes-punter (50–1,955) and kicked 49 field goals. As an infrequent return man, Walker ran back 38 kickoffs 968 yards (25.5 average) and 18 punts 284 yards (15.8 average).

Walker's specialty was the scoreboard. He totaled 534 points, twice winning the NFL scoring title, and a figure that still ranks third on Detroit's career scoreboard. In just six seasons he kicked enough extra points, 183, to place third on the team list.

Walker is still Detroit's top scorer for a season, accounting for 128 points in 1950, and he holds a share of the club record with four touchdowns in one game.

"Well, I'll tell ya," Bobby Layne, Walker's boyhood friend, once said. "If we were ahead 28–0 or somethin', you might not notice Doak on the field.

"But if it was a close game, everybody knew he was there — and he would be the difference."

ALEX WOJCIECHOWICZ

Center/Linebacker · Enshrined 1968

It took Alex Wojciechowicz just four professional games to earn his iron-man reputation. He played them in one week.

"Wojie" played center alongside Vince Lombardi as part of the famed Seven Blocks of Granite at Fordham, where he was unanimous All-America in 1936 and 1937.

The Lions made him their No. 1 draft choice in 1938 and the 6-foot, 235-pound center-linebacker was tagged an iron man right away with his four games in a week exploit.

First came the All-Star game in Chicago against the reigning professional champions. Then came another All-Star game, this one in New York. When Wojciechowicz joined the Lions, it was to suit up for an intra-squad game. He then rounded out his week's work by participating in Detroit's rescheduled season opener September 9 against Pittsburgh.

That game was originally set for early October in Pittsburgh, but was shifted to Detroit because of the possibility the baseball Pirates, who ultimately finished three games behind Chicago's Cubs, would be playing in the World Series.

"When we played 60 minutes, you had to pace yourself," Wojciechowicz said, "and the game was much slower."

Wojciechowicz also left two other calling cards in the world of professional football. He had the leg-span of an albatross — 5-feet, 4-inches — as he hunched over the ball for the center snap. Plus he had difficulty keeping his pants snugged up over his hips. (Hmmmm, maybe there's a connection there . . .)

Wojciechowicz loved to play. One season, he talked his coach into letting him play end part-time in a vain effort to fulfill his desire to score a touchdown.

Although Wojciechowicz is best remembered for his Ambassador Bridge imitation while centering the ball, he actually was a better linebacker. In today's game, he probably would have excelled at outside linebacker because of his excellent pass coverage ability.

Greasy Neale, who picked Wojie up for the Philadelphia Eagles after the Lions cut him in 1946, liked to relate how "the Redskins had Bones Taylor in 1947 and in our opener he caught five touchdown passes.

"So the next time we played Washington, I put Wojie on Bones. He never caught a pass that day and he never caught a pass against us the next three years. Wojie made sure of that."

He had intercepted seven passes for the Lions in 1944, which no defensive back had done to that point. It stood as a club record until defensive back Don Doll picked off 11 in 1949 and a dozen the following season.

Wojciechowicz returned those seven passes 88 yards, second-best figure in the club record books at the time. He ended his career with 16 interceptions.

Early in his rookie season, Wojciechowicz took over the starting center job and he remained a two-way player until being waived after Detroit lost its first three games of the 1946 season.

Neale claimed him for Philadelphia and decided to limit Wojciechowicz play to the defensive side of the line. Wojciechowicz helped them win the Eastern Division championship in 1947, then World Championships the next two seasons.

At the time of his retirement, Wojciechowicz was second only to Sammy Baugh in career longevity. Curiously, he never made an All-NFL team. ❖

Alex Wojciechowicz

12

Your list may not exactly match ours, but you'd have to agree that the greats featured on the following pages, combined with the 11 Hall of Famers, helped shape and define 60 years of Detroit Lions football. So, who would you put on your list?

Some fans argue that Charlie Sanders may be the greatest Lion this side of Canton.

When You Think of the Lions, You Think of...?

Some of pro football's biggest and brightest stars will be forever associated with the Detroit Lions.

by Chuck Klonke

Writing about the greatest Lions in history is the easy part . . . selecting *who* the greatest Lions are is a bit more difficult.

We've profiled Detroit's 11 Pro Football Hall of Famers. But beyond those immortals enshrined in Canton — who are the next Top 20 Lions?

Any list would be purely subjective, of course, so for the purposes of this book, we've tried to draw some parameters.

For starters, let's say we include all players who have been named to four or more Pro Bowl squads. That opens the way for Roger Brown, Lou Creekmur, Jimmy David, Doug English, Ed Flanagan, Alex Karras, Barry Sanders, Charlie Sanders and Harley Sewell. That's a pretty impressive list of nine. No argument there.

Mere Pro Bowl status may not be enough. Add in all the Pro Bowlers who have earned team MVP recognition, say, three times minimum. That brings our grand total to . . . er . . . 11. Hmmm. Only Mike Lucci and Billy Sims meet that tough criteria.

All right, with nine spots remaining, there are still plenty of good players — and coaches — available. That's right, don't forget about the coaches. The Lions have had three skippers lead them to NFL championships: Potsy Clark, Buddy Parker and George Wilson. With three coaches, we now have 14 greats, and six spots left on our Top 20 chart.

There are two men whose contributions to the Lions have been unsurpassed, and for historical reasons, among others, their inclusion is a must. Wayne Walker played for more seasons (15) and in more games (200) than any player in club history; he was also the only player named to Lions' All-Time First Team in both the Golden Era and Modern Era. Russ Thomas served the Detroit Lions for 43 years in every capacity imaginable — as player, scout, assistant coach, director of player personnel, executive vice president and general manager.

Fine, so who are the final four Lions in our Top 20 list? Since the players in Canton are off-limits, maybe we should turn to the State of Michigan Sports Hall of Fame. Twenty-seven Lion greats have been honored by the State Hall, but when you eliminate those in the Pro Football Hall of Fame and the gentlemen mentioned above, the list has been narrowed to 13. Of those, four have been named to one of the Lions' All-Time First Teams.

Four? Enter Les Bingaman, Cloyce Box, Bob Hoernschemeyer and Byron "Whizzer" White and . . . presto! . . . we have our Top 20.

BARRY SANDERS

The Lions knew right from the start that Barry Sanders was something special.

Wayne Fontes knew it the day he timed Sanders in 4.39 seconds for the 40-yard dash during an informal workout. Fontes decided then that Sanders would be the Lions' first pick in the 1989 draft if he was available.

Detroit was so sure Sanders would be a success that he was given jersey No. 20, which had been worn by superstars Billy Sims and Lem Barney.

Sanders showed the fans what was in store when he burst 18 yards on his first NFL carry against the Phoenix Cardinals. He missed winning the league rushing championship by 10 yards as a rookie despite carrying the ball 70 fewer times than Kansas City's Christian Okoye and probably could have beaten out Okoye if he had asked to go back in late in the season finale at Atlanta.

But that's Sanders. He doesn't care about personal glory. He might be the most unassuming superstar in professional sports. He doesn't do any dances or gyrations after scoring a touchdown. He simply hands the ball to the official as if it's something he does all the time — which it is.

"People think Barry is putting on an act with that humble stuff," says teammate William White, "but I'm telling you, he really is that humble. Maybe he's too humble."

Although he's rushed for more than 1,000 yards and has started the Pro Bowl in each of his first four seasons with the Lions, he's the same person he was when he came out of Oklahoma State after winning the Heisman Trophy.

"A lot of people say I don't know how much ability I have, but I know I'm a pretty good football player," Sanders says. "It's just that football is not my whole life. You never know what's going to happen in this business, so you don't want to make it the only thing in your life. But I'll give it 100 percent when I'm playing."

Sanders realizes he can't rush for 1,000-plus yards without some help, and he's quick to credit his blockers for his success. He has been known to give his offensive linemen gifts as thanks for what they've helped him accomplish.

That started when he won the Heisman and was asked to appear at a television studio in Tokyo, where Oklahoma State was scheduled to play later that day. He was reluctant at first, then agreed on the condition that the Cowboys' offensive line and other backs were allowed to come along.

Sanders' combination of speed and the paralyzing ability to stop and start has made him one of the most electrifying runners to hit the NFL. When he stops, defenders are forced to stop with him and none of them can match his first step when he starts up again.

"By the time you get to where Barry is, he isn't there anymore," says former teammate Jerry Ball.

Sanders has already rewritten the Lions' record book, and there's no telling what standards he'll set as his career continues.

BILLY SIMS

One of the best descriptions of Billy Sims' career with the Detroit Lions was "he's a star who approaches the game like a journeyman."

Although he was one of the most exciting runners in the game during his five seasons with the Lions, Sims played hard and practiced hard. His work ethic earned the respect of teammates and coaches. He never hid in the training room nursing injuries to avoid practice.

"For a guy who's in the superstar status, Billy's just a super team player," said his backfield coach, Bill Johnson. "Billy is a football player. Billy does the grubby things that a football player has to do."

Sims' less-heralded teammates also appreciated him.

"I appreciate anybody who goes out and plays hard every day," said offensive lineman Keith Dorney. "He's a fantastic

Barry Sanders

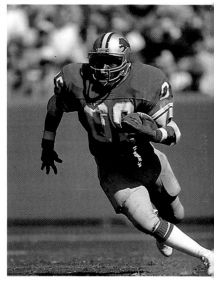

Billy Sims

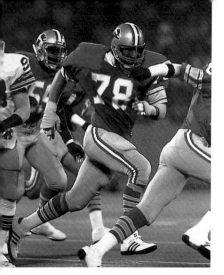

Doug English

runner. As a person, I like Billy, too. He carries his notoriety and superstar status well."

Opponents also respected the former Oklahoma standout, who won the Heisman Trophy as a junior with the Sooners.

"We probably have more respect for him than any other ball carrier and maybe any other player we play against. He's a relentless player," said former San Francisco coach Bill Walsh.

Until Barry Sanders came along, Sims held nearly every Lions' rushing record.

"I like the competition," Sims said after rushing for 1,303 yards as a rookie, which was the third-highest total of any first-year runner. "That's what I like about any game — seeing how well I can do against other guys. I don't like to lose, but if I haven't done my best, winning isn't much fun, either. The competition is what appeals to me."

Sims rushed for 153 yards in his first NFL game against the Los Angeles Rams in 1980 and didn't stop until that fateful game against the Minnesota Vikings in 1984 when he injured his knee.

Sims recently recalled his debut, in which he scored touchdowns on runs of one, 12 and 41 yards and also turned a simple turn-in pattern into a 60-yard gain during the Lions' drive to the winning touchdown.

"It was a great way to break in," he said. "We felt it would be a tough game because the Rams had just gone to the Super Bowl, but we jumped on them and stayed on them.

"It was a tremendous feeling for me and the whole team. I remember thinking, 'It can't get any better than this.'"

But it did.

He was named to the Pro Bowl team in three of his five seasons in Detroit and was the Lions' offensive Most Valuable Player on three occasions.

The year before Sims was drafted by Detroit as the No. 1 pick overall, the Lions struggled to a 2–14 record. The next year, Detroit was 9–7, and by 1983 the Lions were NFC Central Division champions.

 DOUG ENGLISH

It was always easy to tell if the Lions won on Sunday by checking out defensive tackle Doug English.

If English was smiling and having a good time, Detroit was coming off a victory. If there was a grim look on his face during the week, it was a good bet the Lions had lost their last game.

"Winning makes me a lot easier to get along with all week," the big defensive lineman from Texas once explained. "You start to get back to that feeling of accomplishment. I'm elated.

"What's crazy about it, is you can play a heck of a game with sacks, tackles, fumbles and lose and you have that same horrible feeling. I go home and I don't want to go out. Everybody knows I like to go out and have a good time, but I don't feel like I deserve to go out."

The losing bothered English so much that after the Lions won only two of 16 games in 1979, he went into the oil business in his native Texas the following year.

The lure of football proved too much, however, and English returned a year later and played through the 1985 season. He finally quit when doctors advised him that a neck injury could cause permanent disability.

Although he had a lucrative contract with Detroit, English often said he wasn't playing football for the money.

"I don't play on Sunday for the money," he said. "On Monday through Saturday, I'll go through the meetings and the practices and work for you, but on Sundays it's not for the money. It doesn't matter how much they pay me or if I have to pay them to play on Sunday."

English was drafted by the Lions in the second round in 1975 and became a starter two years later. He made the Pro Bowl as a reserve in 1978 and was a starter at defensive tackle from 1981–83.

In 1979, English was the Lions' leading tackler with 90, an unusual feat for a defensive lineman. Bubba Baker was second that year with 69.

English tied for fifth in the NFC in sacks with 13 in 1983 when the Lions won the Central Division championship.

He played his final season in Detroit at nose tackle when Darryl Rogers brought in the 3–4 defensive alignment. At first, English didn't like the move, but after talking to Rogers, his stance softened and he became one of the best in the league until the spinal injury ended his career.

His attitude toward his career with the Lions is best summed up by the remark, "When I'm on the field it means a heck of a lot to me to do well. Money can't pay for the things that players go through in terms of preparation, discipline and playing."

 LES BINGAMAN

Sometimes Les Bingaman's size overshadowed his ability to play football.

Once, the pilot of a chartered DC-9 the Lions were taking asked Bingaman if he would mind moving from the back of the plane to the front so that the pilot could take off.

On another flight, from an exhibition game in Birmingham, Alabama, a worried pilot asked if the 300-pound-plus Bingaman and 260-pound Leon Hart would mind taking another plane.

"There's a short runway here and I'm not sure the plane will take off with those two aboard," he said.

Another time, in training camp, head coach Buddy Parker turned to assistant Buster Ramsey and remarked, "Les is looking a little heavier this year. I'll bet he weighs close to 400 pounds."

Ramsey replied, "No, he's closer to 300."

The Lions didn't have a scale that went high enough to get an accurate reading on Bingaman, so Parker and Ramsey loaded him into a car and drove to the Ypsilanti Farm Bureau where they weighed him on one of the scales that went up to 1,000 pounds.

When the needle stopped it showed

349 pounds, eight ounces. Ramsey had won the bet.

It was nothing for Bingaman to devour 14 hot dogs at a sitting. A typical meal was three steaks, polished off with a quart of ice cream.

One year, Bingaman spent the off-season working on an asphalt finishing machine and reported to camp weighing under 300 pounds. Instead of dominating the middle of the line like he usually did, Bingaman was getting pushed around.

"I had to eat my way onto the team that year," Bingaman said with a chuckle.

A native of Tennessee, Bingaman grew up in Gary, Indiana, and became an All-American middle guard at the University of Illinois. He was drafted by the Lions in the third round in 1948 and played six seasons with the club. He retired at age 28 in 1954.

Bingaman anchored the middle of the line during Detroit's championship seasons in 1952 and 1953. When he retired, the Lions changed the defense to a four-man front with a middle linebacker instead of a middle guard.

The man known as "Bing" was one of the most popular Lions with both the fans and his teammates.

Bingaman returned to coach the Lions from 1960 through 1964 and later moved to the Miami Dolphins as an assistant under George Wilson and later Don Shula.

He died of a heart attack at the age of 44 in November 1970.

 **CLOYCE BOX**

One can only wonder what kind of NFL career Cloyce Box would have had if it hadn't been interrupted twice by stints in the Marines.

Box, who was an outstanding player at West Texas State, was a halfback for the Washington Redskins in 1948 and came to the Lions a year later. His pro career got a late start because he served four years in the Marines.

Les Bingaman

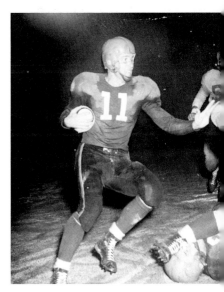

Cloyce Box

Roger Brown

Bo McMillin, who was coaching the Lions when Box arrived on the scene, converted the 6-foot-4, 220-pound Texan to an end when Detroit traded its leading receiver, Bob Mann, to the New York Bulldogs in the deal that brought Bobby Layne to the Lions.

It was an excellent move because Box, who went to college on a basketball scholarship, was a fine athlete and made the adjustment quite easily.

In 1950, Box caught 50 passes for 1,009 yards, second only to Tom Fears of the Los Angeles Rams. Box had his greatest day on December 3, 1950, when he caught 12 passes for 302 yards and four touchdowns against the Baltimore Colts. Layne threw three of the TD passes and Fred Enke connected on the fourth.

Box returned to active duty in the Marines after the 1950 season, despite the efforts of the Lions to obtain a deferment for him.

He hadn't slowed down when he returned, because he made the All-Pro team in 1952 with 42 receptions for 924 yards and 15 touchdowns. Box's scoring total of 90 points was second in the league and made a prophet of coach Buddy Parker.

Box had signed a hefty contract with the Lions after many hours of haggling with general manager Nick Kerbawy. When he finally signed, for a reported $12,000, Parker said, "Now if you can catch 15 touchdown passes, everything will be all right."

During his career with the Lions, which ended after the 1954 season, Box averaged 20.7 yards-per-reception.

After his retirement from football, Box became a successful lawyer and oil baron in Texas.

 ROGER BROWN

When Roger Brown joined the Lions as an unheralded fourth-round draft pick out of Maryland State in 1960, folks talked more about his weight — some-thing well over 300 pounds — than his football ability.

Six years later, when he was traded to the Los Angeles Rams, he was a four-time Pro Bowl selection and one of the premier defensive linemen in the NFL.

Brown's feats of strength, while playing on a defensive line that included Alex Karras, Darris McCord and Sam Williams and was the first to carry the nickname "Fearsome Foursome," are legendary.

Once during the 1962 campaign, which was probably Brown's finest with the Lions, he got a safety against Chicago Bears' quarterback Billy Wade that left everyone who saw it amazed.

Wade faded into his own end zone to pass and as he maneuvered around behind the goalposts, Brown realized he wouldn't be able to get to the quarterback. But then the big Detroit tackle also realized the shortest distance between two points is a straight line.

There was only one problem. Standing in that straight line was Bears' guard Ted Karras, Alex's brother. Brown lifted the 243-pound Karras off his feet and hurled him at Wade, dropping the quarterback for a safety.

When asked about the play after the game, Brown smiled and replied, "I think I just shoved him hard."

Although he played collegiately at a small black school in Princess Anne, Maryland, Brown was known by pro scouts. Most of them, including the neighboring Baltimore Colts, felt they could wait and tap him in one of the later rounds.

However, Lions' scout Bob Nussbaumer warned the club to "grab him early," and Detroit took him with the fourth-round pick it obtained from Pittsburgh in the Bobby Layne trade.

Brown reported to the college All-Star camp and finished third in the 50-yard sprint trials, behind two backs. When he joined the Lions, he immediately became a starter and held that spot throughout his six seasons in Detroit.

Brown's finest day might have been

the Thanksgiving Day game in 1962 when Detroit sacked Green Bay quarterback Bart Starr 10 times in a 26–14 victory; Brown was credited with six of the sacks.

In his first exhibition game with the Lions in 1960, he intercepted a pass against the Cleveland Browns and rambled 23 yards, most of the way with four tacklers clinging to him.

That earned him the nickname "Crazylegs" from his teammates.

In addition to tackling quarterbacks, Brown had a penchant for tackling big meals. It's been said that Lions' coach George Wilson once had four of Brown's teammates sit with him at the dinner table in training camp to make sure he didn't eat more than three steaks at a sitting.

Following his career with the Lions, Brown had several productive seasons with the Rams, teaming with David Jones, Merlin Olsen and Lamar Lundy to form a second "Fearsome Foursome."

POTSY CLARK

George "Potsy" Clark came to Detroit along with the Portsmouth Spartans when the franchise made its shift before the 1934 season.

Clark, who had played for the great Bob Zuppke at the University of Illinois and was a member of the 1914 team that Zuppke called his best ever, was a rugged taskmaster. It wasn't unusual for him to stop the team bus during a lengthy trip and order the players into a cornfield for an impromptu practice.

He was a wry, caustic man who usually wore a battered hat. Dutch Clark, who was no relation to Potsy, but was the star player on those first Lions' teams, once compared the old coach to former Michigan State coach Duffy Daugherty.

"Potsy kept you ready," Dutch Clark said. "But he always had a few jokes. He'd get you in the huddle and tell you

a few jokes, but he'd work you hard. He'd get you ready for the ballgame."

It was cold and snowy when the Lions played New York in the 1935 NFL championship game, but Potsy Clark wouldn't let his players complain about the elements.

"He'd run you around the track if you hollered, so nobody said anything." Dutch Clark recalled.

Potsy Clark coached at Michigan State, Minnesota and Butler before taking the reins at Portsmouth in 1931. He guided the Spartans to an 11–3 record that first season and followed with 6–2–4 and 6–5 campaigns before the move to Detroit.

In his first year in Detroit, Clark led the Lions to a second-place finish with a 10–3 mark, then won the championship in 1935, posting a 7–3–2 record after a slow start that saw them in last place in the Western Conference in mid-November.

The Lions dropped to third place in 1936 with an 8–4 record, and after the season, Potsy Clark quit and was replaced by Dutch Clark. Potsy had actually quit before the season, but reconsidered.

His departure was punctuated by some ill feeling between him and owner George Richards and Clark suggested that the owner should get out of football.

Richards replied by saying, "I'll pick Dutch Clark's Lions to beat Potsy Clark's (Brooklyn) Dodgers every time they meet."

Potsy coached Brooklyn from 1937–39 and returned to the Lions in 1940 after Fred Mandel had bought the club from Richards. Clark posted a 5–5–1 record in 1940 and left a second time to pursue a more relaxing life as an athletic director. He was AD at Nebraska from 1945–1953.

Clark had a 58–31–11 record in his two stints with the Lions but was only 11–17–5 in his three seasons in Brooklyn.

He died November 8, 1972, in LaJolla, California.

Potsy Clark

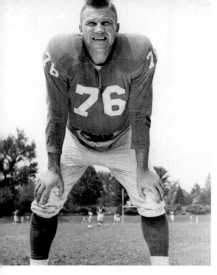

Lou Creekmur

Jim David

 LOU CREEKMUR

Offensive linemen are usually anonymous to the general public, but they're appreciated by their teammates and coaches and are integral parts of winning football teams.

When the Lions were winning championships with regularity in the 1950s, Detroit had a solid offensive line led by tackle Lou Creekmur and guard Harley Sewell.

As the protector of quarterback Bobby Layne and the blocker for runners like Bob Hoernschemeyer, Gene Gedman, John Henry Johnson and Doak Walker, Creekmur earned All-Pro status every season but one from 1951 through 1957. The year he missed, 1955, he spent half the time on the defensive line, but still was invited to play in the Pro Bowl.

Creekmur played in all four of the Lions' championship games against the Cleveland Browns during the 1950s.

He played 10 seasons with the Lions, beginning in 1950 and continuing through 1959. He retired after the 1958 campaign, but came out of retirement after four games in 1959.

Creekmur played collegiately at William & Mary and was drafted by the Philadelphia Eagles of the NFL and the Los Angeles Dons of the All-America Conference in 1948. Although his college class graduated, he still had a year of eligibility and completed that while working on his master's degree.

After the 1949 season, he played in the first Senior Bowl and impressed Lions' coach Bo McMillin when he blocked a punt. McMillin asked Creekmur if he would be interested in playing for Detroit if he was drafted. He said yes, and the Lions made him one of their selections.

Creekmur said it never bothered him that he and his fellow linemen didn't receive the recognition that Layne, Walker or Cloyce Box received.

"I don't think we ever dwelled on it," he said after his career ended. "We knew that we got it from Aldo Forte, our offensive line coach, and from Buddy Parker, and from Layne and the backfield. We were as proud as could be when a guy like Hoernschemeyer or Walker scored, knowing that we helped him over the goal line. We were such a close team; there were no guilt feelings that another guy was getting the publicity."

Creekmur brought a physical style of play to the offensive line. He wasn't afraid to throw an elbow and he once told *Detroit News* columnist Doc Greene, "I probably held on every other play.

"I never really held much with my hands, but I developed a knack of holding with my elbows, knees, feet, head — any place where I could make a junction with my body and the other guy's."

Creekmur said he learned to use his elbows from Marvin Bass, his line coach at William & Mary.

One of his best hits came against San Francisco's Hardy Brown, who had a reputation as the NFL's meanest player because of the way he'd drive his shoulder into an opponent's face.

"It knocked him cold," Creekmur recalled. "We must have run that film back 20 times, watching Hardy Brown get knocked out cold."

 **JIM DAVID**

A few years ago, a reporter asked former Lions' cornerback Jim David how he would have reacted to a receiver dancing and spiking the ball in front of him after a catch.

"I'd have been thrown out of the game," replied David, who was called "The Hatchet" during his career with Detroit. He earned the nickname for the devastating hits he delivered despite his slight build (5-feet-10, 170 pounds).

David, who played for the Lions from 1952 through 1959 and went to the Pro Bowl six times, didn't take kindly to ball-carriers coming into his territory.

He also loved being part of the action.

"Sometimes I get hungry out there," he said. "I make up my mind it's going to be me that brings the next one down. Once I even shouted at the other team to call the play to my side."

While David was popular in Detroit, his hard-nosed style of play didn't earn him many friends around the NFL. Once in 1953, he put San Francisco's Y.A. Tittle and Los Angeles' Tom Fears out of commission on consecutive Sundays.

A jarring tackle fractured Tittle's jaw and a hit on Fears gave the Rams' receiver two broken vertebrae. Those plays sent shock waves throughout the league, asking for then commissioner Bert Bell to mete out some type of punishment for the Lions' cornerback.

"Tittle was an accident, but I kinda went after Fears because he went after our Yale Lary earlier in the game," David later explained. "We policed our own game in those days."

David was the Lions' 22nd-round pick out of Colorado State in 1952. He was second in the nation in pass receptions in 1951, so he knew something about playing both sides of the field. He quickly moved into the lineup as a regular and started in four NFL championship games.

David's love of contact amused former teammate Jack Christiansen.

"He was the only player I could remember who would constantly get up from a really bruising tackle with a smile on his face," Christiansen said.

Buster Ramsey, who was an assistant coach during David's career with Detroit, said the Hatchet was an inspirational player.

"When the other players watch David day in and day out, some of his drive has to rub off on them," Ramsey said. "I'd take 11 guys like him on any team I coached."

David coached the Lions' defensive backs from 1967 through 1972 when former teammate Joe Schmidt was the head coach. He was also an assistant coach with the Rams.

David finished his career with 36 interceptions, ranking him fifth on Detroit's all-time list behind Dick LeBeau (62), Lem Barney (56), Lary (50) and Christiansen (46).

ED FLANAGAN

During the late 1960s and early 1970s, the Lions and Chicago Bears staged some bitter battles, and the focal point of many of those games was the matchup between Bears' linebacker Dick Butkus and Detroit center Ed Flanagan.

It was the continuation of a rivalry that began in college when Flanagan was playing for Purdue and Butkus was with Illinois.

"He was my most troublesome opponent," Flanagan said, adding, "the highlight of my year is playing against Butkus."

Flanagan was drafted by the Lions in the fifth round in 1965 and immediately moved in as a starter when Bob Scholtz was traded to the New York Giants and Bob Whitlow was injured in training camp.

Flanagan started 139 of the next 140 games for Detroit before he was traded to San Diego after the 1974 season. He was a four-time Pro Bowl selection and was named to the All-Pro team once.

Flanagan was the anchor of one of the best offensive lines in the game under former Lions' assistant coach Chuck Knox.

"I guess I came in at a good time," Flanagan once said. "When I broke in we were ranked as one of the worst lines and took a lot of bad press, but we started getting better and now we're considered one of the best. Credit Chuck Knox for that.

"He taught me steps I never had before, like how to play the percentages in the middle linebacker blitz. He also taught me little tricks about sitting back on the ball and how to set up for pass protection," Flanagan said.

Flanagan was born in California, but

Ed Flanagan

Bob Hoernschemeyer

grew up in the rugged steel and coal country of Pennsylvania. He was a junior high school fullback, but was soon converted to the offensive line because of his lack of speed.

Flanagan never complained about the lack of recognition a center receives.

"They can't start without me and I can never be offside," he said with a smile.

Flanagan credited some of his success against Butkus to the practice workouts against Joe Schmidt, who later became Flanagan's coach with the Lions.

"Schmidt has some moves I still haven't seen," he once said.

The chubby, crewcut Flanagan had several nicknames during his Lions' career, including B.F. Goodrich (for his spare tire) and Fluffy.

 BOB HOERNSCHEMEYER

Bob "Hunchy" Hoernschemeyer played only four seasons with the Lions, but they were among the four best in club history.

Hoernschemeyer was a key member of Detroit's championship teams in 1952 and 1953. The former Indiana and Navy standout was the man the Lions looked to when they needed a yard or two on the ground.

"Hunchy isn't one of the name players in the league, but he's certainly one of the most underrated," said coach Buddy Parker.

"When it comes to picking up those all-important two or three yards that can be the difference between winning and losing a game, he's invariably the most reliable man," Parker continued.

The 6-foot, 190-pounder led the Lions in rushing his four seasons with the team and made the Pro Bowl in 1952 and 1953. His most productive year was 1951 when he rushed for 678 yards and caught 23 passes for another 263 yards.

Hoernschemeyer retired as the second-leading rusher in club history with 2,439 yards, only five fewer than Ace Gutowsky.

Hoernschemeyer had a remarkable day against the old New York Yankees in 1950 when he rushed for a club-record 198 yards, including a 96-yard touchdown run.

He joined the Lions before the 1950 season as the club's top choice in the frozen player pool that was used to disperse the talent from the All-American Football Conference. Hoernschemeyer had played for Brooklyn and Chicago in the AAFC and rushed for 2,109 yards.

Parker called him "the best third-down back in the game." In addition to his talents as a short-yardage runner, Hoernschemeyer was a good blocker and an effective receiver.

After his retirement from football, he ran a well-known restaurant-lounge in the Detroit area.

Hoernschemeyer died of cancer at the age of 54 on June 17, 1980.

 ALEX KARRAS

Somebody once described Alex Karras as "Spanky MacFarland grown up into a man-sized monster," and the comparison fit the Lions' defense tackle perfectly.

He had a baby face framed by thick, horn-rimmed glasses and a quick wit that made him a popular guest on the late-night talk shows long before he made acting his second career.

Karras played 12 seasons for the Lions — he sat out the 1963 campaign when he was suspended by commissioner Pete Rozelle after admitting he bet on football games — after being the club's No. 1 draft pick in 1958.

Karras had a brilliant career at the University of Iowa, making All-American two years and winning the Outland Trophy as the nation's top lineman in 1957.

Alex Karras

Although he was a fun-loving sort who fit right in with the Lions' rollicking crew of the '50s, Karras was all business when he stepped on the field.

"To me, football is a contest of embarrassments," he once said. "The quarterback is out there to embarrass me in front of my friends, my teammates, my coaches, my wife, my daughter and my three boys. The quarterback doesn't leave me any choice. I've got to embarrass him."

Les Bingaman coached the Lions' defensive linemen when Karras joined the team, and he had high praise for his tackle, who would be named to the Pro Bowl squad four times.

"Karras doesn't want anybody to get the best of him," Bingaman said. "He's the best pass-rusher in football, bar none. He's awfully quick on his feet and quick with his hands. That, plus he's mean and tough."

Karras was just as much a free thinker on the field as he was off of it. He shunned the classical style of rushing the passer and did what had to be done at the moment, whether it was sliding, scratching, bulling, dancing or operating entirely on feel.

"Having Alex next to you means a lot," said Roger Brown, who played the other tackle in the Lions' Fearsome Foursome. "They have to put two men on him. That leaves me with only one guy to beat most of the time."

Karras didn't lose his sense of humor after his one-year hiatus. As co-captain of the Lions, he participated in the coin flip before one of his first games back.

"Captain Karras," the referee said, "while I flip this coin, would you please call heads or tails."

"I'm sorry, sir," Karras replied. "I'm not permitted to gamble."

Karras signed a seven-year contract with the Lions in 1966, when he was 31 years old, becoming one of the first NFL players to sign a multi-year pact. In 1970 he had surgery on his right knee and began to show signs of slowing down. He was placed on waivers the week before the 1971 season opened.

 MIKE LUCCI

Mike Lucci happened to come along at the wrong time for a middle linebacker in the NFL.

Instead of getting the recognition he deserved, the former Tennessee star had to watch Chicago's Dick Butkus and Green Bay's Ray Nitschke get most of the press clippings and post-season honors.

Although his play was on a par with Butkus and Nitschke, Lucci wasn't as menacing or ferocious as Butkus or as frightening in appearance as Nitschke.

"I think one article made Butkus an animal and another made Nitschke a madman," Lucci once said. "I think I'm a competitive football player. Middle linebacker is a position that warrants toughness, so you're going to be described like that sometimes. It's not up to me to describe myself. I get paid for playing."

Lucci was drafted by the Cleveland Browns after a fine career at Tennessee and was a member of the special teams when the Browns won the NFL championship in 1964. The following year he was traded to Detroit in a three-club deal.

Joe Schmidt retired after the 1965 season and spent the next year as linebackers coach for Detroit, tutoring Lucci as his successor. Lucci couldn't have had a better teacher because Schmidt is generally considered the inventor of the middle linebacker position.

By the time the Lions opened the 1970 season, Schmidt was the head coach and telling anyone who cared to listen that Lucci was the best middle linebacker in the league.

"The best overall middle linebacker, taking into account direction of the team, pass coverage, mobility and toughness, is Mike Lucci," Schmidt declared.

Browns' quarterback Bill Nelson also spoke highly of Lucci when he was at the peak of his career.

Mike Lucci

Buddy Parker

Charlie Sanders

"Lucci isn't one of the top ones physically, but he does a fantastic job," Nelson said. "He's strong against both the run and the pass and is excellent in coordinating the defense."

Lucci was the Lions' defensive Most Valuable Player from 1969–71 and in 1972 he was named to the Pro Bowl squad. His final season was 1973.

 BUDDY PARKER

Raymond "Buddy" Parker was instrumental in each of the Lions' four NFL championships.

He played for the 1935 champions, coached the 1952 and 1953 title squads and coached the 1957 champions in training camp before stunning everyone in the organization by quitting two days before the pre-season opener.

"I'm getting out," Parker declared at the club's annual Meet the Lions dinner. "I can't handle this team anymore. It's the worst team I've ever seen in training camp. They have no life; no go; they're just a dead team. The team got away from me, got beyond me."

"I've been in football a long time. I know the situation. I don't want to get in the middle of another losing season. Materialwise, it's a good team. Maybe somebody else can handle it better than I can," Parker said as players and fans sat in stunned silence.

Parker is probably remembered more for that turbulent incident than any other in his career with the Lions, which is unfortunate.

The tall Texan played two seasons for Detroit and scored a touchdown in the Lions' first championship game in 1935.

Two years later, he was traded to the Chicago Cardinals for Bob Reynolds, who had been an All-American tackle at Stanford.

Parker learned the coaching ropes from Jimmy Conzelman, one of the legendary coaches from the early days of pro football, and in 1950 he was hired by Bo McMillin as an assistant coach with Detroit.

A year later, when McMillin was fired, Parker was elevated to head coach of the Lions. In 1951, he guided Detroit to its first winning record in six years and the following year won the club's first championship since 1935.

One of the innovations Parker brought to the NFL was the use of the two-minute drill. In Bobby Layne, he had the perfect quarterback to engineer the hectic drive against the clock.

"I had noticed how many teams let down the two minutes before the half and the two minutes at the end of the game," Parker said. "It seemed that you could get things done that you couldn't do in the other 56 minutes of play. So we drilled on it — every day. But what made it work is that I had the Big Guy (Layne)."

The Lions' players were never close to Parker, but they respected him. A group of players met with club management when it was deciding whether to fire McMillin and they said they felt they could win if Parker was elevated to the top job.

"I respected the man. I thought he was a fine football mind," Joe Schmidt said. "He'd never say much to you. In fact, we would go out of our way to stay away from him."

Shortly after leaving the Lions, Parker became head coach of the Pittsburgh Steelers and stayed there through the 1964 season.

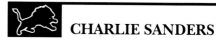 **CHARLIE SANDERS**

Charlie Sanders paid the price for being the best tight end in the NFL during most of his 10-year career with the Lions.

He suffered major injuries to a knee and shoulder, not to mention the other bumps, bruises and concussions he received while being double and triple-teamed by enemy defenses.

Despite the constant attention,

Sanders became the Lions' all-time leading receiver with 336 catches, second in yards gained with 4,817 and fourth in touchdown receptions with 31.

And despite the injuries, he missed only nine regular-season games in his 10 years with the Lions.

"In one sense the coverage makes me feel good," Sanders once remarked, "but in another sense it makes me mad. Why don't they leave me alone like any other tight end?"

Sanders was simply too good to leave alone. As soon as he'd leave the huddle, the opposing defense would maul, poke, punch, trip and jostle him. They'd commit any act — legal or otherwise — to keep him from running his prescribed pass route.

Most of the time Sanders was good-natured about his weekly muggings. Once Sanders caught a pass against Chicago and collided with Bears' middle linebacker Dick Butkus. Butkus then poked his fingers through Sanders' face mask as he brought the Lions' tight end down.

After the game, Sanders shrugged off the incident.

"Dick's just a maladjusted kid," Sanders said with a grin.

Detroit drafted Sanders out of Minnesota in the third round in 1968. The reason he lasted so long was that he was just a skinny kid when he played for the Gophers and didn't become a tight end until his senior year.

Even after he joined the Lions, Sanders was drinking a homemade concoction of raw eggs, honey, malt, ice cream, bananas, syrup and milk in hopes of adding weight.

"There must be 3,000 calories in a quart and the more you drink, the worse it tastes," he said. "I had to drink it three times a day in college."

Sanders was named to the Pro Bowl squad seven times, including his rookie season when he was the only first-year player on the team. He was also an All-Pro twice. Sanders was inducted into the Michigan Sports Hall of Fame in 1990.

He attributed much of his success to his high school basketball competition against former NBA standout Lou Hudson while both were growing up in Greensboro, North Carolina.

"Going one-on-one with him all those years helped me develop my theory for catching a football," Sanders said. "There's no safetyman in the league that big (6-foot-5, 235) or that agile. I learned a lot about the use of the body. I try to use my body to get between the safety and the ball once it's thrown. If I get position on him, like in the pivot, he has to come through me for the ball and that's interference."

Sanders has been an assistant coach with the Lions since 1989.

HARLEY SEWELL

The high school coach watching a Lions' practice session at their Cranbrook training camp couldn't take his eyes off the lineman wearing No. 66.

"He's got more hustle and works harder than any player I have on my squad," the camp visitor said. "It's no wonder he's such a great football player."

The coach wasn't talking about some young rookie who was trying to win a job with the Lions. The fellow that caught his eye was All-Pro guard Harley Sewell.

"I never feel like I have a job cinched." Sewell said during the peak of his career with Detroit.

Sewell's work ethic also impressed his coaches.

"Harley has hustled for us every minute since he joined the Lions," said former offensive line coach Aldo Forte.

In addition to playing guard, Sewell was a fixture on many special teams. One season he made 85 percent of the tackles on Detroit's kickoff team. He was on the punting team and the kickoff receiving unit, and when the Lions brought back a kickoff it wasn't surprising to see Sewell deliver the lead block.

Harley Sewell

Russ Thomas

The guitar-playing Texan began his career with Detroit in 1953 when he was the club's first-round draft pick after earning All-American honors at the University of Texas.

He became an immediate starter on the Lions' offensive line, although he was better known for his defensive play in college. To make matters more difficult, the Longhorns played a split-T offense so he had never played pulling guard until he joined Detroit.

Sewell once recalled how he learned to pull during his first Lions' camp.

"(Assistant coach Buster) Ramsey got me out there and fussed at me by the hour, and then Aldo Forte would come along and fuss at me some more," Sewell said.

"They used to have me practice pulling right by the goalposts so that if I didn't do it right, I'd run into the steel posts. A guy could get killed like that, so I had to do it right."

Because of Sewell's talent at pulling, the Lions used many plays which required the guards to pull out and execute blocks downfield. Sewell would be out of the line in a flash and moments later would blast some unsuspecting defensive back.

Sewell was a fixture at guard through the 1962 campaign and was on the Pro Bowl squad from 1958–60. He was also a Pro Bowl pick in 1963 after he was traded to the Los Angeles Rams.

RUSS THOMAS

Probably no one fits the description "Mr. Detroit Lion" more than Russ Thomas.

During his 43 years with the organization, he served it in nearly every capacity imaginable.

He was an All-Pro tackle and captain until knee surgery abruptly ended his career in 1949. He then became an assistant coach and scout, helping Detroit win three championships during the 1950s.

Thomas scouted the colleges and was also responsible for scouting the Lions' upcoming opponent. His reports were instrumental in Detroit's three NFL championships during the 1950s.

He also spent several seasons as Van Patrick's color man on the Lions' broadcasts.

When William Clay Ford became president of the club, he named his longtime friend director of player personnel. Thomas eventually moved up the ladder to executive vice president and general manager before retiring after the 1989 season.

Thomas headed up the club's college draft each season and had the thankless task of negotiating contracts.

Thomas suffered in silence when fans and critics in the media blamed him for many of the Lions' problems during the 1970s and 1980s, but the losing records hurt him as much as anyone.

His successor, Chuck Schmidt, said that Thomas' gruff image "was all style. Deep down, he was much more sensitive than people could see. He had a very big tender side to him. Very few players ever found it, but when they did they saw a different side to Russ Thomas."

Ford paid Thomas a similar tribute after Thomas died at the age of 66 on March 19, 1991.

"Russ always had the best interests of his players at heart," Ford said. "He tried to look at the human side of each player and do what was best for that individual."

Thomas was respected around the NFL and was the Lions' representative at most league meetings. His experience at all levels of the game led many executives from rival clubs to seek Thomas out for advice.

He was instrumental in the move of the Lions to the Silverdome and led the effort to bring Super Bowl XVI to Pontiac, the first time the game had been held in a cold weather city.

A native of Griffithsville, West Virginia, Thomas was one of the most recruited high school athletes in that state's history.

In addition to his prowess as a football lineman, Thomas was a state champion in the discus and shot put. In 1983, he was inducted into the West Virginia Sports Hall of Fame.

He was recruited to Ohio State by the legendary Paul Brown and was All-Big Ten and All-American and helped the Buckeyes win the 1944 national championship. He lettered in football, track and wrestling during his years at Ohio State.

Thomas was an early draft choice of the Lions in 1946 and became an All-Pro selection in his rookie season with Detroit.

WAYNE WALKER

Wayne Walker arrived a year too late to enjoy the Lions' last NFL championship in 1957, but when he retired after the 1972 season he had no regrets.

"Lots of guys have played on two or three championship teams who haven't had half the career I've had," Walker said at his retirement party.

Detroit's No. 4 draft pick out of Idaho in 1957, Walker carved quite a niche for himself as an outside linebacker playing next to the great Joe Schmidt. When Walker retired, his 200 regular-season games and 15 seasons were both Lions' records — and those marks still stand today.

He was an All-Pro selection in 1964 and 1965 and was named to the Pro Bowl squad from 1964–66. At the time of his retirement, he was third on the club's all-time scoring list.

Walker scored his only two NFL touchdowns in his rookie season, but handled the Lions' place-kicking for four seasons. He made 172 of 175 extra points and booted 53 field goals.

"I think I could have developed into a real good kicker if I'd had the practice time to do it," Walker said, "but I never wanted to do that alone."

The first time Walker touched the ball in an NFL game, he picked off a

Billy Wade pass and returned it 37 yards for a touchdown against the Los Angeles Rams.

That same trip to Los Angeles, Walker experienced his most embarrassing moment as a Lion.

He and Jim Martin went out to the field at Hollywood High School to get some kicking practice before the rest of the squad was scheduled to report. When they arrived, the gate was locked. Since Walker was the rookie, he had to scale the 10-foot fence surrounding the field to look for the caretaker to open the gate.

There were about 200 people at the field, waiting to watch the Detroit club work out.

"I got hooked on the top of the fence and my shorts were ripped right off," Walker later recalled with a laugh. "Worst of all, I twisted my ankle when I fell. I was up all night because of the pain, but that was going to be just the second game I started, so there was no way I was going to tell anybody."

Walker missed only four games in his 15-year career with the Lions. That was probably a throwback to his early days with the team.

"It's a wonder I didn't get an ulcer. I worried so much about making the team," Walker said. "It was tough for a rookie in those days. They didn't get in with the veterans like they do now."

Walker's fondest memories are the mini-wars the Lions staged against the Green Bay Packers and Chicago Bears during the 1960s.

"I played 30 times against the Packers and 30 times against the Bears," he said. "I'd get up a little bit more and have better games against the Packers than any other team."

After his playing career, Walker went into broadcasting and is currently a sports reporter for a San Francisco television station. Walker also currently serves as the radio announcer for the San Francisco Forty-Niners.

Wayne Walker

Byron White

George Wilson

 BYRON WHITE

Football was only a small chapter in Byron White's remarkable life story, but it is one that is always mentioned when the former Supreme Court Justice's name comes up.

White, who served on the Supreme Court from 1962 until 1993, played only three seasons of professional football, but they were memorable ones.

He led the NFL in rushing as a rookie with the Pittsburgh Steelers in 1938, but sat out the 1939 campaign while he studied at Oxford as a Rhodes Scholar. Later he took the $15,000 he earned during his first season in the NFL and used it to put himself through law school at Yale.

The Lions obtained White's rights from the Steelers before the 1940 season and eventually persuaded him to return to professional football.

It was an excellent move for the Lions because White led the NFL in rushing again with 514 yards in 12 games. He scored five touchdowns.

White's final season with Detroit was 1941. He again led the club in rushing and was also the Lions' leading passer.

White entered the Navy in 1942 and won two bronze stars in Pacific combat during World War II. When he returned from service duty, he announced his retirement from football to pursue his career in law.

White — who was known as Whizzer, a nickname he detested — made quite an impression during his brief football career.

His center at the University of Colorado, Gene Moore, once said, "all you had to do was block the extra man. White would beat anybody one-on-one."

"He never had much to say in the huddle, but when he told you he'd be someplace or do something, he was there and he did it."

White's intelligence impressed his teammates and coaches with the Lions.

"I was amazed that a fellow playing with you could know so much about what everyone else did or didn't do on a certain play," said Lions' guard Augie Lio.

White didn't engage in the usual horseplay during trips with the club.

"While the other guys were playing cards for 5 cents a point, White would get out his glasses, his pipe and his law books and start studying," said Potsy Clark, White's coach with the Lions in 1940.

The former All-American running back at Colorado was just taking the advice of his father who once said, "I would rather see you win one medal for scholarship than win 40 ballgames."

 GEORGE WILSON

George Wilson might have been the perfect man to step in as head coach of the Lions when Buddy Parker abruptly quit shortly before the pre-season opener in 1957.

A former receiver with the Chicago Bears during their championship years in the 1940s, the easy-going Wilson took the best qualities of what Parker termed a playboy ball club and molded it into Detroit's last NFL championship squad.

Wilson didn't have a lot of rules away from the field as long as the team performed on Sunday, but when it didn't, the halftime oratory got hot and heavy.

Wilson blew his stack at halftime of the Thanksgiving Day game in '57 when the Lions came off the field trailing the lowly Green Bay Packers 6–3.

"You guys are a disgrace," Wilson screamed. "You ought to be ashamed. You're supposed to be a football team and you're nothing. I'm sick of watching you."

Wilson read the players the riot act for nearly 10 minutes, then sent them back on the field.

The outburst worked. John Henry Johnson ran 62 yards for a touchdown early in the third quarter and the Lions came back for an 18–6 victory.

"He was so mad," said offensive tackle Lou Creekmur, "I wanted to leave. I was afraid he'd hit somebody and I'd be held as a witness."

The coach also made an impression on running back Gene Gedman.

"It was Thanksgiving, but it was no place for Puritans," he said.

Wilson admitted it was the maddest he'd been all year.

"They were fumbling the championship away and it really burned me," he said.

Wilson made another fiery halftime speech during a game with Chicago when the Bears led 10–0 at the intermission, but he used a different kind of rhetoric when Bobby Layne suffered a broken ankle in the first half of the game with Cleveland; the coach appealed to the team to win one for its fallen leader.

Wilson downplayed his reputation as a halftime orator.

"Most halftime talks aren't fiery," he said. "We ate the boys out a little bit against Green Bay. We had Layne's injury to talk about against Cleveland. All I said in Chicago was we had only 30 minutes to do the job or the season was over."

Wilson experienced several years of frustration after guiding the Lions to the title as a rookie head coach. The team had losing seasons in 1958 and 1959, then finished second to Green Bay from 1960–62.

After a losing season in 1963, the Lions rebounded to a 7–5–2 mark the following year, but Wilson resigned after the season and was named the first head coach of the expansion Miami Dolphins in 1967.

Wilson's career record with the Lions was 55–45–6. His eight seasons at the helm are the most by any Detroit coach and his 106 games are only one less than the record held by Monte Clark. ❖

13

The History Book

A year-by-year review of the teams, players and games marking the Lions' first six decades.

by Dan Arthur

1934

Date	Opponent	Crowd	W-L-T	Score
9/23	NEW YORK	12,000	W	9 – 0
9/30	at Cardinals	18,000	W	6 – 0
10/7	at Green Bay	7,500	W	3 – 0
10/14	at Philadelphia	9,860	W	10 – 0
10/17	BOSTON	12,000	W	24 – 0
10/21	BROOKLYN	11,000	W	28 – 0
10/28	at Cin.-St. Louis	4,800	W	38 – 0
11/4	PITTSBURGH	6,000	W	40 – 7
11/11	CARDINALS	11,000	W	17 – 13
11/18	CIN.-ST. LOUIS	15,000	W	40 – 7
11/25	GREEN BAY	12,000	L	0 – 3
11/29	CHICAGO	26,000	L	16 – 19
12/2	at Chicago	34,412	L	7 – 10

HOME GAMES IN CAPS

1934 LION LEADERS

RUSHING Dutch Clark • 122 att. • 763 yds.

PASSING Dutch Clark • 49 att. • 23 comp. • 383 yds.

RECEIVING Harry Ebding • 9 rec. • 257 yds.

SCORING Dutch Clark • 73 points (8 TDs, 4 FGs, 13 PATs)

Dutch Clark

- The transfer of the Portsmouth, Ohio, franchise to Detroit was formally ratified by the National Football League on June 30, 1934.

- A headline in the July 22, 1934, edition of the *Detroit News* read "Pro Grid Team Called 'Lions.'" The official colors of the team were determined as blue and silver.

- George "Potsy" Clark was the Lions' first head coach, moving with the team from Portsmouth where he had coached the Spartans from 1931–33.

- Forty-five players reported to the Lions' first training camp in Detroit. Head Coach Potsy Clark trimmed the roster to the league limit of 25 players three weeks later, before the first regular season game.

- The Lions defeated the New York Giants, 9–0, in their first game as a Detroit franchise.

- Detroit shutout its first eleven opponents of the 1934 season. Overall, the Lions outscored their opponents, 238–59. In their three defeats, the Lions were outscored by a total of nine points.

- Glenn Presnell booted a team-record 54-yard field goal, providing the margin of victory in a 3–0 triumph over the Green Bay Packers. Presnell currently shares the record for the longest field goal in Lions' history with Eddie Murray.

- Earl "Dutch" Clark rushed for 194 yards against Cincinnati on Oct. 28, 1934. Fifty-nine years later, his effort still ranks as the fourth-greatest rushing performance in Lions' history.

- Playing their first Thanksgiving Day game, the Lions lost to the Chicago Bears, 19–16. The loss knocked Detroit out of contention for the Western Division Title.

1935

- The Lions were the only team in the National Football League to score at least one touchdown in each of their 12 games in 1935.

- Dutch Clark was the leading scorer in the National Football League in 1935, scoring 55 points (6 TDs, 1 FG and 16 PATs) in 12 games.

- The Detroit defense held Philadelphia without a first down in the Lions' opening day victory against the Eagles in 1935.

- With four games remaining in the 1935 season, the Lions found themselves in last place in the Western Division, but rebounded by winning three contests and tying another.

- The Lions defeated the Boston Redskins in Boston, 17–7 on Oct. 13, 1935. Detroit was undefeated against the Redskins in Boston (1–0), but the Lions have never won in Washington (0–15).

- Detroit defeated the New York Giants, 26–7, claiming its first NFL Title. Detroit Lions players received $300 each for winning the 1935 NFL Championship.

- After the 1935 Championship game, the Lions went on a 12,000-mile, five-game exhibition trip, culminating in a 30–6 victory over Pop Warner's All-Stars in Hawaii. The Lions won the five games, scoring a total of 182 points.

1935 RESULTS
7–3–2 (1st)
George "Potsy" Clark, Coach

Date	Opponent	Crowd	W-L-T	Score
9/20	PHILADELPHIA	12,000	W	35 – 0
9/29	CARDINALS	8,200	T	10 – 10
10/6	at Brooklyn	12,000	L	10 – 12
10/13	at Boston	18,737	W	17 – 7
10/20	at Green Bay*	9,000	L	9 – 13
10/30	BOSTON	17,000	W	14 – 0
11/3	at Cardinals	5,000	W	7 – 6
11/10	at Green Bay	1,200	L	7 – 31
11/17	GREEN BAY	12,000	W	20 – 10
11/24	at Chicago	14,624	T	20 – 20
11/28	CHICAGO	18,000	W	14 – 2
12/1	BROOKLYN	15,000	W	28 – 0
World Championship				
12/15	NEW YORK	15,000	W	26 – 7

* Milwaukee

HOME GAMES IN CAPS

1935 LION LEADERS

RUSHING   Ernie Caddel • 87 att. • 450 yds.

PASSING   Bill Shepherd • 64 att. • 28 comp. • 417 yds.

RECEIVING Ernie Caddel • 10 rec. • 171 yds.

SCORING   Dutch Clark • 55 points (6 TDs, 1 FG, 16 PATs)

1936 RESULTS
8–4–0 (3rd)
George "Potsy" Clark, Coach

Date	Opponent	Crowd	W-L-T	Score
9/27	CARDINALS	15,000	W	39 – 0
10/11	at Philadelphia	15,000	W	23 – 0
10/14	at Brooklyn	8,000	W	14 – 7
10/18	at Green Bay	13,500	L	18 – 20
10/25	at Chicago	27,424	L	10 – 12
11/1	at New York	25,000	L	7 – 14
11/8	PITTSBURGH	20,000	W	26 – 3
11/15	NEW YORK	20,000	W	38 – 0
11/22	at Cardinals	7,579	W	14 – 7
11/26	CHICAGO	22,000	W	13 – 7
11/29	GREEN BAY	22,000	L	17 – 26
12/6	BROOKLYN	10,000	W	14 – 6

HOME GAMES IN CAPS

1936 LION LEADERS

RUSHING   Ernie Caddel • 87 att. • 450 yds.

PASSING   Dutch Clark • 71 att. • 38 comp. • 467 yds.

RECEIVING   Ernie Caddel • 19 rec. • 150 yds.

SCORING   Dutch Clark • 73 points (7 TDs, 4 FGs, 19 PATs)

Ernie Caddel

- The Lions rushed for a team-record 2,885 yards in 1936.

- Ace Gutowsky's 827 yards rushing remained a Lions record for 24 years until Nick Pietrosante gained 872 yards in 1960.

- Detroit played five consecutive road games in 1936, traveling to, in order, Philadelphia, Brooklyn, Green Bay, Chicago and New York. It stands as the longest such road trip in team history. The Lions lost three of the five contests, knocking the team out of title contention.

- Bill Shepherd booted a team-record 85-yard punt on Nov. 15, 1936, in a 38–0 thrashing of the New York Giants.

- The Lions' 39–0 drubbing of the Chicago Cardinals remained Detroit's most lopsided victory until a 48–7 win over the San Francisco 49ers on Nov. 14, 1954.

- Dutch Clark was named to the all-league team for the third straight year. He was joined on the 1936 honor squad by teammate Ox Emerson.

- The Lions boasted one of football's most potent offensive teams in 1936. Detroit averaged 308.6 yards per game, including 240.4 rushing yards per contest.

1937

- George "Potsy" Clark resigned as head coach and general manager of the Detroit Lions to become head coach of the NFL's Brooklyn Dodgers. Clark was replaced by Lions backfield star Earl "Dutch" Clark.

- Vern Huffman returned an interception 100 yards for a touchdown against Brooklyn on Oct. 17, 1937. The interception return currently stands as the second-longest in team history.

- The Detroit defense held the Pittsburgh Pirates to zero yards passing in a 7–3 victory on Oct. 10, 1937.

- The Lions' four losses came at the hands of their arch-rivals, the Green Bay Packers and Chicago Bears.

- The Lions played their final full slate of games at the University of Detroit Stadium. An ever-increasing demand for tickets prompted the club's decision to move home games to spacious Briggs Stadium for the 1938 season.

- For the fourth consecutive year, Dutch Clark led the Lions in scoring. It is a feat that was unequalled until Errol Mann paced the Lions in scoring in seven straight seasons (1969–75).

"The Detroit Lions"
CRANBROOK SCHOOL
...1937...

1937 RESULTS
7–4–0 (3rd)
Earl "Dutch" Clark, Coach

Date	Opponent	Crowd	W-L-T	Score
9/10	at Cleveland	24,800	W	28 – 0
9/19	CARDINALS	17,000	W	16 – 7
10/3	at Green Bay	17,553	L	6 – 26
10/10	PITTSBURGH	16,000	W	7 – 3
10/17	BROOKLYN	18,000	W	30 – 0
10/24	at Chicago	34,530	L	20 – 28
10/31	GREEN BAY	23,000	L	13 – 14
11/7	CLEVELAND	15,500	W	27 – 7
11/14	at New York	35,000	W	17 – 0
11/21	at Cardinals	8,576	W	16 – 7
11/25	CHICAGO	24,173	L	0 – 13

HOME GAMES IN CAPS

1937 LION LEADERS

RUSHING Dutch Clark • 96 att. • 468 yds.

PASSING Bill Shepherd • 46 att. • 19 comp. • 297 yds.

RECEIVING Ernie Caddel • 9 rec. • 80 yds.

SCORING Dutch Clark • 45 points (6 TDs, 1 FG, 6 PATs)

1938

1938 RESULTS
7–4–0 (2nd)
Earl "Dutch" Clark, Coach

Date	Opponent	Crowd	W-L-T	Score
9/9	PITTSBURGH	17,000	W	16 – 7
10/2	at Cleveland	8,012	L	17 – 21
10/9	at Green Bay	21,968	W	17 – 7
10/18	WASHINGTON	42,855	L	5 – 7
10/23	CARDINALS	17,917	W	10 – 0
10/30	at Chicago	24,356	W	13 – 7
11/8	CLEVELAND	30,140	W	6 – 0
11/13	GREEN BAY	45,139	L	7 – 28
11/20	at Cardinals	8,279	W	7 – 3
11/24	CHICAGO	26,200	W	14 – 7
12/4	PHILADELPHIA	19,000	L	7 – 21

HOME GAMES IN CAPS

1938 LION LEADERS

RUSHING	Bill Shepherd • 100 att. • 455 yds.
PASSING	Vern Huffman • 85 att. • 27 comp. • 382 yds.
RECEIVING	Lloyd Cardwell • 9 rec. • 138 yds.
SCORING	Lloyd Cardwell • 30 points (5 TDs)

- The Lions moved the site of their home games from the University of Detroit Stadium to Briggs Stadium in 1938.

Alex Wojciechowicz

- Player-coach Dutch Clark switched from drop-kicking to place-kicking in 1938. Clark was the last drop-kicker in the league.

- Future Hall of Famer Alex Wojciechowicz joined the Lions in 1938 out of Fordham.

- The Lions were upset by the Cleveland Rams, 21–17, giving Cleveland its second victory in as many seasons. Detroit bounced back the following week, upsetting the powerful Packers in Green Bay, 17–7.

- Detroit defeated the Chicago Bears, 14–7, on Thanksgiving Day. After this game, the Thanksgiving Day series was discontinued during World War II but was eventually resumed in 1945.

- The Lions lost to the Philadelphia Eagles, 21–7, on the final game of the 1938 season, eliminating Detroit from a shot at the Western Division Championship.

- Earl "Dutch" Clark resigned as head coach and player for the Detroit Lions to accept the head coaching position with the Cleveland Rams. Clark was replaced by Gus Henderson, former coach of the Los Angeles Bulldogs.

1939

- Quarterback Dwight Sloans' three interceptions on 102 attempts in 1939 established a Detroit-record for fewest passes intercepted. That record still stands today.

- The Detroit Lions defeated the New York Giants, 18–14, with the help of 4 field goals (Philip Martinovick 3, Chuck Hanneman 1), while the Giants failed in four field goal attempts. The loss snapped the Giants' 15-game undefeated streak.

Bill Shepherd

- After winning their first four games and six of their first seven contests, the Lions dropped their final four games to keep the team out of contention for the Western Division title chase.

- With 420 yards, Bill Shepherd became the first player in team history to lead the Lions in rushing in back-to-back seasons. Shepherd had paced the club with 455 yards (on 100 attempts) in 1938.

- In his only year as head coach, Gus Henderson's 6–5 record gave Detroit its sixth consecutive winning season. It is a string of winning seasons unequalled in club history.

1939 RESULTS
6–5–0 (3rd)
Gus Henderson, Coach

Date	Opponent	Crowd	W-L-T	Score
9/10	CARDINALS	15,075	W	21 – 13
9/24	BROOKLYN	15,515	W	27 – 7
10/1	at Cardinals	11,000	W	17 – 3
10/15	CLEVELAND	30,096	W	15 – 7
10/22	at Green Bay	22,558	L	7 – 26
10/29	at Chicago	30,903	W	10 – 0
11/5	NEW YORK	47,492	W	18 – 14
11/12	CHICAGO	42,684	L	13 – 23
11/19	at Cleveland	28,142	L	3 – 14
11/26	at Washington	36,183	L	7 – 31
12/3	GREEN BAY	30,699	L	7 – 12

HOME GAMES IN CAPS

1939 LION LEADERS

RUSHING   Bill Shepherd • 85 att. • 420 yds.

PASSING   Dwight Sloan • 102 att. • 45 comp. • 658 yds.

RECEIVING   Monk Moscrip • 14 rec. • 176 yds.

SCORING   Chuck Hanneman • 29 points (2 TDs, 4 FGs, 5 PATs)

1942 RESULTS
0–11–0 (5th)

William "Bill" Edwards, Coach (0–3–0)

Date	Opponent	Crowd	W-L-T	Score
9/20	at Cardinals	14,742	L	0 – 13
9/27	CLEVELAND	14,646	L	0 – 14
10/4	BROOKLYN	12,598	L	7 – 28

John Karcis, Coach (0–8–0)

Date	Opponent	Crowd	W-L-T	Score
10/11	at Green Bay*	19,500	L	7 – 38
10/18	CARDINALS	14,100	L	0 – 7
10/25	GREEN BAY	19,097	L	7 – 28
11/1	at Chicago	12,205	L	0 – 16
11/8	PITTSBURGH	16,675	L	7 – 35
11/15	at Cleveland	4,029	L	7 – 27
11/22	CHICAGO	17,348	L	0 – 42
11/29	WASHINGTON	6,044	L	3 – 15

* Milwaukee

HOME GAMES IN CAPS

1942 LION LEADERS

RUSHING Mickey Sanzotta • 71 att. • 268 yds.

PASSING Harry Hopp • 68 att. • 20 comp. • 258 yds.

RECEIVING Bill Fisk • 15 rec. • 177 yds.

SCORING Elmer Hackney • 12 points (2 TDs)

1942

- The United States' entry into World War II devastated the country and impacted heavily on professional sports. The National Football League lost over 100 players to the armed forces from 1941 to 1942. The Lions were struck hard by the war as only eight players returned from the 1941 team.

Bill Fisk

- The Detroit Lions scrimmaged the Army All-Stars prior to the 1942 season. All proceeds, after expenses, went to the Army Relief Fund. The Army All-Stars defeated the Lions, 12–0, netting $29,000 for the fund.

- Head Coach Bill Edwards was fired following a 28–7 drubbing by the Brooklyn Dodgers on Oct. 4, 1942, the Lions' third consecutive loss of the season. In less than one and a half years, Edwards compiled a 4–9–1 mark (4–6–1 in 1941, 0–3 in 1942). Edwards was replaced by backfield coach John Karcis.

- The 1942 Detroit Lions established several unspectacular records in the 0–11 campaign including: first and only winless season, least points in a season (38 points in 11 games) and most times shut out (5).

- The Lions' two losses to the Chicago Cardinals were Detroit's first to them in nine seasons.

- Elmer Hackney's 78-yard run against Pittsburgh established a new team record for longest rushing play.

1943

- Charles "Gus" Dorais left the University of Detroit after 18 years of guiding the Titan football team to join the Detroit Lions as head coach.

- The Lions drafted Frank Sinkwich, the 1942 Heisman Trophy winner, with their first pick in the 1943 college draft.

- End Ben Hightower was lost for the 1943 season due to an attack of malaria.

- In a defensive battle, the New York Giants and Detroit Lions struggled to a 0–0 tie on Nov. 7, 1943. The teams managed a combined nine first downs (Detroit 6, New York 3) while the Lions' defense forced New York's Carl Kinscherf to punt 14 times, the most ever by a Detroit opponent.

- The Lions won their first two contests and three of the first five, only to go winless the remainder of the season.

- Detroit quarterbacks threw a team-record nine interceptions against Green Bay on Oct. 24, 1943, with Frank Sinkwich setting an individual record with seven interceptions.

- Despite his performance against the Packers, Frank Sinkwich led the team in rushing and passing while tossing 20 TDs (3rd best in Lions history).

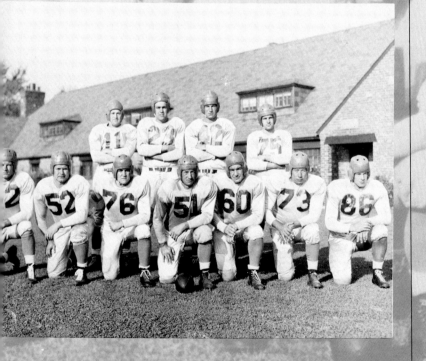

1943 LION LEADERS

RUSHING	Frank Sinkwich • 93 att. • 266 yds.
PASSING	Frank Sinkwich • 126 att. • 50 comp. • 699 yds.
RECEIVING	Harry Hopp • 17 rec. • 229 yds.
SCORING	Harry Hopp • 54 points (6 TDs)

1944

Date	Opponent	Crowd	W-L-T	Score
10/1	at Green Bay*	18,566	L	6 – 27
10/8	at Brooklyn	15,702	W	19 – 14
10/15	CLEVELAND	21,115	L	17 – 20
10/22	at Chicago	23,835	T	21 – 21
10/29	GREEN BAY	30,844	L	0 – 14
11/5	at Card.-Pitt.	17,743	W	27 – 6
11/12	CARD.-PITT.	13,239	W	21 – 7
11/19	CHICAGO	21,960	W	41 – 21
11/26	at Cleveland	7,462	W	26 – 14
12/3	BOSTON	15,027	W	38 – 7

* Milwaukee

HOME GAMES IN CAPS

1944 LION LEADERS

RUSHING   Frank Sinkwich • 150 att. • 563 yds. • 6 TD

PASSING   Frank Sinkwich • 148 att. • 58 comp. • 1060 yds. • 12 TD • 20 int

RECEIVING Jack Matheson • 23 rec. • 361 yds. • 3 TD

SCORING   Frank Sinkwich • 66 points (6 TDs, 2 FGs, 24 PATs)

PUNT RET   Frank Sinkwich • 11 ret. • 148 yds. • 13.5 avg. • 0 TD

KO RET   Arthur Van Tone • 9 ret. • 227 yds. • 25.2 avg. • 1 TD

PUNTING   Frank Sinkwich • 45 punts • 1845 yds. • 41.0 avg.

INTS   Alex Wojciechowicz • 7 int. • 88 yds. • 0 TD

Charley Fenebock and Frank Sinkwich

- Frank Sinkwich led the Lions in rushing, passing, scoring punt returns and punting in 1944, his last season with Detroit.

- Detroit's 41–21 victory over the Chicago Bears on Nov. 19, 1944, at Briggs Stadium marked Detroit's first victory over the Bears in the last eight confrontations. In the win, Sinkwich became the first Lion to pass for four TDs.

- Behind the rushing and passing of their backfield aces Sinkwich and Bob Westfall, the Lions won their last five games. The string was the team's longest winning streak since the 1934 season when the Lions won 10 in a row to start the season.

- Former Lions Alex Ketzko and Chester Wetterland were killed in World War II in 1944. Ketzko played for the Lions in 1943 while Wetterland suited up for the team in 1942.

- Frank Sinkwich became the first Lion in four years to be named to football's all-league team. Byron "Whizzer" White and John Wiethe earned all-league honors in 1940.

1945

- The Lions held training camp in 1945 at Assumption College in Windsor, Canada.

- The Detroit Lions won six of their first seven games but dropped two of their final three contests, knocking the club out of title contention in the Western Division.

- Detroit played on Thanksgiving Day for the first time since 1938, losing to the Cleveland Rams, 28–21. The Thanksgiving Day series had been discontinued from 1939–44 during World War II.

Bill Callihan

- With a 14–3 victory over the Green Bay Packers, the Lions defeated the Packers for the first time in 11 games.

- Guard Bill Radovich returned from three years of military service to earn All-League honors in 1945.

1945 RESULTS
7–3–0 (2nd)
Charles "Gus" Dorais, Coach

Date	Opponent	Crowd	W-L-T	Score
9/23	at Cardinals	5,461	W	10 – 0
10/7	at Green Bay	20,463	L	21 – 57
10/14	PHILADELPHIA	22,580	W	28 – 24
10/21	at Cardinals	32,644	W	26 – 0
10/28	CHICAGO	37,260	W	16 – 10
11/4	at Boston	17,631	W	10 – 9
11/11	at Chicago	24,798	W	35 – 28
11/18	at New York	38,215	L	14 – 35
11/22	CLEVELAND	40,017	L	21 – 28
12/2	GREEN BAY	23,468	W	14 – 3

* Milwaukee

HOME GAMES IN CAPS

1945 LION LEADERS

RUSHING	Bob Westfall • 82 att. • 234 yds. • 6 TD
PASSING	Charles Fenenbock • 110 att. • 45 comp. • 752 yds. • 7 TD • 11 int
RECEIVING	John Greene • 26 rec. • 550 yds. • 5 TD
SCORING	Bob Westfall • 54 points (9 TDs)
PUNT RET	Dave Ryan • 15 punts • 221 yds. • 14.7 avg.
KO RET	Andrew Farkas • 8 ret. • 165 yds. • 20.6 avg. • 0 TD
PUNTING	Charles Fenenbock • 29 punts • 1067 yds. • 36.8 avg.
INTS	Dave Ryan, Charles DeShane, Damon Tassos, John Greene, Ivan Trebotich • 3 each

1946

Date	Opponent	Crowd	W-L-T	Score
9/30	at Cardinals	14,667	L	14 – 34
10/6	at Washington	33,569	L	16 – 17
10/13	CARDINALS	21,939	L	14 – 36
10/20	at Los Angeles	27,928	L	14 – 35
10/27	at Green Bay	17,073	L	7 – 10
11/3	LOS ANGELES	34,447	L	20 – 41
11/10	PITTSBURGH	13,621	W	27 – 7
11/17	GREEN BAY	21,055	L	0 – 9
11/24	at Chicago	24,470	L	6 – 42
11/28	BOSTON	13,010	L	10 – 34
12/8	CHICAGO	19,579	L	24 – 45

* Milwaukee

HOME GAMES IN CAPS

1946 LION LEADERS

RUSHING   Camp Wilson • 64 att. • 207 yds. • 3 TD

PASSING   Dave Ryan • 154 att. • 73 comp. • 965 yds. • 6 TD • 17 int

RECEIVING   John Greene • 20 rec. • 289 yds. • 2 TD

SCORING   Bob Cifers • 24 points (4 TDs)

PUNT RET   Dave Ryan • 7 ret. • 57 yds. • 8.1 avg. • 0 TD

KO RET   Dave Ryan • 15 ret. • 308 yds. • 20.5 avg. • 0 TD

PUNTING   Bob Cifers • 30 punts • 1368 yds. • 45.6 avg.

INTS   Dave Ryan • 4 int. • 105 yds. • 0 TD

- Before the 1946 season began, the Detroit Lions learned they would not retain the services of three former backfield stars returning from military service. Byron "Whizzer" White returned to Yale to finish his law degree, Frank Sinkwich suffered a career-ending injury while in the service and Harry "Hippity" Hopp signed with Buffalo in the All-American Conference.

- The Lions drafted Russell Thomas out of Ohio State in 1946. Thomas was an All-Pro tackle and captain with the Lions until a knee injury ended his career in 1949. He remained with the Lions as an assistant coach and scout. Thomas later served as the Lions' director of player personnel before moving up to executive vice president and general manager.

Chuck DeShane (#17)

- The Lions drafted Glenn Davis, a Heisman Trophy winner out of Army, with their first selection in the NFL Draft following the 1946 season. Davis had a prior commitment with the U.S. Army and never played for the Lions.

- Charles "Gus" Dorais became the first Detroit mentor to coach the team for four consecutive seasons.

- The Lions' only win of the 1946 season came on the arm of quarterback Dave "Gabby" Ryan. In Detroit's 17–7 victory over the Pittsburgh Steelers at Briggs Stadium, Ryan threw just seven passes, connecting on six. But he completed two big passes as Bill DeCorrevont was on the receiving end of a 78-yard touchdown and Johnny Greene caught an 88-yard pass from Ryan that set up another score. The Ryan-to-Greene connection is the fifth-longest pass play in Lions history.

- Bill DeCorrevont's 81-yard punt at Washington still stands as the longest boot in Detroit Lions history.

1947

- Bill Dudley, acquired in a trade with Pittsburgh, led the Lions in scoring (66 points), punt returns (11 returns, 182 yards, a 16.5 yard average and 1 TD), kickoff returns (15 returns, 359 yards and a 23.9 yard average) and interceptions (five).

- Mired in the NFL's powerful Western Division, Detroit finished fifth in 1947, the only team in its division to finish with a losing record.

- Bill Dudley returned a punt 84 yards for a touchdown in a 33–24 loss to the Chicago Bears on Oct. 19, 1947. That punt return shattered the club record and currently stands as the fourth-longest punt return in Lions history.

- This was truly a season of ups and downs for Detroit: The Lions averaged 31 points in their three victories and 15 points in their nine losses.

John Greene

1947 RESULTS
3–9–0 (5th)
Charles "Gus" Dorais, Coach

Date	Opponent	Crowd	W-L-T	Score
9/21	at Pittsburgh	34,861	L	10 – 17
9/28	at Cardinals	22,245	L	21 – 45
10/5	at Boston	16,097	W	21 – 7
10/12	LOS ANGELES	42,955	L	13 – 27
10/19	at Chicago	31,960	L	24 – 33
10/26	at Green Bay	23,100	L	17 – 34
11/2	NEW YORK	28,812	W	35 – 7
11/9	CARDINALS	25,296	L	7 – 17
11/16	WASHINGTON	17,003	W	38 – 21
11/23	at Los Angeles	17,693	L	17 – 28
11/27	CHICAGO	27,214	L	14 – 34
12/7	GREEN BAY	14,055	L	14 – 35

HOME GAMES IN CAPS

1947 LION LEADERS

RUSHING	Camp Wilson • 89 att. • 412 yds. • 0 TD
PASSING	Clyde LeForce • 175 att. • 94 comp. • 1384 yds. • 13 TD • 20 int
RECEIVING	John Greene • 38 rec. • 621 yds. • 5 TD
SCORING	Bill Dudley • 66 points (11 TDs)
PUNT RET	Bill Dudley • 11 ret. • 182 yds. • 16.5 avg. • 1 TD
KO RET	Bill Dudley • 15 ret. • 359 yds. • 23.9 avg. • 0 TD
PUNTING	Leroy Zimmerman • 49 punts • 2077 yds. • 42.4 avg.
INTS	Bill Dudley • 5 int. • 104 yds. • 1 TD

1948 RESULTS
2–10–0 (5th)
Alvin "Bo" McMillin, Coach

Date	Opponent	Crowd	W-L-T	Score
9/22	at Los Angeles	12,941	L	7 – 44
10/3	at Green Bay	21,403	L	21 – 33
10/9	BOSTON	18,747	L	14 – 17
10/17	at Chicago	35,425	L	0 – 28
10/24	LOS ANGELES	17,444	L	27 – 34
10/31	GREEN BAY	15,045	W	24 – 20
11/7	at Cardinals	22,311	L	20 – 56
11/14	at Washington	32,528	L	21 – 46
11/21	PITTSBURGH	13,646	W	17 – 14
11/25	CARDINALS	22,099	L	14 – 28
12/5	CHICAGO	25,781	L	14 – 42
12/12	at Philadelphia	15,322	L	21 – 45

HOME GAMES IN CAPS

1948 LION LEADERS

RUSHING	Camp Wilson • 157 att. • 612 yds. • 2 TD
PASSING	Fred Enke • 221 att. • 100 comp. • 1328 yds. • 11 TD • 17 int
RECEIVING	Joe Margucci • 36 rec. • 450 yds. • 2 TD
SCORING	Bill Dudley • 42 points (6 TDs)
PUNT RET	Joe Margucci • 10 ret. • 100 yds. • 10.0 avg. • 0 TD
KO RET	Camp Wilson • 10 ret. • 228 yds. • 22.8 avg. • 0 TD
PUNTING	George Grimes • 28 punts • 1005 yds. • 35.9 avg.
INTS	Jim Gillette • 6 int. • 17 yds. • 0 TD

1948

- A syndicate headed by Edwin J. Anderson purchased the Detroit franchise for $165,000 and named Alvin "Bo" McMillin general manager and head coach.

- Camp Wilson paced the Lions in rushing for the third straight year. Wilson, who had gained 207 yards in 1946 and 612 yards in '47, ran for a career-high 612 yards on 157 carries in 1948.

- Bob Mann and Mel Groomes joined the Lions in 1948, becoming the first black players to play with Detroit.

- For the fifth consecutive season, a different player led the Lions in passing as Fred Enke passed for 1,328 yards in 1948.

Mel Groomes

- The Lions finished in last place for the third year in a row, their longest stay in the basement in the history of the club.

Bob Mann

1949

- The Lions trained at Michigan Normal College in Ypsilanti prior to the 1949 season.

- Bob Mann led the NFL in receiving yardage and became the first Detroit Lion to surpass 1,000 yards in receiving (1,014 on 66 receptions).

- Don Doll intercepted an NFL-record four passes against the Chicago Cardinals on Oct. 23, 1949. Doll led the Lions with 11 interceptions in 1949 and returned two for touchdowns.

- Bob Smith returned an interception 102 yards for a touchdown against the Chicago Cardinals on Oct. 23, 1949. The interception is the longest in team history and the second-longest in the history of the league.

- For the third consecutive season, Bill Dudley led the Lions in scoring with 81 points.

- Edwin J. Anderson was named president of the Detroit Lions in 1949.

- The Lions won three of their final four contests to climb out of last place in the Western Division.

Bo McMillin and Bill Dudley

1949 RESULTS
4–8–0 (4th)
Alvin "Bo" McMillin, Coach

Date	Opponent	Crowd	W-L-T	Score
9/23	at Los Angeles	17,878	L	24 – 27
10/3	PHILADELPHIA	20,163	L	14 – 22
10/8	at Pittsburgh	21,594	L	7 – 14
10/16	LOS ANGELES	19,839	L	10 – 21
10/23	at Cardinals	19,490	W	24 – 7
10/30	at Green Bay*	6,177	L	14 – 16
11/6	CARDINALS	19,465	L	19 – 42
11/13	at Chicago	32,716	L	24 – 27
11/20	at New York	14,661	W	45 – 21
11/24	CHICAGO	22912	L	7 – 28
12/4	NY BULLDOGS	11,956	W	28 – 27
12/11	GREEN BAY	9,722	W	21 – 7

* Milwaukee

HOME GAMES IN CAPS

1949 LION LEADERS

RUSHING	Bill Dudley • 125 att. • 402 yds. • 4 TD
PASSING	Frank Tripucka • 145 att. • 62 comp. • 833 yds. • 9 TD • 14 int
RECEIVING	Bob Mann • 66 rec. • 1014 yds. • 4 TD
SCORING	Bill Dudley • 81 points (6 TDs, 5 FGs, 30 PATs)
PUNT RET	Bill Dudley • 11 ret. • 199 yds. • 18.1 avg. • 1 TD
KO RET	Don Doll • 21 ret. • 536 yds. • 25.5 avg. • 0 TD
PUNTING	Bill Dudley • 32 punts • 1277 yds. • 39.9 avg.
INTS	Don Doll • 11 int. • 301 yds. • 2 TD

1950 RESULTS
6–6–0 (4th)
Alvin "Bo" McMillin, Coach

Date	Opponent	Crowd	W-L-T	Score
9/17	at Green Bay	20,285	W	45 – 7
9/24	PITTSBURGH	19,600	W	10 – 7
10/2	at NY Yanks	11,096	L	21 – 44
10/8	SAN FRANCISCO	26,000	W	24 – 7
10/15	LOS ANGELES	28,000	L	28 – 30
10/22	at San Francisco	26,252	L	27 – 38
10/29	at Los Angeles	21,700	L	24 – 65
11/5	CHICAGO	32,000	L	21 – 35
11/19	GREEN BAY	18,000	W	24 – 21
11/23	NY YANKS	28,000	W	49 – 14
12/3	at Baltimore	12,058	W	45 – 21
12/10	at Chicago	34,604	L	3 – 6

HOME GAMES IN CAPS

1950 LION LEADERS

RUSHING   Bob Hoernschemeyer • 84 att. • 471 yds. • 1 TD

PASSING   Bobby Layne • 336 att. • 152 comp. • 2323 yds. • 16 TD • 18 int

RECEIVING   Cloyce Box • 50 rec. • 1009 yds. • 11 TD

SCORING   Doak Walker • 128 points (11 TDs, 8 FGs, 38 PATs)

PUNT RET   Clarence Self • 12 ret. • 129 yds. • 10.8 avg. • 0 TD

KO RET   Doak Walker • 10 ret. • 225 yds. • 22.5 avg. • 0 TD

PUNTING   Bob Smith • 32 punts • 1309 yds. • 40.9 avg.

INTS   Don Doll • 12 int. • 163 yds. • 1 TD

- The Lions traded Bill Dudley to the Washington Redskins for halfback Daniel Sandifer in January 1950.

- Prior to the start of the 1950 season, the Lions began building a dynasty that would last almost a decade. The team acquired Heisman Trophy winners Doak Walker (1948) and Leon Hart (1949) and Hall of Fame quarterback Bobby Layne. Layne was obtained in a trade that sent Camp Wilson to Washington.

- Don Doll intercepted a team-record 12 passes in 1950.

- Doak Walker scored 128 points (11 TDs, 8 FGs and 38 PATs) in 1950, establishing a Detroit record.

- Cloyce Box caught 50 passes for 1,009 yards and 11 TDs. His best effort of the season came against the Baltimore Colts on Dec. 3, 1950, as he established Detroit records for receptions, receiving yards and receiving TDs with 12 catches for 302 yards and four TDs.

- Bobby Layne passed for a team-record 374 yards against the Chicago Bears on Nov. 5, 1950. In 1950 Layne became the first Detroit quarterback to surpass 2,000 yards.

- Bob Hoernschemeyer rushed for 198 yards against the New York Yanks on Nov. 23, 1950, including a team-record 96-yard gallop. The run is the third longest in league history.

- The Lions defeated the New York Yanks on Thanksgiving Day, earning the Lions their first Thanksgiving Day victory since 1938. In the game, Detroit gained a team-record 582 yards.

- Wally Triplett returned four kickoffs for an NFL-record 294 yards, including a 97-yard return. Triplett averaged an NFL-record 73.5 yards on four returns.

- Alvin "Bo" McMillin resigned as head coach of the Detroit Lions in December 1950; replacing McMillin was assistant coach Raymond "Buddy" Parker. Parker played for the Lions from 1935–36 and was a member of the 1935 Championship team.

Cloyce Box

1951

- The Lions lost Cloyce Box, Wally Triplett and Jim Cain before the 1951 season. Box was recalled for active duty in the U.S. Marines while Triplett and Cain were inducted into the U.S. Army.

- The Lions lost guard Dick Stanfel, the team's first draft pick in 1951, for the '51 season after he suffered a knee injury in training camp.

- Detroit acquired fullback Pat Harder from the Chicago Cardinals in exchange for fullback Johnny Panelli.

- The Lions defeated the Los Angeles Rams for the first time in 12 contests and won for the first time against the Rams since the team moved from Cleveland to Los Angeles.

- Detroit recorded its first winning season since 1945, but the Lions failed to capture the Western Division crown after two losses to the San Francisco 49ers in the final three weeks of the season.

Jack Christiansen

- Bobby Layne passed for a Detroit record 26 touchdowns in 1951.

- Jack Christiansen set a Lions record against Los Angeles as he returned two punts for touchdowns. He repeated the feat on Nov. 22, 1951, against the Green Bay Packers, including an 89-yard return for a touchdown (second longest in team history). Christiansen's four punt return TDs are the most ever by a Lion.

- Bob Hoernschemeyer ran 85 yards for a touchdown against the Green Bay Packers on Nov. 22, 1951, the second-longest run in team history. Hoernschemeyer established the team record, a 96-yard run in 1950.

- The Lions' 41–28 victory over the Chicago Bears was Detroit's first victory over the Bears since 1946, snapping a 12-game Chicago winning streak.

1951 RESULTS
7– 4 –1 (2nd)
Raymond "Buddy" Parker, Coach

Date	Opponent	Crowd	W-L-T	Score
9/30	WASHINGTON	27,831	W	35 – 17
10/7	NY YANKS	24,194	W	37 – 10
10/14	LOS ANGELES	50,567	L	21 – 27
10/21	NY YANKS	21,807	T	24 – 24
10/28	CHICAGO	34,778	L	23 – 28
11/4	at Green Bay	18,165	W	24 – 17
11/11	at Chicago	43,709	W	41 – 28
11/18	at Philadelphia	25,098	W	28 – 10
11/22	GREEN BAY	32,247	W	52 – 35
12/2	SAN FRANCISCO	45,757	L	10 – 20
12/9	at Los Angeles	52,937	W	24 – 22
12/16	at San Francisco	26,465	L	17 – 21

HOME GAMES IN CAPS

1951 LION LEADERS

RUSHING	Bob Hoernschemeyer • 132 att. • 678 yds. • 2 TD
PASSING	Bobby Layne • 332 att. • 152 comp. • 2403 yds. • 26 TD • 23 int
RECEIVING	Leon Hart • 35 rec. • 544 yds. • 12 TD
SCORING	Doak Walker • 97 points (6 TDs, 6 FGs, 43 PATs)
PUNT RET	Jack Christiansen • 18 ret. • 343 yds. • 19.1 avg. • 4 TD
KO RET	Doak Walker • 15 ret. • 408 yds. • 27.2 avg. • 0 TD
PUNTING	Bob Smith • 49 punts • 2083 yds. • 42.5 avg.
INTS	Bob Smith • 3 int. • 70 yds. • 0 TD

1952 RESULTS
9–3–0 (1st)
Raymond "Buddy" Parker, Coach

Date	Opponent	Crowd	W-L-T	Score
9/28	at San Francisco	54,761	L	3 – 17
10/3	at Los Angeles	42,743	W	17 – 14
10/12	SAN FRANCISCO	56,822	L	0 – 28
10/19	LOS ANGELES	40,152	W	24 – 18
10/26	at Green Bay	24,656	W	52 – 17
11/2	CLEVELAND	56,029	W	17 – 6
11/9	at Pittsburgh	26,170	W	31 – 6
11/16	DALLAS	33,304	W	43 – 13
11/23	at Chicago	37,508	L	23 – 24
11/27	GREEN BAY	39,101	W	48 – 24
12/7	CHICAGO	50,410	W	45 – 21
12/13	at Dallas	12,252	W	41 – 6

Playoff

12/21	LOS ANGELES	47,645	W	31 – 21

World Championship

12/28	at Cleveland	50,934	W	17 – 7

HOME GAMES IN CAPS

1952 LION LEADERS

RUSHING Bob Hoernschemeyer • 106 att. • 457 yds. • 4 TD

PASSING Bobby Layne • 287 att. • 139 comp. • 1999 yds. • 19 TD • 20 int

RECEIVING Cloyce Box • 42 rec. • 924 yds. • 15 TD

SCORING Cloyce Box • 90 points (15 TDs)

PUNT RET Jack Christiansen • 15 ret. • 322 yds. • 21.5 avg. • 2 TD

KO RET Jack Christiansen • 16 ret. • 409 yds. • 25.6 avg. • 0 TD

PUNTING Bob Smith • 61 punts • 2727 yds. • 44.7 avg.

INTS Bob Smith • 9 int. • 184 yds. • 1 TD

1952

- Former Detroit coach Alvin "Bo" McMillin, 57, died March 31, 1952.

- Cloyce Box returned to the Lions from the U.S. Marines in 1952, catching a team-record 15 receiving TDs. Box had a trio of three-TD games in 1952.

Pat Harder

- Defensive end Jim Doran was voted by his teammates as the Lions' Most Valuable Player. Doran became the first player to receive the President's Trophy offered by Edwin J. Anderson, the Lions president, in honor of the team's MVP.

- After losing two of their first three games in 1952 (both to the San Francisco 49ers), the Lions won eight of their last nine games to earn a playoff game against the Los Angeles Rams. Detroit defeated the Rams, 31–21, earning a place in the title game against the Cleveland Browns.

- In the Lions' 31–21 playoff victory over the Los Angeles Rams, Pat Harder scored an NFL playoff record 19 points (2 TDs, 1 FG and 4 PATs).

- Detroit defeated the Cleveland Browns in the 1952 Championship game to earn its first title in 17 seasons.

- The 1952 Detroit Lions boasted a high-powered offense as the team scored 40 points or more five times and scored a regular-season Detroit record 52 points in a victory over the Green Bay Packers. The Lions defense contributed to the team's success in 1952, coming up big when necessary. The Detroit defense had four important goal line stands in the 1952 Championship game, and the Lions' defense held the Pittsburgh Steelers to a Detroit-record 3 yards rushing on Nov. 9, 1952.

1953

- Lewis Carpenter became the third Detroit player to play baseball and football in the same season, joining Bob Hoernschemeyer and Yale Lary.

- Don Doll was traded by the Lions to the Washington Redskins for two draft choices.

- On Thanksgiving Day 1953, Bobby Layne hooked up with Cloyce Box for a 97-yard touchdown pass play in a 34–15 victory over the Green Bay Packers. The pass play stands as the second-longest in team history.

- The Detroit defense intercepted a team-record 38 passes in 1953, including 12 steals by Jack Christiansen, also a team record.

- Tragedy struck the Lions in 1953 as Mary Lou Torgeson, 24, the wife of Lions linebacker LaVern Torgeson, died of a liver ailment.

- With slightly more than two minutes remaining in the 1953 NFL Championship game, Doak Walker's conversion kick after a Bobby Layne-to-Jim Doran 33-yard touchdown pass provided the Lions with a 17–16 victory over the Cleveland Browns. The Lions became only the third team in NFL history to win back-to-back titles, joining the Chicago Bears (1940–41) and the Philadelphia Eagles (1948–49).

- Bob Hoernschemeyer became the first Lion to lead the team in rushing for four consecutive seasons (1950–53).

Vince Banonis

1953 RESULTS
10–2–0 (1st)
Raymond "Buddy" Parker, Coach

Date	Opponent	Crowd	W-L-T	Score
9/27	PITTSBURGH	44,587	W	38 – 21
10/3	at Baltimore	25,259	W	27 – 17
10/11	SAN FRANCISCO	58,079	W	24 – 21
10/18	LOS ANGELES	55,772	L	19 – 31
10/25	at San Francisco	54,662	W	14 – 10
11/1	at Los Angeles	93,751	L	24 – 37
11/7	BALTIMORE	46,508	W	17 – 7
11/15	at Green Bay	20,834	W	14 – 7
11/22	at Chicago	36,165	W	20 – 16
11/26	GREEN BAY	52,547	W	34 – 15
12/6	CHICAGO	58,056	W	13 – 7
12/13	at New York	28,390	W	27 – 16
	World Championship			
12/27	CLEVELAND	54,577	W	17 – 16

HOME GAMES IN CAPS

1953 LION LEADERS

RUSHING	Bob Hoernschemeyer • 101 att. • 482 yds. • 7 TD
PASSING	Bobby Layne • 273 att. • 125 comp. • 2088 yds. • 16 TD • 21 int
RECEIVING	Doak Walker • 30 rec. • 502 yds. • 3 TD
SCORING	Doak Walker • 93 points (5 TDs, 12 FGs, 27 PATs)
PUNT RET	Yale Lary • 13 ret. • 115 yds. • 8.8 avg. • 1 TD
KO RET	Jack Christiansen • 10 ret. • 183 yds. • 18.3 avg. • 0 TD
PUNTING	Bob Smith • 40 punts • 1648 yds. • 41.2 avg.
INTS	Jack Christiansen • 12 int. • 238 yds. • 1 TD

1954

9–2–1 (1st)

Raymond "Buddy" Parker, Coach

Date	Opponent	Crowd	W-L-T	Score
9/26	CHICAGO	52,343	W	48 – 23
10/10	LOS ANGELES	56,523	W	21 – 3
10/16	BALTIMORE	48,272	W	35 – 0
10/24	at San Francisco	60,500	L	31 – 37
10/31	at Los Angeles	74,342	W	27 – 24
11/6	at Baltimore	25,287	W	27 – 3
11/14	SAN FRANCISCO	58,431	W	48 – 7
11/21	at Green Bay	20,767	W	21 – 17
11/25	GREEN BAY	55,532	W	28 – 24
12/5	PHILADELPHIA	54,939	T	13 – 13
12/12	at Chicago	37,240	L	24 – 28
12/19	at Cleveland	34,168	W	14 – 10

World Championship

12/26	at Cleveland	43,827	L	10 – 56

HOME GAMES IN CAPS

1954 LION LEADERS

RUSHING Lew Carpenter • 104 att. • 476 yds. • 3 TD

PASSING Bobby Layne • 246 att. • 135 comp. • 1818 yds. • 14 TD • 12 int

RECEIVING Dorne Dibble • 46 rec. • 768 yds. • 6 TD

SCORING Doak Walker • 106 points (5 TDs, 11 FGs, 43 PATs)

PUNT RET Jack Christiansen • 23 ret. • 225 yds. • 9.8 avg. • 1 TD

KO RET Jug Girard • 12 ret. • 248 yds. • 20.7 avg. • 0 TD

PUNTING Jug Girard • 63 punts • 2583 yds. • 41.0

INTS Jack Christiansen • 8 int. • 84 yds. • 1 TD

- Charles "Gus" Dorais, the Lions' head coach from 1943–47, died of a circulatory ailment in January 1954.

- The Lions lost Yale Lary and Gene Gedman to military service in 1954.

- Detroit rookie Bill Bowman, playing in his first game as a Lion, returned a kickoff 100 yards for a touchdown in the Lions' opening-game victory over the Chicago Bears on Sept. 26, 1954.

- Detroit's 35–0 shutout of the Baltimore Colts was the team's first shutout since 1945 when the Lions beat the Chicago Cardinals, 26–0.

- With the Lions' two victories over the Packers in 1954, Detroit extended its winning streak over Green Bay to 12 games.

- After defeating the Cleveland Browns, 14–10, in the season finale, Detroit and Cleveland staged a rematch in the 1954 NFL Title game. The Browns blasted the Lions, 56–10, keeping Detroit Coach Raymond "Buddy" Parker from becoming the first NFL coach to win three consecutive NFL Championships. The Cleveland defense baffled Bobby Layne the entire game, forcing the Detroit signal caller to throw six interceptions.

Lew Carpenter, Lou Creekmur and Dick Stanfel

1955

- Detroit's six consecutive losses at the start of the 1955 season equaled the team's longest losing streak in 10 years. Fortunately, the Lions rebounded to win three of the remaining six contests. The team's losing record was its first since 1949 when the Lions were 4–8.

Jug Girard

- Hall of Fame halfback Doak Walker retired following the 1955 season. Walker was the Lions' leading scorer in five of his six seasons in Detroit and his 534 career points currently rank third on the Lions' all-time scoring list.

- The Lions lost seven key members of the 1954 Western Division Championship team prior to the start of the 1955 season, including end Cloyce Box (retired), middle guard Les Bingaman (retired), defensive tackle Thurman McGraw (retired), quarterback Tom Dublinski (signed with Canadian League), back Dick Kercher (military service), tackle Gerald Perry (military service) and fullback Bill Bowman (military service).

- Detroit's 24–10 victory over the Green Bay Packers in the 1955 Thanksgiving Day game was the Lions' sixth consecutive victory in Thanksgiving Day games, the team's longest winning streak in the series.

- Bob Hoernschemeyer, Detroit's leading rusher from 1950–53, retired after the 1955 season.

1955 RESULTS
3–9–0 (6th)
Raymond "Buddy" Parker, Coach

Date	Opponent	Crowd	W-L-T	Score
9/27	at Green Bay	22,217	L	17 – 20
10/1	at Baltimore	40,030	L	13 – 28
10/9	LOS ANGELES	54,836	L	10 – 17
10/16	SAN FRANCISCO	51,438	L	24 – 27
10/23	at Los Angeles	68,690	L	13 – 24
10/30	at San Francisco	47,431	L	21 – 36
11/5	BALTIMORE	53,874	W	24 – 14
11/13	at Pittsburgh	34,441	W	31 – 28
11/20	CHICAGO	53,610	L	14 – 24
11/24	GREEN BAY	51,685	W	24 – 10
12/4	at Chicago	39,388	L	20 – 21
12/11	NEW YORK	45,929	L	19 – 24

HOME GAMES IN CAPS

1955 LION LEADERS

RUSHING	Lew Carpenter • 137 att. • 543 yds. • 6 TD
PASSING	Bobby Layne • 270 att. • 143 comp. • 1830 yds. • 11 TD • 17 int
RECEIVING	Dave Middleton • 44 rec. • 663 yds. • 3 TD
SCORING	Doak Walker • 96 points (7 TDs, 9 FGs, 27 PATs)
PUNT RET	Lee Riley • 14 ret. • 107 yds. • 7.6 avg. • 0 TD
KO RET	Dave Middleton • 11 ret. • 188 yds. • 17.1 avg. • 0 TD
PUNTING	Jug Girard • 56 punts • 2313 yds. • 41.3 avg.
INTS	Jack Christiansen, Jim David and Bill Stits • 3 each

1956 RESULTS
9–3–0 (2nd)
Raymond "Buddy" Parker, Coach

Date	Opponent	Crowd	W-L-T	Score
9/30	at Green Bay	24,668	W	20 – 16
10/6	at Baltimore	42,622	W	31 – 14
10/14	LOS ANGELES	56,281	W	24 – 21
10/21	SAN FRANCISCO	55,662	W	20 – 17
10/28	at Los Angeles	76,758	W	16 – 7
11/4	at San Francisco	46,708	W	17 – 13
11/11	at Washington	28,003	L	17 – 18
11/18	BALTIMORE	55,788	W	27 – 3
11/22	GREEN BAY	54,087	L	20 – 24
12/2	CHICAGO	57,024	W	42 – 10
12/9	PITTSBURGH	52,124	W	45 – 7
12/16	at Chicago	49,086	L	21 – 38

HOME GAMES IN CAPS

1956 LION LEADERS

RUSHING	Gene Gedman • 135 att. • 479 yds. • 7 TD
PASSING	Bobby Layne • 244 att. • 129 comp. • 1909 yds. • 9 TD • 17 int
RECEIVING	Dave Middleton • 39 rec. • 606 yds. • 5 TD
SCORING	Bobby Layne • 99 points (5 TDs, 12 FGs, 33 PATs)
PUNT RET	Howard Cassady • 13 ret. • 83 yds. • 6.4 avg. • 0 TD
KO RET	Howard Cassady • 16 ret. • 382 yds. • 23.9 avg. • 0 TD
PUNTING	Yale Lary • 42 punts • 1697 yds. • 40.4 avg.
INTS	Yale Lary • 8 int. • 182 yds. • 1 TD

1956

- The Lions acquired Ohio State halfback Howard "Hopalong" Cassady, winner of the 1955 Heisman Trophy.

- Yale Lary, Oliver Spencer and Gene Gedman, members of Detroit's 1953 Championship team, returned to the Lions in 1956 after finishing military commitments.

- The Detroit Lions faced the Chicago Bears in the 1956 season finale, with the winner representing the Western Division in the NFL Title game. After Detroit quarterback Bobby Layne was knocked out of the game in the second quarter with a concussion, Detroit's title hopes dwindled and Chicago turned a 3–0 lead into a 38–21 trouncing of the Lions.

- Raymond "Buddy" Parker signed a two-year contract with the Lions after the 1956 season.

- Detroit jumped out to a quick start in 1956, winning the first six games of the season en route to a 9–3 finish.

Leon Hart

1957

- Raymond "Buddy" Parker, who guided the Lions to two NFL Championship victories in the 1950s, resigned suddenly and unexpectedly at a "Meet the Lions" banquet in Detroit during the 1957 training camp. Parker cited the players' lack of motivation as the reason for his leaving.

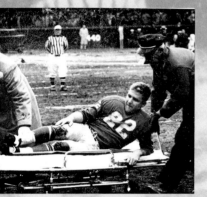

Bobby Layne

  "I can't handle this team anymore. It is the worst team I've ever seen in training camp," said Parker. "They have no life, no go; just a completely dead team."
  Parker was replaced by assistant coach George Wilson, who took the so-called "dead team" to an NFL World Championship.

- The Lions traded fullback Bill Bowman and defensive back Bill Stits to the San Francisco 49ers for Hall of Fame fullback John Henry Johnson. Johnson led the Lions in rushing in 1957 with 621 yards and five touchdowns on 129 carries.

- The Detroit Lions acquired quarterback Tobin Rote and halfback Val Joe Walker from the Green Bay Packers in a six-player deal that sent halfback Don McIlhenny, tackle Oliver Spencer, guard Jim Salisbury and tackle Norm Masters to Green Bay.

- Quarterback Bobby Layne suffered a broken leg in Detroit's 20–7 victory against Cleveland, the second-to-last game of the season. However, Tobin Rote picked up the slack, passing Detroit to wins over Chicago, San Francisco and Cleveland to earn an NFL Championship.

- Down by 20 points early in the second half in the 1957 playoff game, the Detroit Lions stormed back and scored three touchdowns in a span of four minutes and 29 seconds late in the game to give the Lions a 31–27 come-from-behind victory. The comeback is the second-largest in NFL playoff history.

- Detroit's 59 points in a 59–14 trouncing of the Cleveland Browns in the 1957 NFL Championship game are the most points scored by a Detroit Lion team. Tobin Rote tossed four touchdowns, helping the Lions avenge a 56–10 blowout to the Browns in the 1954 title game.

1957 RESULTS

8–4–0 (1st)

George W. Wilson, Coach

Date	Opponent	Crowd	W-L-T	Score
9/29	at Baltimore	40,112	L	14 – 34
10/6	at Green Bay	32,132	W	24 – 14
10/13	LOS ANGELES	55,914	W	10 – 7
10/20	BALTIMORE	55,764	W	31 – 27
10/27	at Los Angeles	77,314	L	17 – 35
11/3	at San Francisco	59,702	L	31 – 35
11/10	at Philadelphia	29,302	W	27 – 16
11/17	SAN FRANCISCO	56,915	W	31 – 10
11/24	CHICAGO	55,769	L	7 – 27
11/28	GREEN BAY	54,301	W	18 – 6
12/8	CLEVELAND	55,814	W	20 – 7
12/15	at Chicago	41,088	W	21 – 13
	Playoff			
12/22	at San Francisco	60,118	W	31 – 27
	World Championship			
12/29	CLEVELAND	55,263	W	59 – 14

HOME GAMES IN CAPS

1957 LION LEADERS

RUSHING	John Henry Johnson • 129 att. • 621 yds. • 5 TD
PASSING	Bobby Layne • 179 att. • 87 comp. • 1169 yds. • 6 TD • 10 int
RECEIVING	Jim Doran • 33 rec. • 624 yds. • 5 TD
SCORING	Bobby Layne • 43 points (6 FGs, 25 PATs)
PUNT RET	Yale Lary • 25 ret. • 139 yds. • 5.6 avg. • 0 TD
KO RET	Howard Cassady • 10 ret. • 232 yds. • 23.2 avg. • 0 TD
PUNTING	Yale Lary • 54 punts • 2155 yds. • 39.9 avg.
INTS	Jack Christiansen • 10 int. • 137 yds. • 1 TD

1958 RESULTS

4–7–1 (5th)

George W. Wilson, Coach

Date	Opponent	Crowd	W-L-T	Score
9/28	at Baltimore	48,377	L	15 – 28
10/5	at Green Bay	32,035	T	13 – 13
10/12	LOS ANGELES	55,648	L	28 – 42
10/19	BALTIMORE	55,190	L	14 – 40
10/26	at Los Angeles	81,703	W	41 – 24
11/2	at San Francisco	59,213	L	21 – 24
11/9	at Cleveland	75,363	W	30 – 10
11/16	SAN FRANCISCO	54,523	W	35 – 21
11/23	CHICAGO	55,280	L	7 – 20
11/27	GREEN BAY	50,971	W	24 – 14
12/7	NEW YORK	50,115	L	17 – 19
12/14	at Chicago	38,346	L	16 – 21

HOME GAMES IN CAPS

1958 LION LEADERS

RUSHING Tobin Rote • 77 att. • 351 yds. • 3 TD

PASSING Tobin Rote • 257 att. • 118 comp. • 1678 yds. • 14 TD • 10 int

RECEIVING Dave Middleton • 29 rec. • 506 yds. • 3 TD

SCORING Jim Martin • 49 points (7 FGs, 28 PATs)

PUNT RET Yale Lary • 27 punts • 196 yds. • 7.3 avg. • 1 TD

KO RET Ken Webb • 7 ret. • 154 yds. • 22.0 avg. • 0 TD

PUNTING Yale Lary • 59 punts • 2525 yds. • 42.8 avg.

INTS Joe Schmidt • 6 int • 69 yds. • 0 TD

1958

- Detroit's 28–15 loss to the eventual NFL Champion Baltimore Colts set the tone for the 1958 season as the Lions went without a victory in their first four contests and finished the season at 4–7–1.

- Tobin Rote led the Detroit Lions in both rushing (351 yards on 77 attempts) and passing (118-of-257 for 1,678 yards). Rote joined Dutch Clark (1934), Byron "Whizzer" White (1940–41) and Frank Sinkwich (1943–44) as the only players in Detroit history to accomplish this feat.

- Nick Kerbawy resigned as general manager of the Detroit Lions in 1958 to accept a similar position with the Detroit Pistons.

- Alex Karras, the colorful defensive tackle out of Iowa, joined the Lions in 1958.

- The Lions traded Hall of Fame quarterback Bobby Layne to the Pittsburgh Steelers in exchange for quarterback Earl Morrall and draft choices on Oct. 6, 1958.

- In one of the lone bright spots of the 1958 season, the Lions defeated the Los Angeles Rams, 41–24, with the help of seven interceptions and a 104-yard kickoff return. Linebacker Joe Schmidt led the assault with three interceptions while Terry Barr (92 yards) and Gene Gedman (12 yards) combined for the third-longest return in NFL-history and the longest in team history.

- Hall of Fame defensive back Jack Christiansen played his last season in Detroit, ending his eight-year career in Detroit with 46 interceptions, currently fourth on the Lions' all-time list. Christiansen's eight touchdowns on punt returns are an NFL record.

Tobin Rote

1959

- Fullback Nick Pietrosante joined the Lions in 1959 out of Notre Dame.

- Head Coach George Wilson inserted Earl Morrall at quarterback in the fifth game of the season, replacing the ineffective Tobin Rote. Morrall responded to the promotion, leading Detroit to its first victory of the season, a 17–7 win over Los Angeles.

- The Lions acquired Dick LeBeau off of waivers early in the 1959 season and moved him into the Detroit starting defensive backfield by the end of the season. The acquisition of LeBeau paid dividends as he intercepted a team-record 62 passes in 14 seasons in Detroit.

- In a game that pitted mentor against student and starter against backup, the result was a 10–10 stalemate. The Buddy Parker-coached Pittsburgh Steelers were guided by former Detroit quarterback Bobby Layne while George Wilson had Tobin Rote at the helm for the Lions.

- Howard Cassady hauled in three passes, all touchdowns, against Baltimore in a 31–24 loss to the Colts on Oct. 11, 1959.

1959 Coaching Staff

1959 RESULTS
3–8–1 (5th)
George W. Wilson, Coach

Date	Opponent	Crowd	W-L-T	Score
9/29	at Baltimore	55,588	L	9 – 21
10/4	at Green Bay	32,150	L	10 – 28
10/11	BALTIMORE	54,197	L	24 – 31
10/18	SAN FRANCISCO	52,585	L	13 – 34
10/25	at Los Angeles	74,288	W	17 – 7
11/1	at San Francisco	59,064	L	7 – 33
11/8	at Pittsburgh	24,614	T	10 – 10
11/15	LOS ANGELES	52,217	W	23 – 17
11/22	CHICAGO	54,059	L	14 – 24
11/26	GREEN BAY	49,221	L	17 – 24
12/6	CARDINALS	45,811	W	45 – 21
12/13	at Chicago	40,890	L	14 – 25

HOME GAMES IN CAPS

1959 LION LEADERS

RUSHING	Nick Pietrosante • 76 att. • 447 yds. • 3 TD
PASSING	Earl Morral • 137 att. • 65 comp. • 1102 yds. • 5 TD • 6 int
RECEIVING	Jim Gibbons • 31 rec. • 431 yds. • 1 TD
SCORING	Howard Cassady • 30 points (5 TDs)
PUNT RET	Terry Barr • 16 ret. • 102 yds. • 0 TD
KO RET	Ken Webb • 16 ret. • 352 yds. • 0 TD
PUNTING	Yale Lary • 45 punts • 2118 yds. • 47.1 avg.
INTS	Gary Lowe • 5 int. • 130 yds.

1960

1960 RESULTS

7 – 5 – 0 (2nd)

George W. Wilson, Coach

Date	Opponent	Crowd	W-L-T	Score
10/2	at Green Bay	32,150	L	9 – 28
10/9	SAN FRANCISCO	49,825	L	10 – 14
10/16	at Philadelphia	38,065	L	10 – 28
10/23	BALTIMORE	53,854	W	30 – 17
10/30	at Los Angeles	53,295	L	35 – 48
11/6	at San Francisco	48,447	W	20 – 0
11/13	LOS ANGELES	54,019	W	12 – 10
11/20	at Chicago	46,267	L	7 – 28
11/24	GREEN BAY	54,123	W	23 – 10
12/4	at Baltimore	57,808	W	20 – 15
12/11	DALLAS	43,272	W	23 – 14
12/18	CHICAGO	51,017	W	36 – 0

Runner-Up

1/7	at Cleveland	34,981	W	17 – 16

HOME GAMES IN CAPS

1960 LION LEADERS

RUSHING   Nick Pietrosante • 161 att. • 872 yds. • 8 TD

PASSING   Jim Ninowski • 283 att. • 134 comp. • 1599 yds. • 2 TD • 18 int

RECEIVING   Jim Gibbons • 51 rec. • 604 yds. • 2 TD

SCORING   Jim Martin • 65 points (13 FGs, 26 PATs)

PUNT RET   Terry Barr • 14 ret. • 104 yds. • 7.4 avg. • 0 TD

KO RET   Jim Steffen • 8 ret. • 225 yds. • 28.1 avg. • 0 TD

PUNTING   Yale Lary • 64 punts • 2802 yds. • 43.8 avg. • 0 TD

INTS   Dick Lane • 5 int. • 102 yds. • 1 TD

- The Detroit Lions lost top draft pick Jimmy Robinson, halfback from Louisiana State, to the Dallas Texans of the newly-formed American Football Conference.

- Tobin Rote left the Detroit Lions and signed a contract with the Toronto Argonauts of the Canadian Football League.

- Don Shula joined the Lions in 1960 as defensive backs coach. In later years, Shula would go on to become one of the league's most successful head coaches, winning a pair of Super Bowls with the Miami Dolphins.

- The Lions sent linebacker Bob Long to the Cleveland Browns in exchange for quarterback Jim Ninowski.

- In a spectacular finish, the Detroit Lions and Baltimore Colts combined for two touchdowns in the final 14 seconds of the game on Dec. 12, 1960. With 14 seconds left, John Unitas connected with Lenny Moore on a 37-yard touchdown pass. But after the ensuing kickoff, Earl Morrall hit Jim Gibbons for a 65-yard TD as time expired to give Detroit a 20–15 win.

- The Lions lost to the San Francisco 49ers, 14–10, with the 49ers scoring the game winning touchdown as time ran out on a John Brodie to R.C. Owens 18-yard pass.

- Detroit defeated Baltimore for its first victory of the 1960 season with the help of an 80-yard interception return by Dick "Night Train" Lane. The Hall of Fame defensive back was obtained in 1960 by the Lions and Lane contributed immediately, leading the team in interceptions in 1960 with five.

- The Lions' 20–0 victory over the San Francisco 49ers marked the Lions' first shutout since 1954 when Detroit defeated Baltimore, 35–0.

- Detroit won seven of its last nine games and four straight at the end of the season to earn a berth in the Runner-Up Bowl where the Lions defeated Cleveland, 17–16.

- Nick Pietrosante's 872 yards established a new Detroit rushing record, breaking the mark set by Ace Gutowsky (827 yards) in 1936.

1961

- William Clay Ford was elected president of the Detroit Lions by the board of directors on Jan. 23, 1961. Ford replaced Edwin J. Anderson as president, but Ford allowed Anderson to remain as general manager.

- A heavy-hearted Jim Martin kicked three field goals, including a game-winning 49-yarder with less than four minutes remaining, in the Lions' 16–15 victory over the Baltimore Colts on Sept. 24, 1961. Just six days earlier, Martin's eight-month-old son, Michael, died of leukemia and his father-in-law died of a heart attack.

- Detroit's 49–0 thrashing at the hands of the San Francisco 49ers on Oct. 1, 1961, was the first time the Lions had been shutout since 1952 when San Francisco jolted the Lions, 28–0.

- Replacing the ineffective Jim Ninowski, Earl Morrall sparked the Lions to a 37–10 victory after trailing 10–0. Morrall connected on 13 of his 17 passes for 154 yards and three touchdowns in the Lions' win over Minnesota.

- Detroit played in the Runner-Up Bowl for the second consecutive season, defeating the Philadelphia Eagles, 38–10.

- The Lions defeated Green Bay in Milwaukee, 17–13, earning their first victory in Milwaukee.

- Joe Schmidt was voted Most Valuable Player by his teammates in 1960, becoming the first Lion to win the award four seasons (1955, '57, '58 and '61).

Lion Receivers

1961 RESULTS
8–5–1 (2nd)
George W. Wilson, Coach

Date	Opponent	Crowd	W-L-T	Score
9/17	at Green Bay*	44,307	W	17 – 13
9/24	at Baltimore	54,259	W	16 – 15
10/1	SAN FRANCISCO	53,155	L	0 – 49
10/8	CHICAGO	50,521	L	17 – 31
10/15	LOS ANGELES	45,873	W	14 – 13
10/22	BALTIMORE	53,106	L	14 – 17
10/29	at Los Angeles	49,123	W	28 – 10
11/5	at San Francisco	56,878	T	20 – 20
11/12	at St. Louis	20,320	W	45 – 14
11/19	at Minnesota	32,296	W	37 – 10
11/23	GREEN BAY	55,662	L	9 – 17
12/3	at Chicago	47,394	W	16 – 15
12/10	MINNESOTA	42,655	W	13 – 7
12/17	PHILADELPHIA	44,231	L	24 – 27

Runner-Up

1/6	at Philadelphia	25,612	W	38 – 10

* Milwaukee

HOME GAMES IN CAPS

1961 LION LEADERS

RUSHING — Nick Pietrosante • 201 att. • 841 yds. • 5 TD

PASSING — Jim Ninowski • 247 att. • 117 comp. • 1921 yds. • 7 TD • 18 int.

RECEIVING — Gail Cogdill • 45 rec. • 956 yds. • 6 TD

SCORING — Jim Martin • 70 points (15 FGs, 25 PATs)

PUNT RET — Howard Cassady • 16 ret. • 159 yds. • 9.9 avg. • 0 TD

KO RET — Pat Studstill • 16 ret. • 448 yds. • 28.1 avg. • 1 TD

PUNTING — Yale Lary • 52 punts • 2517 yds. • 48.4 avg.

INTS — Dick Lane and Yale Lary • 6 int. each

1962

Date	Opponent	Crowd	W-L-T	Score
9/16	PITTSBURGH	46,641	W	45 – 7
9/23	SAN FRANCISCO	51,032	W	45 – 24
9/30	at Baltimore	57,966	W	29 – 20
10/7	at Green Bay	38,669	L	7 – 9
10/14	LOS ANGELES	53,714	W	13 – 10
10/21	at New York	62,856	L	14 – 17
10/28	CHICAGO	53,342	W	11 – 3
11/4	at Los Angeles	44,241	W	12 – 3
11/11	at San Francisco	43,449	W	38 – 24
11/18	at Minnesota	31,257	W	17 – 6
11/22	GREEN BAY	57,598	W	26 – 14
12/2	BALTIMORE	53,012	W	21 – 14
12/9	MINNESOTA	42,256	W	37 – 23
12/16	at Chicago	44,948	L	0 – 3
Runner-Up				
1/6	at Pittsburgh	36,284	W	17 - 10

HOME GAMES IN CAPS

1962 LION LEADERS

RUSHING	Dan Lewis • 120 att. • 488 yds. • 6 TD
PASSING	Milt Plum • 325 att. • 179 comp • 2378 yds • 15 TD • 20 int
RECEIVING	Gail Cogdill • 53 rec. • 991 yds. • 7 TD
SCORING	Wayne Walker • 64 points (9 FGs, 37 PATs)
PUNT RET	Pat Studstill • 29 ret. • 457 yds. • 15.8 avg.
KO RET	Tommy Watkins • 17 ret. • 452 yds. • 26.6 avg.
PUNTING	Yale Lary • 52 punts • 2402 yds. • 45.3 avg.
INTS	Yale Lary • 8 int. • 51 yds. • 0 TD

- The Detroit Lions engineered a deal with the Cleveland Browns that sent quarterback Jim Ninowski, halfback Howard "Hopalong" Cassady and defensive end Bill Glass to the Browns in return for quarterback Milt Plum, halfback Tommy Watkins and linebacker Dave Lloyd. Plum was the NFL's top-ranked passer in 1960 and 1961.

- The Lions' "Fearsome Foursome," consisting of Darris McCord, Alex Karras, Roger Brown and Sam Williams, sacked Green Bay quarterback Bart Starr 11 times in a Thanksgiving Day win over the Packers in 1962. The 26–14 victory avenged an early-season 9–7 loss to the Packers.

- Unfortunately for the Lions, their Thanksgiving Day win over the Packers was Green Bay's only loss of the season. The Lions (11–3) played in the Runner-Up Bowl for the third consecutive season, beating the Pittsburgh Steelers, 17–10.

- Relegated to bench duty for most of the 1962 season, Earl Morrall rescued the Lions from defeat in four games after replacing Milt Plum in wins over Baltimore, Minnesota, San Francisco and Los Angeles.

- The Lions defeated the Minnesota Vikings, 37–23, with the help of a team-record 10 takeaways (five interceptions, five fumble recoveries).

Dan Lewis

1963

- Former Lion great Earl "Dutch" Clark was voted in as a charter member of the Pro Football Hall of Fame.

- The Detroit Lions organization and six Detroit players

Tommy Watkins

  were reprimanded by NFL Commissioner Pete Rozelle for the players' alleged involvement in gambling. Lions management was fined $4,000 for neglecting action on a Detroit police report which revealed player associations with "known hoodlums." Joe Schmidt, Gary Lowe, Wayne Walker, John Gordy and Sam Williams were fined $2,000 each for betting on the 1962 Championship game between Green Bay and New York. Alex Karras received an "indefinite suspension" for betting on at least six games. Karras was reinstated for the 1964 season.

- In the third game of the season, defensive back Gary Lowe was lost for the season after suffering a torn Achilles' tendon.

- The Detroit Lions' game against the Green Bay Packers on Thanksgiving Day in 1963 marked the 13th consecutive game the two teams had played on Thanksgiving Day. The game ended, fittingly, in a 13–13 tie. Detroit and Green Bay would not meet on Thanksgiving Day again until 1984.

- Earl Morrall passed for 2,621 yards and 24 touchdowns, the second-highest TD total in Lions history.

- Terry Barr (13 TDs) and Gail Cogdill (10 TDs) combined for 23 touchdown receptions in 1963. Barr's 1,086 yards on 66 receptions ranks third on Detroit's all-time list.

- Yale Lary averaged 48.9 yards on 35 punts, establishing a Detroit record and ranking second in NFL history.

- Tom Watkins returned five punts for a team-record 184 yards against the San Francisco 49ers on Oct. 6, 1963. Included in the the third-best punt returning performance in NFL history was a team-record 90-yard punt return for a touchdown.

1963 RESULTS
5–8–1 (4th)
George W. Wilson, Coach

Date	Opponent	Crowd	W-L-T	Score
9/14	at Los Angeles	49,342	W	23 – 2
9/22	at Green Bay*	45,912	L	10 – 31
9/29	CHICAGO	55,400	L	21 – 37
10/6	SAN FRANCISCO	44,088	W	26 – 3
10/13	at Dallas	27,264	L	14 – 17
10/20	BALTIMORE	51,901	L	21 – 25
10/27	MINNESOTA	44,509	W	28 – 10
11/3	at San Francisco	33,511	W	45 – 7
11/10	at Baltimore	59,758	L	21 – 24
11/17	LOS ANGELES	44,951	L	21 – 28
11/24	at Minnesota	28,763	L	31 – 34
11/28	GREEN BAY	54,016	T	13 – 13
12/8	CLEVELAND	51,382	W	38 – 10
12/15	at Chicago	45,317	L	14 – 24

* Milwaukee

HOME GAMES IN CAPS

1963 LION LEADERS

RUSHING	Dan Lewis • 133 att. • 528 yds. • 2 TD
PASSING	Earl Morrall • 328 att. • 174 comp. • 2621 yds. • 24 TD • 14 int
RECEIVING	Terry Barr • 66 rec. • 1086 yds. • 13 TD
SCORING	Terry Barr • 78 points (13 TDs)
PUNT RET	Tommy Watkins • 32 ret. • 399 yds. • 12.5 avg. • 1 TD
KO RET	Tommy Watkins • 21 ret. • 447 yds. • 0 TD
PUNTING	Yale Lary • 35 punts • 1713 yds. • 48.9 avg.
INTS	Dick LeBeau and Dick Lane • 5 ints.

1964 RESULTS
7–5–2 (4th)
George W. Wilson, Coach

Date	Opponent	Crowd	W-L-T	Score
9/13	at San Francisco	33,204	W	26 – 17
9/19	at Los Angeles	52,001	T	17 – 17
9/28	GREEN BAY	59,203	L	10 – 14
10/4	NEW YORK	54,836	W	26 – 3
10/11	at Minnesota	40,840	W	24 – 20
10/18	at Chicago	47,567	W	10 – 0
10/25	BALTIMORE	57,814	L	0 – 34
11/1	LOS ANGELES	52,064	W	37 – 17
11/8	at Green Bay	42,327	L	7 – 30
11/15	at Cleveland	83,064	L	21 – 37
11/22	MINNESOTA	48,291	T	23 – 23
11/26	CHICAGO	52,231	L	24 – 27
12/6	at Baltimore	60,213	W	31 – 14
12/13	SAN FRANCISCO	41,854	W	24 – 7

HOME GAMES IN CAPS

1964 LION LEADERS

RUSHING	Nick Pietrosante • 147 att. • 536 yds. • 4 TD
PASSING	Milt Plum • 287 att. • 154 comp. • 2241 yds • 18 TD • 15 int
RECEIVING	Terry Barr • 57 rec. • 1030 yds. • 9 TD
SCORING	Wayne Walker • 74 points (14 FGs, 32 PATs)
PUNT RET	Tommy Watkins • 16 ret. • 238 yds. • 14.9 yds. • 2 TD
KO RET	Pat Studstill • 29 ret. • 708 yds. • 24.4 avg.
PUNTING	Yale Lary • 67 punts • 3102 yds. • 46.3 avg.
INTS	Yale Lary • 6 int. • 101 yds. • 0 TD

1964

- William Clay Ford took over as the Lions sole owner after purchasing the franchise for $4.5 million on Jan. 10, 1964. After buying the Lions, Ford gave Edwin J. Anderson a three-year contract and a new title of vice president to go with general manager. In another front office move, Ford appointed former Lion player Russ Thomas to director of player personnel; His duties included supervising all talent scouting and signing of all players.

- Detroit offensive tackle Lucien Reeberg died on Jan. 31, 1964, after suffering heart failure due to uremic poisoning. Reeberg, 21, entering his second season with the Lions, was at the Detroit Osteopathic Hospital when he collapsed and suffered a cardiac arrest. He had been in the hospital for six days at the suggestion of the Lions to begin a program of weight reduction when he died. The Lions wanted the 305-pound Reeberg to reduce his weight to 265. He started eight games for Detroit in 1963 despite being selected in the 19th round of the NFL draft in 1963.

- Detroit Lion halfback coach Ray "Scooter" McLean, 48, died after a battle with cancer on March 4, 1964. McLean, the Lions' backfield coach since 1959, had been hospitalized since October 1963 with the illness.

- Alex Karras, the Lions defensive tackle, was reinstated by the NFL after serving one year of an "indefinite" ban from the league. Karras, who was suspended for gambling, was allowed back in the NFL on the condition he sell his interests in the Lindell A.C. Lounge in Detroit.

- The Lions lost quarterback Earl Morrall early in the season to a shoulder injury, but Milt Plum performed well in his absence, passing for 2,241 yards and 18 TDs. Plum also connected with Dan Lewis for a 92-yard touchdown pass at Cleveland on Nov. 15, 1964.

Lion Defense

- George Wilson resigned as head coach of the Lions after all five of his assistant coaches were fired. Wilson had been with the team since 1949 when he was named an assistant under Bo McMillin. He was head coach of the team from 1957–64.

- Terry Barr's 1,030 yards on 57 receptions made him the only Lion in team history to have two 1,000-yard receiving seasons.

1965

- Detroit hired Harry Gilmer, a Minnesota Viking assistant coach, as the team's head coach in early January. Gilmer played for the Lions in 1955–56 but played sparingly behind Bobby Layne. He was an assistant under Buddy Parker with the Pittsburgh Steelers before joining the Vikings in 1960.

- Detroit obtained tight end Ron Kramer from the Green Bay Packers in exchange for the Lions' number one pick in 1965.

- The Lions sent veteran quarterback Earl Morrall to the New York Giants in a three-way trade involving the Lions, Giants and Cleveland Browns. The transaction was initiated with Cleveland sending linebacker Mike Lucci and a draft choice to New York for defensive back Erich Barnes. Lucci and offensive guard Darrell Dess were then traded to the Lions for Morrall and a draft choice.

- Detroit obtained quarterback George Izo and offensive guard Ted Karras, brother of Lions defensive tackle Alex Karras, from the Washington Redskins. Washington received offensive guard Darrell Dess and a draft choice in return.

- The Lions defeated the Minnesota Vikings, 31–29, scoring the winning touchdown on a 48-yard pass from Milt Plum to Amos Marsh with only 22 seconds remaining in the game. The play culminated a five-play, 75-yard scoring drive that lasted only 47 seconds.

Joe Don Looney

- The Detroit defense ranked number one in the NFL in yards allowed (254 per game) in 1965.

- Detroit tied a team-record with 11 sacks in a 12–7 win at Green Bay on Nov. 7, 1965.

- Tommy Watkins, who led the NFL in punt return average in 1964 with a 14.9 yard average and two TDs on 16 returns, was the league's leading kickoff returner with a team-record 34.4 yard average on 17 returns.

- Joe Don Looney was injured on a touchdown plunge in Detroit's 12–7 win over Green Bay and missed the last half of the 1965 season.

1965 RESULTS
6–7–1 (6th)
Harry Gilmer, Coach

Date	Opponent	Crowd	W-L-T	Score
9/19	LOS ANGELES	46,941	W	20 – 0
9/26	at Minnesota	46,826	W	31 – 29
10/3	WASHINGTON	52,627	W	14 – 10
10/10	at Baltimore	60,238	L	7 – 31
10/17	GREEN BAY	56,712	L	21 – 31
10/24	at Chicago	45,658	L	10 – 38
10/31	at Los Angeles	35,137	W	31 – 7
11/7	at Green Bay	50,852	W	12 – 7
11/14	SAN FRANCISCO	54,534	L	21 – 27
11/21	CHICAGO	51,499	L	10 – 17
11/25	BALTIMORE	55,036	T	24 – 24
12/5	at San Francisco	38,463	L	14 – 17
12/12	MINNESOTA	45,420	L	7 – 29
12/19	at Philadelphia	56,718	W	35 – 28

HOME GAMES IN CAPS

1965 LION LEADERS

RUSHING	Amos Marsh • 131 att. • 405 yds. • 6 TD
PASSING	Milt Plum • 308 att. • 143 comp. • 1710 yds • 12 TD • 19 int
RECEIVING	Pat Studstill • 28 rec. • 389 yds. • 3 TD
SCORING	Wayne Walker • 57 points (8 FGs, 33 PATs)
PUNT RET	Tommy Watkins • 23 ret. • 234 yds. • 0 TD
KO RET	Tommy Watkins • 17 ret. • 584 yds. • 0 TD
PUNTING	Pat Studstill • 78 punts • 3335 yds. • 42.8 avg.
INTS	Dick LeBeau • 7 int. • 84 yds. • 1 TD

1966

1966 RESULTS

4–9–1 (6th)

Harry Gilmer, Coach

Date	Opponent	Crowd	W-L-T	Score
9/11	CHICAGO	52,225	W	14 – 3
9/18	at Pittsburgh	35,473	L	3 – 17
9/25	ATLANTA	47,615	W	28 – 10
10/2	at Green Bay	50,861	L	14 – 23
10/9	LOS ANGELES	52,793	L	7 – 14
10/16	at Baltimore	60,238	L	14 – 45
10/23	at San Francisco	36,745	L	24 – 27
10/30	GREEN BAY	56,954	L	7 – 31
11/6	at Chicago	47,041	T	10 – 10
11/13	at Minnesota	43,939	W	32 – 31
11/20	BALTIMORE	52,383	W	20 – 14
11/24	SAN FRANCISCO	53,189	L	14 – 41
12/4	at Los Angeles	40,039	L	3 – 23
12/11	MINNESOTA	43,022	L	16 – 28

HOME GAMES IN CAPS

1966 LION LEADERS

RUSHING	Tom Nowatzke • 151 att. • 512 yds. • 6 TD
PASSING	Karl Sweetan • 309 att. • 157 comp • 1809 yds. • 4 TD • 14 int
RECEIVING	Pat Studstill • 67 rec. • 1266 yds. • 5 TD
SCORING	Garo Yepremian • 50 points (13 FGs, 11 PATs)
PUNT RET	Tommy Vaughn • 18 ret. • 179 yds. • 9.9 avg. • 0 TD
KO RET	Tommy Vaughn • 23 ret. • 595 yds. • 0 TD
PUNTING	Pat Studstill • 72 punts • 2956 yds. • 41.1 avg.
INTS	Mike Lucci • 5 int. • 118 yds. • 1 TD

- Hall of Fame linebacker Joe Schmidt retired from the Lions after the 1965 season and became an assistant coach.

- Detroit traded running back Joe Don Looney to Washington after several confrontations with Head Coach Harry Gilmer. The Lions received a 1967 draft choice for Looney.

- Rookie Karl Sweetan, starting his first game, tossed two fourth-quarter touchdowns to give the Lions a 24–20 lead over the San Francisco 49ers with 51 seconds remaining in the game on Oct. 23, 1966. However, John Brodie ruined Sweetan's inaugural game as he threw a 21-yard touchdown to Monty Stickles in the closing moments.

- Garo Yepremian booted a team-record six field goals in a 32–31 victory over the Minnesota Vikings on Nov. 13, 1966. Defensively, Mike Lucci supplied a supreme effort, intercepting three passes and returning one 65 yards for a touchdown.

- Karl Sweetan threw an NFL-record 99-yard touchdown to Pat Studstill in a 45–14 victory over Baltimore on Oct. 16, 1966.

- Pat Studstill tallied a team-record 1,266 yards on 67 receptions in 1966.

Milt Plum and Lions offense

1967

- Joe Schmidt replaced Harry Gilmer as head coach of the Detroit Lions on Jan. 11, 1967.

- Mel Farr and Lem Barney, Detroit's top two selections in the 1967 draft, made an immediate impact on the team. Farr was the team's leading rusher (860 yards and three TDs on 206 carries) and receiver (317 yards and three TDs on 39 receptions) while Barney led the league with 10 interceptions.

John Gordy and Mel Farr

- Detroit traded defensive tackle Roger Brown to the Los Angeles Rams in exchange for three draft picks, including the Ram's number one in 1968.

- Detroit fumbled an NFL-record ten times, losing five, in a 10–10 tie against the Minnesota Vikings on Nov. 12, 1967. Despite the fumbles, Mel Farr managed 197 yards, the third highest total in team history.

- For the fifth consecutive season, the Lions had a different leading rusher: In order, they had been Dan Lewis (1963), Nick Pietrosante (1964), Amos Marsh (1965), Tom Nowatzke (1966) and Mel Farr (1967).

1967 RESULTS
5–7–2 (3rd)
Joe Schmidt, Coach

Date	Opponent	Crowd	W-L-T	Score
9/17	at Green Bay	50,861	T	17 – 17
9/24	CLEVELAND	57,383	W	31 – 14
10/1	at St. Louis	43,821	L	28 – 38
10/8	GREEN BAY	57,877	L	17 – 27
10/15	at Chicago	46,024	L	3 – 14
10/22	ATLANTA	50,601	W	24 – 3
10/29	at San Francisco	37,990	W	45 – 3
11/5	CHICAGO	55,606	L	13 – 27
11/12	at Minnesota	40,032	T	10 – 10
11/19	at Baltimore	60,238	L	7 – 14
11/23	LOS ANGELES	54,389	L	7 – 31
12/3	PITTSBURGH	47,713	L	14 – 24
12/10	at New York	63,011	W	30 – 7
12/17	MINNESOTA	44,874	W	14 – 3

HOME GAMES IN CAPS

1967 LION LEADERS

RUSHING	Mel Farr • 206 att. • 860 yds. • 3 TD
PASSING	Milt Plum • 172 att. • 86 comp • 925 yds • 4 TD • 8 int
RECEIVING	Mel Farr • 39 rec. • 317 yds. • 3 TD
SCORING	Mel Farr and Tom Nowatzke • 36 points each (6 TDs)
PUNT RET	Tommy Watkins • 15 ret. • 57 yds. • 3.8 avg. -0 TD
KO RET	Tommy Vaugh • 16 ret. • 446 yds. • 27.9 avg. • 0 TD
PUNTING	Pat Studstill • 36 punts • 1602 yds. • 44.5 avg.
INTS	Lem Barney • 10 int. • 232 yds. • 3 TD

1970 RESULTS
10–4–0 (2nd)
Joe Schmidt, Coach

Date	Opponent	Crowd	W-L-T	Score
9/20	at Green Bay	56,263	W	40 – 0
9/27	CINCINNATI	58,202	W	38 – 3
10/5	CHICAGO	58,210	W	28 – 14
10/11	at Washington	50,414	L	10 – 31
10/18	at Cleveland	83,577	W	41 – 24
10/25	at Chicago	45,632	W	16 – 10
11/1	MINNESOTA	58,210	L	17 – 30
11/8	at New Orleans	66,910	L	17 – 19
11/15	at Minnesota	47,900	L	20 – 24
11/22	SAN FRANCISCO	56,232	W	28 – 7
11/26	OAKLAND	56,597	W	28 – 14
12/6	ST. LOUIS	56,362	W	16 – 3
12/14	at Los Angeles	79,441	W	28 – 23
12/20	GREEN BAY	57,387	W	20 – 0

NFC Playoff

Date	Opponent	Crowd	W-L-T	Score
12/26	at Dallas	73,167	L	0 – 5

HOME GAMES IN CAPS

1970 LION LEADERS

RUSHING	Mel Farr • 166 att. • 717 yds. • 9 TD
PASSING	Bill Munson • 158 att. • 84 comp. • 1049 yds. • 7 int • 10 TD
RECEIVING	Charlie Sanders • 40 rec. • 544 yds. • 6 TD
SCORING	Errol Mann • 101 points (20 FGs, 41 PATs)
PUNT RET	Lem Barney • 25 ret. • 259 yds. • 10.4 avg. • 1 TD
KO RET	Bobby Williams • 25 ret. • 544 yds. • 21.7 avg. • 1 TD
PUNTING	Herman Weaver • 62 punts • 2483 yds. • 40.0 avg.
INTS	Dick LeBeau • 9 int. • 96 yds. • 0 TD

1970

- Detroit selected fullback Steve Owens, the 1969 Heisman Trophy winner out of Oklahoma, in the first round of the 1970 college draft.

- The Lions defeated their first two opponents in 1970 by a combined score of 78–3, beating Green Bay 40–0 and Cincinnati 38–3.

Bill Munson and Ed Flanagan

- Quarterback Greg Landry had a 76-yard run against Green Bay in the Lions' 40–0 win over the Packers in the opening game.

- Detroit intercepted five Cleveland passes and Larry Walton caught five passes for 158 yards and two touchdowns in a 41–24 victory over the Browns in Cleveland.

- Tom Dempsey booted an NFL-record 63-yard field goal, providing the New Orleans Saints with a 19–17 victory over the Lions on Nov. 8, 1970, in Tulane Stadium.

- Former Detroit player and coach Les Bingaman, 44, died on Nov. 20, 1970.

- Mel Farr's 121 yards on 21 carries led the Lions to a 28–14 victory over the Oakland Raiders after trailing 14–0 early in the game. The victory was Detroit's first win on Thanksgiving Day since 1962.

- Lem Barney had an outstanding game in a victory over the Green Bay Packers, helping the Lions clinch a playoff berth. Barney returned a kickoff 74 yards to set up an Errol Mann field goal, ran 65 yards on a punt return to set up a touchdown, and returned an interception 49 yards for a TD.

- Detroit won five straight games at the end of the regular season to earn its first trip to the playoffs since 1957. Unfortunately, the Lions lost to the Dallas Cowboys, 5–0, in the opening round.

1971

- Detroit placed perennial all-pro defensive tackle Alex Karras on waivers prior to the start of the 1971 season, ending his 12-year career in Detroit.

- Greg Landry passed for 302 yards and four touchdowns in a 31–28 victory over Green Bay on Oct. 10, 1971.

- In the fourth quarter of Detroit's 28–23 loss to Chicago, Lions wide receiver Chuck Hughes collapsed on the field at Tiger Stadium and died of a heart attack on Oct. 24, 1971.

- Ron Jessie returned a kickoff 102 yards for a touchdown, the second-longest return in team history, in a game against Chicago on Oct. 24, 1971. Earlier in the season, Jessie returned a kickoff 97 yards for a touchdown against the Atlanta Falcons.

- Charlie Sanders earned his third straight Pro Bowl selection.

- Steve Owens rushed for 1,035 yards and eight TDs on 246 carries, becoming the first Lion to rush for 1,000 yards in a season.

- Errol Mann scored 103 points, breaking the 100-point barrier for the third consecutive season.

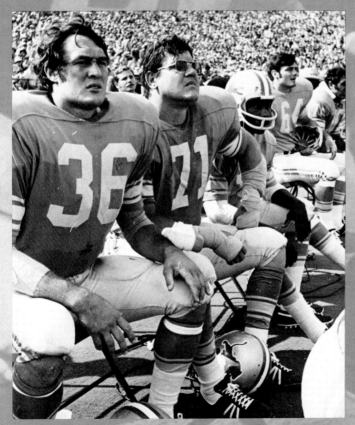

Steve Owens, Alex Karras and Lem Barney

1971 RESULTS
7–6–1 (2nd)
Joe Schmidt, Coach

Date	Opponent	Crowd	W-L-T	Score
9/20	MINNESOTA	54,418	L	13 – 16
9/26	at New England	61,057	W	34 – 7
10/3	ATLANTA	54,418	W	41 – 38
10/10	GREEN BAY	54,418	W	31 – 28
10/17	at Houston	45,885	W	31 – 7
10/24	CHICAGO	54,418	L	23 – 28
11/1	at Green Bay*	47,961	T	14 – 14
11/7	at Denver	51,200	W	24 – 20
11/14	LOS ANGELES	54,418	L	13 – 21
11/21	at Chicago	55,049	W	28 – 3
11/25	KANSAS CITY	54,418	W	32 – 21
12/5	PHILADELPHIA	54,418	L	20 – 23
12/11	at Minnesota	49,784	L	10 – 29
12/19	at San Francisco	45,580	L	27 – 31

* Milwaukee

HOME GAMES IN CAPS

1971 LION LEADERS

RUSHING	Steve Owens • 246 att. • 1035 yds. • 8 TD
PASSING	Greg Landry • 261 att. • 136 comp • 2237 yds • 16 TD • 13 int
RECEIVING	Steve Owens • 32 rec. • 350 yds. • 2 TD
SCORING	Errol Mann • 103 points (22 FGs, 37 PATs)
PUNT RET	Lem Barney • 14 ret. • 122 yds. • 8.7 avg. • 0 TD
KO RET	Ron Jessie • 16 ret. -470 yds. • 29.4 avg. • 2 TD
PUNTING	Herman Weaver • 42 punts • 1752 yds. • 41.7 avg.
INTS	Dick LeBeau • 6 int. • 76 yds. • 0 TD

1972 RESULTS
8–5–1 (2nd)
Joe Schmidt, Coach

Date	Opponent	Crowd	W-L-T	Score
9/17	NY GIANTS	54,418	W	30 – 16
9/24	MINNESOTA	54,418	L	10 – 34
10/1	at Chicago	55,701	W	38 – 24
10/8	at Atlanta	58,850	W	26 – 23
10/16	GREEN BAY	54,418	L	23 – 24
10/22	SAN DIEGO	54,371	W	34 – 20
10/30	at Dallas	65,378	L	24 – 28
11/5	CHICAGO	54,418	W	14 – 0
11/12	at Minnesota	49,784	L	14 – 16
11/19	NEW ORLEANS	53,752	W	27 – 14
11/23	NY JETS	54,418	W	37 – 20
12/3	at Green Bay	55,263	L	7 – 33
12/10	at Buffalo	41,583	T	21 – 21
12/17	at Los Angeles	71,761	W	34 – 17

HOME GAMES IN CAPS

1972 LION LEADERS

RUSHING — Altie Taylor • 154 att. • 658 yds. • 4 TD

PASSING — Greg Landry • 268 att. • 134 comp. • 2066 yds. • 18 TD • 17 int.

RECEIVING — Altie Taylor • 29 rec. • 250 yds. • 2 TD

SCORING — Errol Mann • 98 points (20 FGs, 38 PATs)

PUNT RET — Lem Barney • 15 ret. • 108 yds. • 7.2 avg. • 0 TD

KO RET — Ron Jessie • 23 ret. • 558 yds. • 24.3 avg. • 0 TD

PUNTING — Herman Weaver • 43 punts • 1734 yds. • 40.3 avg.

INTS — Lem Barney • 3 int. • 88 yds. • 0 TD

1972

- Jerry Rush, the Lions' starting defensive tackle the previous five seasons, was traded to the Cleveland Browns in exchange for a 1973 draft choice.

- All-pro tight end Charlie Sanders missed five games in 1972 after injuring his shoulder in the preseason.

- Third-string tight end John Hilton caught three passes for 120 yards, including a 66-yard touchdown, in a 30–16 opening game win over the New York Giants.

- Greg Landry rushed for three touchdowns and threw for another in a 38–24 victory over the Chicago Bears on Oct. 1, 1972. For the season, Landry rushed for nine TDs while throwing 18 scoring strikes on his way to becoming the first Detroit quarterback since Bobby Layne to earn a trip to the Pro Bowl.

- Potsy Clark, 78, the Lions' first head coach, died on Nov. 8, 1972, of a heart attack.

- The Lions lost to the Minnesota Vikings for the 10th consecutive time as Errol Mann's 33-yard field goal was blocked as time expired.

- Detroit's 33–7 loss to the Green Bay Packers in Week 12 knocked the Lions out of playoff contention. The Lions finished with an 8–5–1 record, their fourth consecutive winning record under Joe Schmidt.

- Wayne Walker and Dick LeBeau, two of Detroit's leading defensive players, retired following the 1972 season. The players are atop the Lions longevity list with Walker playing 15 seasons and 200 games and LeBeau playing 14 seasons and 185 games. LeBeau holds the Lions' career interception record with 62 pickoffs.

Chuck Walton and Altie Taylor

1973

- On Jan. 12, 1973, Joe Schmidt resigned as head coach of the Detroit Lions. Don McCafferty, former head coach of the Baltimore Colts, replaced Schmidt on Jan. 26, 1973.

- Lions assistant coach Raymond Berry and former Detroit player and coach Joe Schmidt were elected to the Pro Football Hall of Fame.

- Altie Taylor rushed for 160 yards on 23 carries in a 34–0 victory over the Green Bay Packers on Oct. 28, 1973.

- Quarterback Greg Landry was lost for the last seven games of the season after injuring his left knee.

- Detroit intercepted five Chicago passes and returned them for a team-record 192 yards in a 30–7 triumph over the Bears on Nov. 18, 1973. Dick Jauron picked off three passes, including one that he returned 95 yards for a touchdown.

- Linebacker Mike Lucci retired following the 1973 season.

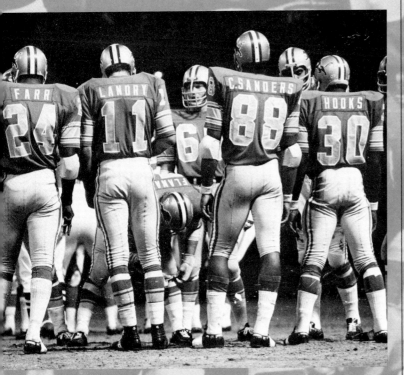

Offensive huddle

1973 RESULTS
6–7–1 (2nd)
Don McCafferty, Coach

Date	Opponent	Crowd	W-L-T	Score
9/16	at Pittsburgh	48,913	L	10 – 24
9/23	at Green Bay	56,267	T	13 – 13
10/1	ATLANTA	54,418	W	31 – 6
10/7	MINNESOTA	54,418	L	9 – 23
10/14	at New Orleans	57,810	L	13 – 20
10/21	BALTIMORE	53,688	L	27 – 29
10/28	GREEN BAY	53,859	W	34 – 0
11/4	SAN FRANCISCO	54,348	W	30 – 20
11/11	at Minnesota	48,503	L	7 – 28
11/18	at Chicago	55,701	W	30 – 7
11/22	WASHINGTON	54,418	L	0 – 20
12/2	at St. Louis	47,712	W	20 – 16
12/9	CHICAGO	52,641	W	40 – 7
12/15	at Miami	80,047	L	7 – 34

HOME GAMES IN CAPS

1973 LION LEADERS

RUSHING   Altie Taylor • 176 att. • 719 yds. • 5 TD

PASSING   Bill Munson • 187 att. • 95 comp. • 1129 yds. • 9 TD • 8 int.

RECEIVING   Charlie Sanders • 28 rec. • 433 yds. • 2 TD

SCORING   Errol Mann • 53 points (13 FGs, 14 PATs)

PUNT RET   Lem Barney • 27 ret. • 231 yds. • 8.6 avg. • 0 TD

KO RET   Dick Jauron • 17 ret. • 405 yds. • 23.8 avg. • 0 TD

PUNTING   Herman Weaver • 54 punts • 2333 yds. • 43.2 avg.

INTS   Levi Johnson • 5 int. • 82 yds.

TACKLES   Charlie Weaver • 55 total

QB SACKS   Larry Hand • 11.0 • sacks

1974

Date	Opponent	Crowd	W-L-T	Score
9/15	at Chicago	55,202	L	9 – 17
9/22	MINNESOTA	49,703	L	6 – 7
9/29	at Green Bay*	47,292	L	19 – 21
10/6	at Los Angeles	64,987	L	13 – 16
10/14	SAN FRANCISCO	49,756	W	17 – 13
10/20	at Minnesota	48,501	W	20 – 16
10/27	GREEN BAY	54,418	W	19 – 17
11/3	NEW ORLEANS	49,127	W	19 – 14
11/10	at Oakland	54,020	L	13 – 35
11/17	NY GIANTS	45,859	W	20 – 19
11/24	CHICAGO	47,376	W	34 – 17
11/28	DENVER	53,314	L	27 – 31
12/8	at Cincinnati	59,575	W	23 – 19
12/15	at Philadelphia	66,052	L	17 – 28

* Milwaukee

HOME GAMES IN CAPS

1974 LION LEADERS

RUSHING	Altie Taylor • 150 att. • 532 yds. • 5 TD
PASSING	Bill Munson • 292 att. • 166 comp. • 1874 yds. • 8 TD • 7 int.
RECEIVING	Ron Jessie • 54 rec. • 761 yds. • 3 TD
SCORING	Errol Mann • 92 points (23 FGs, 23 PATs)
PUNT RET	Dick Jauron • 17 ret. • 286 yds. • 16.8 avg. • 0 TD
KO RET	Jimmie Jones • 38 ret. • 927 yds. • 24.4 avg. • 0 TD
PUNTING	Herman Weaver • 72 punts • 2772 yds. • 38.5 avg.
INTS	Levi Johnson • 5 int. • 139 yds. • 2 TD
TACKLES	Jim Laslavic • 120 total
QB SACKS	Ken Sanders • 6.5 sacks

- Detroit traded running back Mel Farr to the Houston Oilers for a fourth round draft choice while acquiring defensive back Ben Davis from the Cleveland Browns in a trade.

- Head Coach Don McCafferty, 53, died of a heart attack on July 28, 1974. Assistant coach Rick Forzano was named interim head coach.

- Maurie Schubot, Detroit Lions ticket manager, retired after serving the Lions since 1934.

- The Lions swapped quarterbacks with the Washington Redskins, acquiring Sam Wyche in exchange for Bill Cappleman.

- Van Patrick, 58, voice of the Lions since 1950, lost his battle with cancer on Sept. 29, 1974.

- Errol Mann booted a 41-yard field goal with nine seconds left, lifting the Lions over the Packers, 19–17.

- The Thanksgiving Day game of 1974 marked the end of an era. Detroit's 31–27 loss to the Denver Broncos was the Lions' final game in Tiger Stadium.

- Bill Munson threw just seven interceptions in 292 attempts in 1974.

- The Lions defeated Minnesota on Oct. 20, 1974, breaking Detroit's streak of 13 consecutive losses to the Vikings.

1975

- Ron Jessie, the Lions' leading receiver in 1974, signed with the Los Angeles Rams. NFL Commissioner Pete Rozelle awarded the Lions running back Cullen Bryant as compensation, but a draft pick was given to the Lions when Bryant refused to report to Detroit.

- After 18 years at Cranbrook School, the Lions moved training camp to Oakland University in Rochester, Michigan. The training facility had more meeting rooms and was closer to the Pontiac Silverdome, the Lions' new home.

Mike Weger and Herb Orvis

- Detroit blocked three punts against the Green Bay Packers, resulting in 21 points in a 30–16 opening game win. One blocked punt was recovered in the endzone for a touchdown, another was returned 34 yards for a score and the third blocked punt was recovered at the Green Bay 7-yard line.

- On Oct. 6, 1975, Detroit lost to the Dallas Cowboys, 36–10, in the first regular season game played in the Pontiac Silverdome.

- Detroit's 27–7 victory over the Chicago Bears on Oct. 12, 1975, marked the Lions' 13th win in the last 15 games against Chicago.

- Joe Reed started at quarterback for the final eight games after Greg Landry and Bill Munson both suffered mid-season knee injuries.

- The Lions lost four of their final five contests, including a 24–21 loss to Kansas City in the Detroit's first overtime game.

1975 RESULTS
7–7–0 (2nd)
Rick Forzano, Coach

Date	Opponent	Crowd	W-L-T	Score
9/21	at Green Bay*	50,781	W	30 – 16
9/26	at Atlanta	45,218	W	17 – 14
10/6	DALLAS	#79,784	L	10 – 36
10/12	CHICAGO	74,032	W	27 – 7
10/19	at Minnesota	47,872	L	19 – 25
10/26	at Houston	46,904	L	8 – 24
11/2	at San Francisco	43,209	W	28 – 17
11/9	CLEVELAND	75,283	W	21 – 10
11/16	GREEN BAY	76,946	W	13 – 10
11/23	at Kansas City	55,161	L/OT	21 – 24
11/27	LOS ANGELES	#69,552	L	0 – 20
12/7	at Chicago	37,772	L	21 – 25
12/14	MINNESOTA	#73,130	W	17 – 10
12/21	ST. LOUIS	64,656	L	13 – 24

* Milwaukee
# Silverdome Sellout
HOME GAMES IN CAPS

1975 LION LEADERS

RUSHING	Dexter Bussey • 157 att. • 696 yds. • 2 TD
PASSING	Joe Reed • 191 att. • 86 comp. • 1181 yds. • 9 TD • 10 int.
RECEIVING	Charlie Sanders • 37 rec. • 486 yds. • 3 TD
SCORING	Errol Mann • 67 points (14 FGs, 29 PATs)
PUNT RET	Charlie West • 22 ret. • 219 yds. • 10.0 avg. • O TD
KO RET	Bobby Thompson • 22 ret. • 565 yds. • 25.7 avg. • 0 TD
PUNTING	Herman Weaver • 80 punts • 42.0 avg.
INTS	Lem Barney • 5 int. • 23 yds. • 0 TD
TACKLES	Paul Naumoff • 143 total
QB SACKS	Larry Hand • 7.0 sacks

1976 RESULTS
6–8–0 (3rd)
Rick Forzano, Coach
(1–3–0)

Date	Opponent	Crowd	W-L-T	Score
9/12	at Chicago	54,125	L	3 – 10
9/19	ATLANTA	50,840	W	24 – 10
9/26	MINNESOTA	#77,292	L	9 – 10
10/3	at Green Bay	55,041	L	14 – 24

Tommy Hudspeth, Coach
(5–5–0)

Date	Opponent	Crowd	W-L-T	Score
10/10	NEW ENGLAND	60,174	W	30 – 10
10/17	at Washington	45,906	L	7 – 20
10/24	at Seattle	61,280	W	41 – 14
10/31	GREEN BAY	74,992	W	27 – 6
11/7	at Minnesota	46,735	L	23 – 31
11/14	at New Orleans	42,048	L	16 – 17
11/21	CHICAGO	#78,042	W	14 – 10
11/25	BUFFALO	66,875	W	27 – 14
12/5	at NY Giants	66,068	L	10 – 24
12/11	LOS ANGELES	73,470	L	17 – 20

\# Silverdome Sellout

HOME GAMES IN CAPS

1976 LION LEADERS

RUSHING — Dexter Bussey • 196 att. • 858 yds. • 3 TD

PASSING — Greg Landry • 291 att. • 168 comp. • 2191 yds. • 17 TD • 8 int.

RECEIVING — Ray Jarvis • 39 rec. • 822 yds. • 5 TD

SCORING — Bennie Ricardo • 49 points (10 FGs, 19 PATs)

PUNT RET — Lem Barney • 23 ret. • 191 yds. • 8.3 avg. • 0 TD

KO RET — Bobby Thompson • 22 ret. • 431 yds. • 19.6 avg. • 0 TD

PUNTING — Herman Weaver • 83 punts • 3280 yds. • 39.5 avg.

INTS — James Hunter • 7 int. • 120 yds. • 17.1 avg.

TACKLES — Charlie Weaver • 114 total

QB SACKS — Charlie Weaver • 7 sacks

- The Lions signed quarterback Gary Danielson, formerly of the World Football League and the Purdue Boilermakers.

- Running back Steve Owens retired from the Lions during training camp in 1976. Owens had not played since the 1974 Thanksgiving Day game because of injuries.

- Detroit lost to the Minnesota Vikings, 10–9, after a Detroit extra point attempt was blocked in the fourth quarter.

- Rick Forzano resigned as head coach of the Lions on Oct. 4, 1976, after posting a 1–3 mark in 1976. Tommy Hudspeth, Detroit's coordinator of personnel and scouting, was named interim head coach on Oct. 5, 1976. Hudspeth guided the Lions to a 5–5 record as interim head coach, earning a three-year contract.

- Errol Mann, then the Lions' all-time leading scorer with 636 points, was waived after the fifth game of the 1976 season.

- Despite O.J. Simpson's 273 yards rushing — the second-best single game performance in the history of the NFL — the Lions defeated Buffalo, 27–14, on Thanksgiving Day.

- Detroit allowed a team-record 67 sacks in 1976.

Charlie Weaver and Ken Sanders

1977

- Bob Kowalkowski, an eleven-year veteran offensive guard, was traded to the Cleveland Browns for a draft choice.

- Kicker Benny Ricardo was lost for the entire 1977 season after suffering a shoulder separation. His replacement, Steve Mike-Mayer, led the '77 team in scoring with 43 points.

Paul Naumoff

- Detroit ate up 306 yards on the ground, 150 by Dexter Bussey, in a 23–19 win over the New Orleans Saints on Sept. 25, 1977.

- Gary Danielson started for the first time in Detroit, helping the Lions to their first road victory of the season, a 13–10 win over the Baltimore Colts. Wide receiver Leonard Thompson, however, was the hero of the game as he blocked a punt and returned it for a touchdown with 14 seconds left in the game.

- Eddie Payton scored two touchdowns — one on a 98-yard kickoff return and another on an 87-yard punt return — in a 30–21 loss to the Minnesota Vikings on Dec. 17, 1977. Payton totaled 289 yards in returns (105 in kickoff returns and 184 in punt returns).

1977 RESULTS
6–8–0 (3rd)
Tommy Hudspeth, Coach

Date	Opponent	Crowd	W-L-T	Score
9/18	at Chicago	51,530	L	20 – 30
9/25	NEW ORLEANS	51,458	W	23 – 19
10/2	PHILADELPHIA	57,236	W	17 – 13
10/9	at Minnesota	45,860	L	7 – 14
10/16	GREEN BAY	#78,452	W	10 – 6
10/23	at San Francisco	39,392	L	7 – 28
10/30	at Dallas	63,160	L	0 – 37
11/6	SAN DIEGO	72,559	W	20 – 0
11/13	at Atlanta	47,461	L	6 – 17
11/20	TAMPA BAY	49,751	W	16 – 7
11/24	CHICAGO	71,373	L	14 – 31
12/4	at Green Bay	56,367	L	9 – 10
12/11	at Baltimore	45,124	W	13 – 10
12/17	MINNESOTA	#78,452	L	21 – 30

Silverdome Sellout

HOME GAMES IN CAPS

1977 LION LEADERS

RUSHING	Horace King • 155 att. • 521 yds. • 1 TD
PASSING	Greg Landry • 240 att. • 135 comp. • 6 TD • 7 int.
RECEIVING	Horace King • 40 rec. • 238 yds. • 0 TD
SCORING	Steve Mike-Mayer • 43 points (8 FGs, 19 PATs)
PUNT RET	Eddie Payton • 27 ret. • 273 yds. • 1 TD
KO RET	Eddie Payton • 18 ret. • 457 yds. • 1 TD
PUNTING	Wilbur Summers • 93 punts • 3420 yds. • 36.8 avg.
INTS	James Hunter • 6 int. • 104 yds.
TACKLES	Ed O'Neil • 73 total

1978 RESULTS
7–9–0 (3rd)
Monte Clark, Coach

Date	Opponent	Crowd	W-L-T	Score
9/3	GREEN BAY	51,167	L	7 – 13
9/9	at Tampa Bay	64,445	W	15 – 7
9/17	CHICAGO	65,982	L	0 – 19
9/24	at Seattle	56,781	L	16 – 28
10/1	at Green Bay*	54,601	L	14 – 35
10/8	WASHINGTON	60,555	L	19 – 21
10/15	at Atlanta	51,172	L	0 – 14
10/22	SAN DIEGO	54,031	W	31 – 14
10/29	at Chicago	53,376	W	21 – 17
11/5	at Minnesota	46,008	L	7 – 17
11/12	TAMPA BAY	60,320	W	34 – 23
11/19	at Oakland	44,517	L	17 – 29
11/23	DENVER	71,785	W	17 – 14
12/3	at St. Louis	39,200	L	14 – 21
12/9	MINNESOTA	#78,865	W	45 – 14
12/17	SAN FRANCISCO	56,674	W	33 – 14

* Milwaukee
\# Silverdome Sellout
HOME GAMES IN CAPS

1978 LION LEADERS

RUSHING	Dexter Bussey • 225 att. • 924 yds. • 5 TD
PASSING	Gary Danielson • 351 att.- 199 comp. • 2294 yds. • 18 TD • 17 int
RECEIVING	David Hill • 53 rec. • 633 yds. • 4 TD
SCORING	Bennie Ricardo • 92 points (20 FGs, 32 PATs)
PUNT RET	Jesse Thompson • 16 ret. • 161 yds. • 10.1 avg. • 0 TD
KO RET	Jesse Thompson • 14 ret. • 346 yds. • 24.7 avg. • 0 TD
PUNTING	Tom Skladany • 86 punts • 3654 yds. • 42.5 avg.
INTS	Jimmy Allen • 5 int. • 70 yds.
TACKLES	Ed O'Neil • 85 total • 56 solo • 29 assists
QB SACKS	Al Baker • 23 sacks

1978

Ken Sanders and John Woodcock

- Head Coach Tommy Hudspeth and his staff were fired on Jan. 9, 1978, after a 6–8 mark in 1977. Monte Clark, former coach of the San Francisco 49ers, was named head coach and director of Football Operations on Jan. 11, 1978.

- Safety Levi Johnson suffered a ruptured Achilles' tendon in mini-camp, ending his career in Detroit.

- Tight end Charlie Sanders retired prior to the 1978 training camp after 10 brilliant seasons as a Detriot Lion. Sanders was voted to the Pro Bowl in seven of his 10 seasons and is at the top or near the top of several Detroit all-time lists in receiving. He is first in receptions (336), second in receiving yards (4,817) and third in touchdowns (31). A knee injury that forced Sanders to miss the final five games of the 1977 season never healed sufficiently, forcing his retirement from the game.

- Earl "Dutch" Clark, 71, died on Aug. 6, 1978. Clark led the Lions to their first NFL championship in 1935 and was a charter member of the NFL's Pro Football Hall of Fame.

- Detroit placed Lem Barney on the injured waiver list prior to the 1978 season. Barney's 56 career interceptions are second on the Lions' all-time list and his 10 touchdown returns are also a record.

- The Detroit defense held Tampa Bay to a Detroit-record –31 yards passing in a 15–7 win over the Buccaneers.

- Horace King set a Silverdome record with a 75-yard touchdown run in a 34–23 triumph over Tampa Bay on Nov. 12, 1978.

- The "Silver Rush," a nickname for Detroit's defensive pass rush unit, recorded a team-record 55 sacks in 1978. The group was comprised of Doug English, John Woodcock, Dave Pureifory, Ed O'Neil, Charlie Weaver and rookie Al "Bubba" Baker, who established a team-record with 23 sacks.

1979

- Detroit sent longtime quarterback Greg Landry to the Baltimore Colts in exchange for three draft picks.

- Former Detroit defensive back and punting standout Yale Lary was elected into the Pro Football Hall of Fame. Lary became the eighth Detroit Lion enshrined in Canton.

- Linebacker Paul Naumoff, who led the Lions with 143 tackles in 1975, retired from the Lions before the 1979 season after 12 years in Detroit.

- Gary Danielson suffered a season-ending knee injury during training camp in 1979 while back-up Joe Reed missed most of the season with an abdominal injury. Replacing Danielson and Reed at quarterback, rookie Jeff Komlo played well at certain times and struggled at other times, and threw a team-record 23 interceptions.

- The Lions' 14 losses were the most by a Detroit Lions team.

Bennie Ricardo

1979 RESULTS
2–14–0 (5th)
Monte Clark, Coach

Date	Opponent	Crowd	W-L-T	Score
9/1	at Tampa Bay	68,225	L	16 – 31
9/9	WASHINGTON	54,991	L	24 – 27
9/16	at N.Y. Jets	49,612	L	10 – 31
9/23	ATLANTA	56,249	W	24 – 23
9/30	MINNESOTA	75,295	L	10 – 13
10/7	at New England	60,629	L	17 – 24
10/14	at Green Bay*	53,930	L	16 – 24
10/21	at New Orleans	57,428	L	7 – 17
10/28	BUFFALO	61,911	L	17 – 20
11/4	at Chicago	50,108	L	7 – 35
11/11	TAMPA BAY	70,461	L	14 – 16
11/18	at Minnesota	43,650	L	7 – 14
11/22	CHICAGO	66,219	W	20 – 0
12/2	at Philadelphia	66,128	L	7 – 44
12/9	MIAMI	76,087	L	10 – 28
12/15	GREEN BAY	57,376	L	13 – 18

* Milwaukee

HOME GAMES IN CAPS

1979 LION LEADERS

RUSHING — Dexter Bussey • 144 att. • 625 yds. • 1 TD

PASSING — Jeff Komlo • 368 att. • 183 comp. • 2238 yds. • 11 TD • 23 int.

RECEIVING — Fred Scott • 62 rec. • 929 yds. • 5 TD

SCORING — Bennie Ricardo • 55 points (10 FGs, 25 PATs)

PUNT RET — John Arnold • 19 ret. • 164 yds. • 8.6 avg. • 0 TD

KO RET — John Arnold • 23 ret. • 539 yds. • 23.4 avg. • 0 TD

PUNTING — Larry Swider • 88 punts • 3523 yds. • 40.0 avg.

INTS — Luther Bradley and Jimmy Allen • 4 each

TACKLES — Doug English • 90 total

QB SACKS — Al Baker • 16 sacks

1980

1980 RESULTS
9–7–0 (2nd)
Monte Clark, Coach

Date	Opponent	Crowd	W-L-T	Score
9/7	at Los Angeles	64,892	W	41 – 20
9/14	at Green Bay*	53,099	W	29 – 7
9/21	ST. LOUIS	80,027	W	20 – 7
9/28	MINNESOTA	#80,291	W	27 – 7
10/5	at Atlanta	57,265	L	28 – 43
10/12	NEW ORLEANS	78,147	W	24 – 13
10/19	at Chicago	58,508	L	7 – 24
10/26	at Kansas City	59,391	L	17 – 20
11/2	SAN FRANCISCO	#78,845	W	17 – 13
11/9	at Minnesota	46,264	L	0 – 34
11/16	BALTIMORE	77,677	L	9 – 10
11/23	at Tampa Bay	64,976	W	24 – 10
11/27	CHICAGO	#75,397	L/OT	17 – 23
12/7	at St. Louis	46,966	L	23 – 24
12/14	TAMPA BAY	#77,098	W	27 – 14
12/21	GREEN BAY	#75,111	W	24 – 3

* Milwaukee
# Silverdome Sellout

HOME GAMES IN CAPS

1980 LION LEADERS

RUSHING Billy Sims • 313 att. • 1303 yds. • 13 TD

PASSING Gary Danielson • 417 att. • 244 comp. • 3223 yds. • 13 TD • 11 int

RECEIVING Fred Scott • 53 rec. • 834 yds. • 4 TD

SCORING Ed Murray • 116 points (27 FGs, 35 PATs)

PUNT RET Ray Williams • 27 ret. • 259 yds. • 0 TD

KO RET Rick Kane • 23 ret. • 495 yds. • 0 TD

PUNTING Tom Skladany • 72 punts • 3036 yds. • 42.2 avg.

INTS Jimmy Allen and James Hunter • 6 each

TACKLES Ken Fantetti • 85 total • 45 solo • 40 assists

QB SACKS Al Baker • 18 sacks

- Defensive tackle Doug English announced his retirement from football, accepting a job in the oil business.

- Detroit drafted running back Billy Sims out of Oklahoma with the first pick in the 1980 draft. Sims made an instant impact, rushing for 153 yards and three TDs in his first game in Detroit, a 41–20 win over the Los Angeles Rams.

Billy Sims

- Detroit won its first four games of the 1980 season after winning only two contests in all of 1979.

- On Thanksgiving Day, the Lions blew a 14-point fourth-quarter lead and allowed Vince Evans to score a tying touchdown on the final play of regulation to send the game to overtime. Then, on the kickoff to start overtime, Dave Williams of the Bears returned an Ed Murray kick 95 yards for a touchdown in the shortest overtime game in the history of the NFL.

- As a rookie, Sims enjoyed the greatest single season in Lions history. He rushed for 1,303 yards and 13 touchdowns on 313 attempts, becoming only the second Lion to rush for 1,000 yards.

- Gary Danielson completed 244-of-417 passes for 3,223 yards, establishing club records in attempts and yardage.

- Rookie placekicker Ed Murray scored 116 points on a team-record 27 field goals, including five field goals against Green Bay on Sept. 14, 1980.

1981

- Doug English ended his one-year retirement and returned to the Detroit Lions.

- Gary Danielson threw an interception at the goal line with one second remaining, ending Detroit's comeback bid in a 28–23 loss to the San Diego Chargers.

- Starting his first NFL game, quarterback Eric Hipple threw for 336 yards and four touchdowns and ran for two more TDs in a 48–17 Monday Night blasting of the Chicago Bears.

- Detroit lost a heart-breaker to Tampa Bay in the season finale, 20–17, knocking the Lions out of playoff contention.

- Billy Sims shattered his own single-season rushing record. He ran for 1,437 yards and 13 TDs on 296 attempts, becoming the first Lion to have multiple 1,000-yard rushing seasons.

- Fred Scott gained 1,022 yards receiving, the first Lion to gain 1,000 yards receiving since Pat Studstill totaled 1,266 yards in 1966.

- The Lions established several team records on offense in 1981, including rushing attempts (596), points (397) and total yards gained (5,933).

Russ Bolinger and Eric Hipple

1981 RESULTS
8–8–0 (2nd)
Monte Clark, Coach

Date	Opponent	Crowd	W-L-T	Score
9/6	SAN FRANCISCO	62,123	W	24 – 17
9/13	at San Diego	51,624	L	23 – 28
9/20	at Minnesota	45,350	L	24 – 26
9/27	OAKLAND	#77,919	W	16 – 0
10/4	at Tampa Bay	71,733	L	10 – 28
10/11	at Denver	74,816	L	21 – 27
10/19	CHICAGO	71,273	W	48 – 17
10/25	GREEN BAY	#76,063	W	31 – 27
11/1	at Los Angeles	61,814	L	13 – 20
11/8	at Washington	52,096	L	31 – 33
11/15	DALLAS	#79,694	W	27 – 24
11/22	at Chicago	50,082	W	23 – 7
11/26	KANSAS CITY	#76,735	W	27 – 10
12/6	at Green Bay	54,481	L	17 – 31
12/12	MINNESOTA	#79,428	W	45 – 7
12/20	TAMPA BAY	#80,444	L	17 – 20

Silverdome Sellout

HOME GAMES IN CAPS

1981 LION LEADERS

RUSHING	Billy Sims • 296 att. • 1437 yds. • 13 TD
PASSING	Eric Hipple • 279 att. • 140 comp. • 2358 yds. • 14 TD • 15 int.
RECEIVING	Fred Scott • 53 rec. • 1022 yds. • 5 TD
SCORING	Ed Murray • 121 points (25 FGs, 46 PATs)
PUNT RET	Robbie Martin • 52 ret. • 450 yds. • 1 TD
KO RET	Alvin Hall • 25 ret. • 525 yds. • 0 TD
PUNTING	Tom Skladany • 64 punts • 2784 yds. • 43.5 avg.
INTS	Jimmy Allen • 9 int. • 123 yds. • 0 TD
TACKLES	Ken Fantetti • 148 total
QB SACKS	Dave Pureifory • 11 sacks

1982

Date	Opponent	Crowd	W-L-T	Score
9/12	CHICAGO	71,337	W	17 – 10
9/19	at LA Rams	59,470	W	19 – 14
11/21	at Chicago	46,783	L	17 – 20
11/25	NY GIANTS	64,348	L	6 – 13
12/6	NY JETS	79,361	L	13 – 28
12/12	at Green Bay	51,875	W	30 – 10
12/19	MINNESOTA	73,058	L	31 – 34
12/26	at Tampa Bay	65,997	L	21 – 23
1/2	GREEN BAY	64,377	W	27 – 24

NFC Playoff

Date	Opponent	Crowd	W-L-T	Score
1/8	at Washington	55,045	L	7 – 31

HOME GAMES IN CAPS

1982 LION LEADERS

RUSHING	Billy Sims • 172 att. • 639 yds. • 4 TD
PASSING	Gary Danielson • 197 att. • 100 comp. • 1343 yds. • 10 TD • 14 int
RECEIVING	Billy Sims • 34 rec. • 342 yds. • 0 TD
SCORING	Ed Murray • 49 points (11 FGs, 16 PATs)
PUNT RET	Robbie Martin • 26 ret. • 275 yds. • 10.6 avg. • 0 TD
KO RET	Alvin Hall • 16 ret. • 426 yds. • 26.6 avg. • 1 TD
PUNTING	Tom Skladany • 36 punts • 1483 yds. • 41.2 avg. • 6 In20
INTS	Bobby Watkins • 5 ints. • 22 yds. • 0 TD
TACKLES	Ken Fantetti • 56 total
QB SACKS	Al Baker, William Gay and Dave Pureifory, 6 each

- Raymond "Buddy" Parker, 68, former Lions player and coach, died in March 1982.

- Detroit signed Monte Clark to a five-year contract extension with the Lions through 1987.

- Detroit earned its second win of the season as Billy Sims gained over 100 yards rushing (119) and receiving (103) in a 19–14 victory over the Los Angeles Rams. With the victory, the Lions were 2–0, but the momentum was interrupted by a two-month long players strike.

- James Hunter suffered a neck injury that caused numbness in his arms and legs during a 34–31 loss to Minnesota. Hunter retired to prevent further injury because of a recurring spinal condition.

- Alvin Hall returned a kickoff 96 yards for a touchdown in a 30–10 victory over Green Bay on Dec. 12, 1982.

- Despite a regular season record of 4–5, the Lions found themselves in the playoffs in that strike-shortened season (the top eight teams from each conference made the playoffs). Detroit, playing in its first playoff game since 1970, lost to the eventual Super Bowl Champion Washington Redskins, 31–7.

Silver Rush

1983

- Linebacker Stan White, an 11-year NFL veteran, became the first established NFL player to jump to the rival United States Football League.

- Bob Reynolds left the Lions' broadcast booth in 1983 after a 32-year career as an announcer.

- Defensive end William Gay had five and a half sacks in an 11–0 opening game victory over Tampa Bay.

Ken Fantetti and William Graham

- Detroit rebounded from a 1–4 start and won eight of the final 11 contests to earn a playoff berth.

- The Detroit defense intercepted five Pittsburgh passes and Billy Sims ran for 106 yards and two touchdowns in a 45–3 Thanksgiving Day rout of the Pittsburgh Steelers.

- Ed Murray tied a team-record set by Glenn Presnell (1934), booting a 54-yard field against Cincinnati.

- In a 23–20 win over Green Bay in Milwaukee, Billy Sims carried the ball a team-record 36 times and gained a personal-best 189 yards. Despite missing three games with a broken hand, Sims managed to gain 1,048 yards that season.

- Gary Danielson entered the final regular-season game against Tampa Bay late in the third quarter after starter Eric Hipple left with a sprained left knee. Danielson, who entered the game with the score tied at 13, completed 9 of 12 passes for 143 yards while directing the Lions to a field goal and a touchdown in the Lions' 23–20 victory.

- After kicking field goals from 37, 21, and 54 yards, Ed Murray missed a 43-yard attempt with five seconds remaining as the Lions fell short in a 24–23 loss to the San Francisco 49ers in a first round playoff game. Detroit dominated the game offensively, outgaining San Francisco 412 yards to 291, but Danielson's five interceptions hurt the cause. Sims led the Lions with 114 yards and two touchdowns on 20 carries.

1983 RESULTS
9–7–0 (1st)
Monte Clark, Coach

Date	Opponent	Crowd	W-L-T	Score
9/4	at Tampa Bay	62,154	W	11 – 0
9/11	CLEVELAND	60,095	L	26 – 31
9/18	ATLANTA	54,622	L	14 – 31
9/25	at Minnesota	56,254	L	17 – 20
10/2	at LA Rams	49,403	L	10 – 21
10/9	GREEN BAY	67,738	W	38 – 14
10/16	CHICAGO	66,709	W	31 – 17
10/23	at Washington	43,189	L	17 – 38
10/30	at Chicago	58,764	W	38 – 17
11/7	NY GIANTS	68,985	W	15 – 9
11/13	at Houston	40,060	L	17 – 27
11/20	at Green Bay*	50,050	W/OT	23 – 20
11/24	PITTSBURGH	#77,724	W	45 – 3
12/5	MINNESOTA	#79,169	W	13 – 2
12/11	at Cincinnati	45,728	L	9 – 17
12/18	TAMPA BAY	#78,553	W	23 – 20

NFC Playoff

Date	Opponent	Crowd	W-L-T	Score
12/31	at San Francisco	58,286	L	23 – 24

* Milwaukee # Silverdome Sellout

HOME GAMES IN CAPS

1983 LION LEADERS

RUSHING	Billy Sims • 220 att. • 1040 yds. • 7 TD
PASSING	Eric Hipple • 387 att. • 204 comp. • 2577 yds. • 12 TD • 18 int.
RECEIVING	James Jones • 46 rec. • 467 yds. • 1 TD
SCORING	Ed Murray • 113 points (25 FGs, 38 PATs)
PUNT RET	Ken Jenkins • 23 ret. • 230 yds. • 10.0 avg. • 0 TD
KO RET	Alvin Hall • 23 ret. • 492 yds. • 21.4 avg. • 0 TD
PUNTING	Mike Black • 71 punts • 2911 yds. • 41.0 avg. • 17 In20
INTS	Bruce McNorton • 7 ints. • 30 yds. • 0 TD
TACKLES	Ken Fantetti • 132 total • 82 solo • 50 assists
QB SACKS	William Gay • 13.5 sacks • 103.5 yds.

1984 RESULTS
4–11–1 (4th)
Monte Clark, Coach

Date	Opponent	Crowd	W-L-T	Score
9/2	SAN FRANCISCO	56,782	L	27 – 30
9/9	at Atlanta	49,878	W/OT	27 – 24
9/16	at Tampa Bay	44,560	L	17 – 21
9/23	MINNESOTA	57,511	L	28 – 29
9/30	at San Diego	59,849	L	24 – 27
10/7	DENVER	55,836	L	7 – 28
10/14	TAMPA BAY	44,308	W/OT	13 – 7
10/21	at Minnesota	57,953	W	16 – 14
10/26	at Green Bay	54,289	L	9 – 41
11/4	PHILADELPHIA	59,141	T/OT	23 – 23
11/11	at Washington	50,212	L	14 – 26
11/18	at Chicago	54,911	L	14 – 16
11/22	GREEN BAY	63,696	W	31 – 28
12/2	at Seattle	62,441	L	17 – 38
12/10	LA RAIDERS	66,710	L	3 – 24
12/16	CHICAGO	53,252	L	13 – 30

HOME GAMES IN CAPS

1984 LION LEADERS

RUSHING   Billy Sims • 130 att. • 687 yds. • 5 TD

PASSING   Gary Danielson • 410 att. • 252 comp. • 3076 yds. • 17 TD • 15 int

RECEIVING James Jones • 77 rec. • 662 yds. • 5 TD

SCORING   Ed Murray • 91 points (20 FGs, 31 PATs)

PUNT RET   Robbie Martin • 25 ret. • 210 yds. • 8.4 avg. • 0 TD

KO RET   Pete Mandley • 22 ret. • 390 yds. • 17.7 avg. • 0 TD

PUNTING   Mike Black • 76 punts • 3164 yds. • 41.6 avg. • 13 In20

INTS   Bobby Watkins • 6 int.

TACKLES   Alvin Hall • 147 total • 94 solo • 53 assists

QB SACKS   William Gay • 10 sacks • 72 yds.

1984

- Billy Sims galloped 81 yards, the third-longest run in team history, but the Lions lost to the San Diego Chargers, 27–24.

- Detroit won its second game of the season on a 37-yard TD pass from Gary Danielson to Leonard Thompson at 4:34 of overtime, providing the Lions with a 13–7 win over Tampa Bay. Danielson replaced the injured Eric Hipple in the second quarter and led the Lions to the victory.

- Billy Sims injured his right knee in a 16–14 triumph over Minnesota on Oct. 21, 1984. Surgery was required to repair torn cartilage and two torn ligaments. The injury ended Sims' career in Detroit. The injury came after Sims gained 103 yards in the game, surpassing Dexter Bussey as the Lions all-time leading rusher. Sims finished with 5,106 yards while Bussey had 5,021 yards at the time of the injury.

- Gary Danielson passed for 3,076 yards, his second 3,000-yard season. To date, he is the only Lion to pass for over 3,000 yards.

- Running back James Jones established a team record with 77 receptions.

- Monte Clark and his coaching staff were released on Dec. 19, 1984, after a 4–11–1 record in 1984.

James Jones

1985

- Darryl Rogers, former head coach at Michigan State and Arizona State, was named head coach of the Lions on Feb. 6, 1985.

- Detroit obtained quarterback Joe Ferguson from the Buffalo Bills.

- Lomas Brown, an offensive lineman from Florida, was the Lions' first pick in the 1985 draft.

- Detroit traded quarterback Gary Danielson to the Cleveland Browns for a draft pick in 1986.

- The Lions obtained running back Wilbert Montgomery from the Philadelphia Eagles in a trade that sent Garry Cobb to the Eagles.

- Injuries took their toll on the Lions' defensive unit in 1986: Linebacker Michael Cofer missed the last nine games of the season with a fractured hip, and tackle Doug English was sidelined for the final six games with a ruptured disc in his neck.

- The Lions were knocked out of playoff contention after losing the final three games of the season.

- Ed Murray scored 109 points in 1985, his fourth 100-point season (a team-record).

William Gay and Doug English

1985 RESULTS
7–9–0 (4th)
Darryl Rogers, Coach

Date	Opponent	Crowd	W-L-T	Score
9/8	at Atlanta	37,785	W	28 – 27
9/15	DALLAS	72,985	W	26 – 21
9/22	at Indianapolis	60,042	L	6 – 14
9/29	TAMPA BAY	45,023	W	30 – 9
10/6	at Green Bay	55,914	L	10 – 43
10/13	at Washington	52,845	L	3 – 24
10/20	SAN FRANCISCO	67,715	W	23 – 21
10/27	MIAMI	#75,291	W	31 – 21
11/3	at Minnesota	58,012	L	13 – 16
11/10	at Chicago	53,467	L	3 – 24
11/17	MINNESOTA	54,647	W	41 – 21
11/24	at Tampa Bay	43,471	L/OT	16 – 19
11/28	NY JETS	65,531	W	31 – 20
12/8	at New England	59,078	L	6 – 23
12/15	GREEN BAY	49,379	L	23 – 26
12/22	CHICAGO	#74,042	L	17 – 37

\# Silverdome Sellout

HOME GAMES IN CAPS

1985 LION LEADERS

RUSHING	James Jones • 244 att. • 886 yds. • 6 TD
PASSING	Eric Hipple • 406 att. • 223 comp. • 2952 yds. • 17 TD • 18 int.
RECEIVING	Leonard Thompson • 51 rec. • 736 yds. • 5 TD
SCORING	Ed Murray • 109 points (26 FGs, 31 PATs)
PUNT RET	Pete Mandley • 38 ret. • 403 yds. • 10.6 avg. • 1 TD
KO RET	Alvin Hall • 39 ret. • 886 yds. • 22.7 avg. • 0 TD
PUNTING	Mike Black • 73 punts • 3054 yds. • 41.8 avg. • 18 In20
INTS	Bobby Watkins • 5 int. • 15 yds. • 0 TD
TACKLES	William Graham • 113 total • 75 solo • 38 assists
QB SACKS	Jimmy Williams • 7.5 sacks • 55 yds.

1986 RESULTS
5–11–0 (3rd)
Darryl Rogers, Coach

Date	Opponent	Crowd	W-L-T	Score
9/7	at Minnesota	54,851	W	13 – 10
9/14	DALLAS	73,812	L	7 – 31
9/21	TAMPA BAY	38,453	L	20 – 24
9/28	at Cleveland	72,029	L	21 – 24
10/5	HOUSTON	41,960	W	24 – 13
10/12	at Green Bay	52,290	W	21 – 14
10/19	at LA Rams	50,992	L	10 – 14
10/26	at Chicago	62,064	L	7 – 13
11/2	CINCINNATI	52,423	L	17 – 24
11/9	MINNESOTA	53,725	L	10 – 24
11/16	at Philadelphia	54,568	W	13 – 11
11/23	at Tampa Bay	30,029	W	38 – 17
11/27	GREEN BAY	61,199	L	40 – 44
12/7	at Pittsburgh	45,042	L	17 – 27
12/15	CHICAGO	#75,602	L	13 – 16
12/21	ATLANTA	35,255	L	6 – 20

Silverdome Sellout
HOME GAMES IN CAPS

1986 LION LEADERS

RUSHING	James Jones • 252 att. • 903 yds. • 8 TD
PASSING	Eric Hipple • 305 att. • 192 comp. • 1919 yds. • 9 TD • 11 int.
RECEIVING	James Jones • 54 rec. • 334 yds. • 1 TD
SCORING	Ed Murray • 85 points • (18 FGs, 31 PATs)
PUNT RET	Pete Mandley • 43 ret. • 420 yds. • 9.8 avg. • 1 TD
KO RET	Herman Hunter • 48 ret. • 1007 yds. • 21.0 avg. • 0 TD
PUNTING	Mike Black • 46 punts • 1819 yds. • 39.5 avg. • 11 In20
INTS	Devon Mitchell • 5 int. • 41 yds. • 0 TD
TACKLES	Demetrious Johnson • 112 total • 92 solo • 20 assists
QB SACKS	Keith Ferguson • 9.5 sacks • 73 yds.

- Former Lion halfback Doak Walker was inducted into the Pro Football Hall of Fame.

- Doug English retired prior to training camp in 1986, fearing the possibility of paralysis after suffering a ruptured disc in his neck.

- Billy Sims officially announced his retirement after an unsuccessful comeback attempt from his 1984 knee injury.

- James Jones rushed for 174 yards, tying a team-record with 36 carries in a 13–10 season opening win over Minnesota.

- Jones caught a Detroit-record 12 passes for 85 yards in a 24–21 loss to the Cleveland Browns. Eric Hipple completed a team-record 33 passes in the contest.

- On Nov. 23, 1986, rookie Chuck Long entered the game against Tampa Bay in the fourth-quarter and completed the first pass he threw in his NFL career, hooking up with Leonard Thompson on a 34-yard TD pass.

- Herman Hunter returned 41 kickoffs for 1,007 yards; both marks are Detroit records.

- Jack Christiansen, 57, a member of the Lions' 1952 and 1953 Championship teams and a Hall of Famer, died on March 29, 1986. Hall of Fame quarterback Bobby Layne, 59, died in December 1986 from a heart attack.

- In Week 9, the Lions acquired former NFL punting leader Jim Arnold. In Detroit's final seven games, Arnold averaged 42.6 yards per kick.

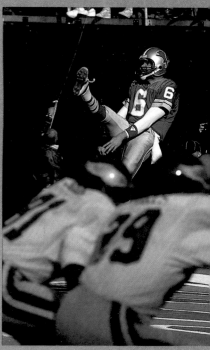
Jim Arnold

1987

- Edwin J. Anderson, 84, former president and general manager of the Detroit Lions, died in February 1987.

- Leonard Thompson was cut by the Lions prior to the 1987 season. Thompson left with 277 receptions for 4,682 yards and 35 TDs, a Detroit-record.

- NFL players went on strike over the issue of free agency following the second game of the 1987 season. After a one week layoff, NFL play resumed with the owners hiring replacement, or "Plan B," players. The "Plan B" team played three games, of which the Lions lost two. Detroit's average home attendance during the strike was 6,614.

- The Lions bounced back from a 24-point second-quarter deficit to take a one-point lead with just over three minutes left in an Oct. 26, 1987, contest against Green Bay. But the Packers responded with a 42-yard drive, resulting in a 45-yard field goal by Al Del Greco. Chuck Long then drove the Lions to the Packer 28-yard line, but Ed Murray missed a 45-yard field goal as time expired. The loss wasted a brilliant effort by Long, who completed 33-of-47 passes for 362 yards and three touchdowns. The 362 yards were a personal best, and the 33 completions tied a team record.

- Former Lions trainer Aid Kushner, 76, died in December 1987. Kushner began as an assistant trainer and equipment manager for the Lions in 1934 and served on the Lions' staff for seven seasons. He remained active with the club until the time of his death, personally engraving every game ball.

- Punter Jim Arnold was voted to the Pro Bowl, becoming the first Lion to be named to the Pro Bowl since William Gay and Doug English in 1983.

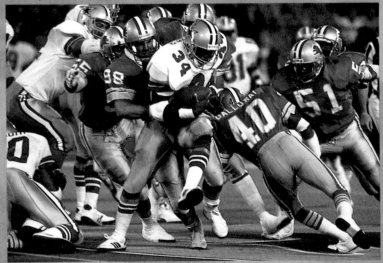

Dennis Gibson

1987 RESULTS
4–11–0 (5th)
Darryl Rogers, Coach

Date	Opponent	Crowd	W-L-T	Score
9/13	at Minnesota	57,061	L	19 – 34
9/20	at LA Raiders	50,300	L	7 – 27
9/27	CHICAGO	Cancelled — Players' Strike		
10/4	TAMPA BAY	4,919	L	27 – 31
10/11	at Green Bay	35,779	W/OT	19 – 16
10/18	SEATTLE	8,310	L	14 – 37
10/25	GREEN BAY	27,278	L	33 – 34
11/1	at Denver	75,172	W	0 – 34
11/8	DALLAS	45,325	W	27 – 17
11/15	at Washington	53,593	L	13 – 20
11/22	at Chicago	63,357	L	10 – 30
11/26	KANSAS CITY	43,820	L	20 – 27
12/6	LA RAMS	33,413	L	16 – 37
12/13	at Tampa Bay	41,699	W	20 – 10
12/20	MINNESOTA	27,693	L	14 – 17
12/27	at Atlanta	13,906	W	30 – 13

HOME GAMES IN CAPS

1987 LION LEADERS

RUSHING	James Jones • 96 att. • 342 yds. • 0 TD
PASSING	Chuck Long • 416 att. • 232 comp. • 2598 yds. • 11 TD • 20 int.
RECEIVING	Pete Mandley • 58 rec. • 720 yds. • 7 TD
SCORING	Ed Murray • 81 points (20 FGs, 21 PATs)
PUNT RET	Pete Mandley • 23 ret. • 250 yds. • 10.9 avg. • 0 TD
KO RET	Gary Lee • 32 ret. • 719 yds. • 22.5 avg. • 0 TD
PUNTING	Jim Arnold • 46 punts • 2007 yds. • 43.6 avg. • In20
INTS	James Griffin • 6 int. • 130 yds. • 0 TD
TACKLES	Dennis Gibson • 82 total • 68 solo • 14 assists
QB SACKS	Michael Cofer • 8.5 sacks • 78 yds.

1988 RESULTS
4–12–0 (4th)
Darryl Rogers, Coach (2–9–0)

Date	Opponent	Crowd	W–L–T	Score
9/4	ATLANTA	31,075	W	31 – 17
9/11	at LA Rams	46,262	L	10 – 17
9/18	NEW ORLEANS	32,943	L	14 – 22
9/25	NY JETS	29,250	L	10 – 17
10/2	at San Francisco	58,285	L	13 – 20
10/9	CHICAGO	64,256	L	7 – 24
10/16	at NY Giants	74,813	L	10 – 30
10/23	at Kansas City	66,926	W	7 – 6
10/30	NY GIANTS	38,354	L/OT	10 – 13
11/6	at Minnesota	55,573	L	17 – 44
11/13	TAMPA BAY	25,956	L	20 – 23

Wayne Fontes, Interim Coach (2–3–0)

Date	Opponent	Crowd	W–L–T	Score
11/20	at Green Bay*	44,327	W	19 – 9
11/24	MINNESOTA	46,479	L	0 – 23
12/4	GREEN BAY	28,124	W	30 – 14
12/11	at Chicago	55,010	L	12 – 13
12/18	at Tampa Bay	37,778	L	10 – 21

* Milwaukee
HOME GAMES IN CAPS

1988 LION LEADERS

RUSHING Garry James • 182 att. • 552 yds. • 5 TDs

PASSING Rusty Hilger • 306 att. • 126 comp. • 1558 yds. • 7 TD • 12 int.

RECEIVING Pete Mandley • 44 rec. • 617 yds. • 4 TDs

SCORING Ed Murray • 82 points (20 FGs, 22 PATs)

PUNT RET Pete Mandley • 37 ret. • 287 yds. • 7.8 avg. • 0 TD

KO RET Gary Lee • 18 ret. • 355 yds. • 19.7 avg. •) TD

PUNTING Jim Arnold • 97 punts • 4110 yds. • 42.4 avg. • 22 In20

INTS Devon Mitchell and George Jamison • 3 each

TACKLES Chris Spielman • 153 total • 118 solo • 35 asst.

QB SACKS Michael Cofer • 12.0 sacks • 88 yds.

- Former Detroit fullback Nick Pietrosante, 50, died in February after a long illness.

- Rookie linebacker Chris Spielman led the Lions in tackles with a team-record 153 tackles.

- Rusty Hilger, signed by the Lions as a free agent when injuries mounted for the club in 1988, was the Lions' top quarterback that year and was named the team's "Offensive Most Valuable Player."

Wayne Fontes

- Defensive end Reggie Rogers was involved in a drunken driving accident that resulted in the deaths of three teenagers on Oct. 20, 1988. Rogers and each of the three teens in the crash had blood-alcohol levels above the state's legal intoxication limit of 0.10 percent. Rogers was convicted of negligent homicide and was sentenced to 16 months to two years in prison.

- Darryl Rogers was released from his duties as head coach on Nov. 13, 1988, after a 2–9 start. Wayne Fontes, defensive coordinator, was named interim head coach. Under Fontes, the Lions rebounded with a 2–3 finish, and in December, Fontes was named Detroit's 17th head coach.

1989

- Darrell "Mouse" Davis brought the Run 'n' Shoot to Detroit as Wayne Fontes renamed the Lions' offense the "Silver Stretch." Davis was brought in for the last four games of the 1988 season when Wayne Fontes was interim head coach.

Mike Cofer and Jerry Ball

- The Lions drafted running back Barry Sanders, the 1988 Heisman Trophy winner, in the first round of the 1989 draft. Sanders signed just three days before the start of the regular season but managed 71 yards on nine carries in the Lions' season opener against Phoenix.

- Quarterback Rodney Peete, the Lions' sixth round draft choice in 1989, earned a starting job in training camp but was injured before the season began. When healthy, Peete was the Lions' starter, but he was available for only eight games and compiled a 4–4 record in those starts.

- Detroit won its first game of the season after five losses. The victory was sealed on a 5-yard run by Rodney Peete with 23 seconds remaining, giving the Lions a 17–16 win. Peete rushed for 78 yards and threw for 268 yards.

- Sanders rushed for 184 yards on 30 carries, but the Lions still lost 23–20 in overtime to the Packers.

- The Lions began the season with a 1–8 record but rebounded to win six out of seven and five straight to finish the season at 7–9.

- Sanders rushed for 1,470 yards, breaking Billy Sims' single-season record of 1,437 yards.

- Receiver Richard Johnson caught 70 passes for 1,091 yards, including a 248-yard performance and a 172-yard game.

- General Manager Russ Thomas retired on Dec. 26, 1989. Replacing him was Chuck Schmidt who became the Lions' executive vice president and chief operating officer. Schmidt, a member of the Lions' front office since 1976, was promoted from vice president for finance.

1989 RESULTS
7–9–0 (3rd)
Wayne Fontes, Coach

Date	Opponent	Crowd	W-L-T	Score
9/10	PHOENIX	36,735	L	13 – 16
9/17	at NY Giants	76,021	L	14 – 24
9/24	CHICAGO	71,148	L	27 – 47
10/1	PITTSBURGH	43,804	L	3 – 23
10/8	at Minnesota	55,380	L	17 – 24
10/15	TAMPA BAY	46,225	W	17 – 16
10/22	MINNESOTA	51,579	L	7 – 20
10/29	at Green Bay*	53,731	L/OT	20 – 23
11/5	at Houston	46,056	L	31 – 35
11/12	GREEN BAY	44,324	W	31 – 22
11/19	at Cincinnati	55,720	L	7 – 42
11/23	CLEVELAND	66,624	W	13 – 10
12/3	NEW ORLEANS	38,550	W	21 – 14
12/10	at Chicago	52,650	W	27 – 17
12/17	TAMPA BAY	40,362	W	33 – 7
12/24	at Atlanta	7,792	W	31 – 24

* Milwaukee
HOME GAMES IN CAPS

1989 LION LEADERS

RUSHING Barry Sanders • 280 att. • 1470 yds. • 14 TDs

PASSING Bob Gagliano • 232 att. • 117 comp. • 1671 yds. • 6 TDs • 12 int.

RECEIVING Richard Johnson • 70 rec. • 1091 yds. • 8 TDs

SCORING Ed Murray • 96 points (20 FGs, 36 PATs)

PUNT RET Walter Stanley • 36 ret. • 496 yds. • 13.8 avg. • 0 TDs

KO RET Mel Gray • 24 ret. • 640 yds. • 26.7 avg. • 0 TDs

PUNTING Jim Arnold • 82 punts • 3538 yds. • 43.1 avg. • 15 In20

INTS Jerry Holmes • 6 int. • 77 yds. • 1 TD

TACKLES Chris Spielman • 125 total • 89 solo • 36 assists

QB SACKS Michael Cofer • 9.5 sacks • 60 yds.

1990 RESULTS
6–10–0 (3rd)
Wayne Fontes, Coach

Date	Opponent	Crowd	W-L-T	Score
9/9	TAMPA BAY	54,728	L	21 – 38
9/16	ATLANTA	48,961	W	21 – 14
9/23	at Tampa Bay	55,075	L	20 – 23
9/30	GREEN BAY	64,509	L	21 – 24
10/7	at Minnesota	57,586	W	34 – 27
10/14	at Kansas City	74,312	L	24 – 43
10/28	at New Orleans	64,368	W	27 – 10
11/4	WASHINGTON	69,326	L/OT	38 – 41
11/11	MINNESOTA	68,264	L	7 – 17
11/18	at NY Giants	76,109	L	0 – 20
11/22	DENVER	73,896	W	40 – 27
12/2	at Chicago	62,313	L/OT	17 – 23
12/10	LA RAIDERS	#72,190	L	31 – 28
12/16	CHICAGO	67,759	W	38 – 21
12/22	at Green Bay	46,700	W	24 – 17
12/30	at Seattle	50,681	L	10 – 30

Silverdome Sellout
HOME GAMES IN CAPS

1990 LION LEADERS

RUSHING Barry Sanders • 255 att. • 1304 yds. • 13 TDs

PASSING Rodney Peete • 271 att. • 142 comp. • 1974 yds. • 13 TDs • 8 int.

RECEIVING Richard Johnson • 64 rec. • 727 yds. • 6 TDs

SCORING Barry Sanders • 96 points (16 TDs)

PUNT RET Mel Gray • 34 ret. • 362 yds. • 10.6 avg. • 0 TDs

KO RET Mel Gray • 41 ret. • 939 yds. • 22.9 avg. • 0 TDs

PUNTING Jim Arnold • 63 punts • 2560 yds. • 40.6 avg. • 10 In20

INTS William White • 5 int's. • 120 yds. • 24.0 avg. • 1 TD

TACKLES Chris Spielman • 108 total • 79 solo • 29 assists

QB SACKS Michael Cofer • 10.0 sacks • 57 yds.

Rodney Peete

- Nick Kerbawy, 77, died of cancer in June. He helped build the Lions into a dynasty in the 1950s at the team's general manager.

- Detroit traded Chuck Long to the Los Angeles Rams for a 1991 draft choice.

- Detroit acquired running back James Wilder from Washington in a trade that sent defensive end Eric Williams to the Redskins.

- Frank Sinkwich, 70, the first Heisman Trophy winner to play for the Lions, died after a long illness.

- Detroit blew a 17-point fourth-quarter lead and eventually lost to the Washington Redskins in overtime, 41–38. The Redskins' offense controlled the ball for over 49 minutes and gained 674 yards, a record against the Lions.

- In a Monday Night match-up between two of the game's greatest runners — the Lions' Barry Sanders and the Raiders' Bo Jackson — Detroit lost a heart-breaker to Los Angeles, 38–31. Sanders won the rushing dual, outgaining Jackson 176 yards to 129 and outscoring him two touchdowns to one.

- Rodney Peete passed the Lions to a 38–21 victory over the Chicago Bears, throwing for 316 yards and four touchdowns.

- Barry Sanders led the NFL in rushing with 1,304 yards on 255 attempts, the lowest rushing total in his first four seasons. Sanders became the first Detroit back to lead the league in rushing since Byron "Whizzer" White rushed for 514 yards in 1940.

1991

- Russ Thomas, 66, former general manager, died in his sleep on March 19, 1991.

- The Lions staged a miraculous comeback against the Vikings on Oct. 6, 1991, scoring three touchdowns in a span of 6:14 to beat the Vikings, 24–20. Barry Sanders culminated the comeback with a 15-yard touchdown run with 36 seconds remaining.

- Ray Crockett returned an interception 96 yards for a touchdown in a 34–10 victory over the Dallas Cowboys. However, the victory was overshadowed by the loss of quarterback Rodney Peete for the season to a torn Achilles' tendon.

- Offensive guard Mike Utley was paralyzed from the chest down in a freakish fall in a 21–10 win over the Los Angeles Rams. Utley suffered a ruptured spinal disc and shattered his sixth cervical vertebra, but as he was wheeled from the playing field, flashed his teammates a "thumbs up" sign which became the team's rallying cry. Riding an emotional wave after Utley's injury, the Lions won the final six games of the season to earn their first playoff game since 1983.

- Barry Sanders rushed for a team-record 220 yards and four touchdowns in a 34–14 rout of the Minnesota Vikings.

George Jamison

- The Lions played their first home playoff game since 1957 and the first in the Silverdome, defeating the Dallas Cowboys, 38–6. Erik Kramer, who guided the Lions in the final eight games of the season, connected on 29-of-38 passes for a Detroit playoff record 341 yards and three touchdowns.

- Detroit ended the 1991 season where it began, in Washington, with a 41–10 NFC Championship game loss to the Redskins.

- Barry Sanders established Detroit records in rushing yards (1,548), rushing attempts (342), rushing TDs (16) and total TDs (17).

- Mel Gray became the first player in NFL history to lead the league in both kickoff (25.8-yard average) and punt return average (15.4-yard average) in the same season.

1991 RESULTS
12–4–0 (1st)
Wayne Fontes, Coach

Date	Opponent	Crowd	W-L-T	Score
9/1	at Washington	52,958	L	0 – 45
9/8	GREEN BAY	43,132	W	23 – 14
9/15	MIAMI	56,896	W	17 – 13
9/22	Indianapolis	53,396	W	33 – 24
9/29	TAMPA BAY	44,479	W	31 – 3
10/6	MINNESOTA	63,423	W	24 – 20
10/20	at San Francisco	61,240	L	3 – 35
10/27	DALLAS	#74,906	W	34 – 10
11/3	at Chicago	57,281	L	10 – 20
11/10	at Tampa Bay	37,742	L	21 – 30
11/17	LA RAMS	60,873	W	21 – 10
11/24	at Minnesota	51,644	W	34 – 14
11/28	CHICAGO	#78,879	W	16 – 6
12/8	NY JETS	69,304	W	34 – 20
12/15	at Green Bay	43,881	W	21 – 17
12/22	at Buffalo	78,059	W/OT	17 – 14

NFC Playoffs

Date	Opponent	Crowd	W-L-T	Score
1/5	DALLAS	#79,835	W	38 – 6
1/12	at Washington	55,585	L	10 – 41

\# Silverdome Sellout
HOME GAMES IN CAPS

1991 LION LEADERS

RUSHING	Barry Sanders • 342 att. • 1548 yds. • 16 TDs
PASSING	Erik Kramer • 265 att. • 136 comp. • 1635 yds. • 11 TDs • 8 int.
RECEIVING	Brett Perriman • 52 rec. • 668 yds. • 1 TD
SCORING	Barry Sanders • 102 points (17 TDs)
PUNT RET	Mel Gray • 25 ret. • 385 yds. • 15.4 avg. • 1 TD
KO RET	Mel Gray • 36 ret. • 929 yds. • 25.8 avg. • 0 TDs
PUNTING	Jim Arnold • 75 punts • 3092 yds. • 41.2 avg. • 27 In20
INTS	Ray Crockett • 6 int's. • 141 yds. • 1 TD
TACKLES	Chris Spielman • 126 total • 84 solo • 42 assists
QB SACKS	Jeff Hunter • 6.0 sacks • 53 yds.

1992 RESULTS
5–11–0 (5th)
Wayne Fontes, Coach

Date	Opponent	Crowd	W-L-T	Score
9/6	at Chicago	63,672	L	24 – 27
9/13	MINNESOTA	57,519	W	31 – 17
9/20	at Washington	55,818	L	10 – 13
9/27	TAMPA BAY	51,374	L	23 – 27
10/4	NEW ORLEANS	66,971	L	7 – 13
10/15	at Minnesota	52,816	L	14 – 31
10/25	at Tampa Bay	53,995	W	38 – 7
11/1	GREEN BAY	60,594	L	13 – 27
11/8	DALLAS	#74,816	L	3 – 37
11/15	at Pittsburgh	52,242	L	14 – 17
11/22	at Cincinnati	48,574	W	19 – 16
11/26	HOUSTON	73,711	L	21 – 24
12/6	at Green Bay*	49,469	L	10 – 38
12/13	CLEVELAND	65,970	W	24 – 14
12/20	CHICAGO	72,777	W	16 – 3
12/28	at San Francisco	55,907	L	6 – 24

* Milwaukee
\# Silverdome Sellout
HOME GAMES IN CAPS

1992 LION LEADERS

RUSHING Barry Sanders • 312 att. • 1352 yds. • 9 TDs

PASSING Rodney Peete • 213 att. • 123 comp. • 1702 yds. • 9 TDs • 9 int.

RECEIVING Brett Perriman • 69 rec. • 810 yds. • 4 TD

SCORING Jason Hanson • 93 points (21 FGs, 30 PATs)

PUNT RET Mel Gray • 18 ret. • 175 yards • 9.7 avg. • 1 TD

KO RET Mel Gray • 42 ret. • 1006 yds. • 24.0 avg. • 1 TD

PUNTING Jim Arnold • 65 punts • 2846 yds. • 43.8 avg. • 12 In20

INTS Ray Crockett, Melvin Jenkins, Kevin Scott and William White • 4 int.

TACKLES Chris Spielman • 146 total • 94 solo • 52 assists

QB SACKS Tracy Scroggins • 7.5 sacks • 41.0 yds.

1992

- The Lions entered the 1992 season with heavy hearts, stemming from three tragedies in less than a year. Mike Utley was paralyzed from the chest down during a game in 1991; assistant coach Len Fontes, 54, the brother of head coach Wayne Fontes, died in May of a heart attack; and guard Eric Andolsek, 25, was killed when a truck ran off the road and struck him in front of his home in Thibodaux, Louisiana.

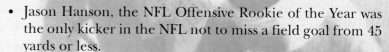
Chris Spielman

- Detroit waived veteran kicker Ed Murray after drafting Jason Hanson in the 1992 draft. Murray is the Lions' all-time leading scorer with 1,113 points.

- Lem Barney became the 11th Lion great inducted into the Pro Football Hall of Fame.

- The opening contest at Chicago set the tone for the 1992 season as the Bears scored a fourth-down TD in the game's final seconds to earn a 27–24 victory.

- Jason Hanson, the NFL Offensive Rookie of the Year was the only kicker in the NFL not to miss a field goal from 45 yards or less.

- With the tragic losses of Andolsek and Utley, the Lions' offensive line was in trouble before the season started. But things did not improve as the season progressed with Detroit starting 10 different offensive linemen, including four different centers. Left tackle Lomas Brown and left guard Shawn Bouwens were the only linemen to start all 16 games.

- Barry Sanders became the Lions' all-time leading rusher in a 19–13 triumph over Cincinnati on Nov. 22, 1992. Sanders passed Billy Sims (5,106 yards) as the Lions' leading ground gainer on an end sweep for 18 yards late in the second quarter. Sanders finished the game with 151 yards and gained 1,352 yards for the season.

- Detroit's 1990 first round draft pick, Andre Ware, started the last three games at quarterback, guiding the Lions to a 2–1 mark. Ware was the third quarterback to start for the Lions in 1992 with Rodney Peete starting 10 games and Erik Kramer starting three.

- Chris Spielman led the Lions in tackles for a club-record fifth consecutive season.

The Motown Charts

DETROIT'S ALL-TIME PLAYER ROSTER

Includes all Lions who have played in at least one regular season game

A

Adams, Ernie, LB, Illinois 1987
Addams, Abraham, E, Indiana 1949
Ahrens, Dave, LB, Wisconsin 1988
Aiello, Anthony, B, Youngstown 1944
Alderman, Grady, G, Detroit 1960
Alexander, Bruce, CB, Stephen F. Austin 1989–91
Alford, Mike, C, Auburn 1966
Allen, Jimmy, DB, UCLA 1978–81
Allen, Nate, DB, Texas Southern 1979
Allerman, Kurt, LB, Penn State 1985
Andersen, Stanley, E, Stanford 1941
Anderson, Gary, G, Stanford 1977–78
Andolsek, Eric,* G, LSU 1988–91
Ane, Charles, T, USC 1953–59
Arena, Anthony, C, Mich. State 1942–46
Arnold, Jim, P, Vanderbilt 1986–
Ashcom, Richard, T, Oregon 1943
Atkins, George, G, Auburn 1955
Atty, Alexander, G, West Virginia 1941
Austin, James, E, St. Mary's 1939

B

Baack, Steve, DE, Oregon 1984
Bailey, Byron, B, Washington St. 1953–54
Baker, Al, DE, Colorado St. 1978–82
Baker, John, DE, N. Carolina College 1968
Baldischwiler, Karl, T, Oklahoma 1978–82
Ball, Jerry, NT, SMU 1987–92
Banas, Stephen, B, Notre Dame 1935
Banjavic, Emil, B, Arizona 1942
Banonis, Vincent, C, Detroit 1951–53
Barle, Louis, B, Duluth 1938
Barnes, Al, WR, New Mexico St. 1971–73
Barnes, Roosevelt, LB, Purdue 1982
Barney, Lem, DB, Jackson St. 1967–77
Barr, Terry, B, Michigan 1957–65
Barrett, Reggie, WR, UTEP 1991–
Barrows, Scott, G-C-T, West Virginia 1986–88
Barton, Greg, QB, Tulsa 1969
Bass, Mike, DB, Michigan 1967
Batinski, Stanley,* G, Temple 1941–47
Batten, Pat, FB, Hardin-Simmons 1964
Baumgartner, Maxie, E, Texas 1948
Beaty, Doug, RB, Appalachian St. 1988
Beemer, Bob, DE, Toledo 1987
Behan, Charles,* E, DeKalb 1942
Belichick, Stephen, B, W. Reserve 1941
Bell, Anthony, LB, Michigan State 1991
Bell, Bob, DT, Cincinnati 1971–73
Benson, Charles, DE, Baylor 1987
Bernard, Charles,* C, Michigan 1934
Bernard, Karl, RB, S.W. Louisiana 1987–88
Berrang, Edward, E, Villanova 1951
Berry, Connie M.,* E, N. Carolina St. 1939
Bingaman, Lester,* G, Illinois 1948–54
Black, Mike, P, Arizona State 1983–87
Blades, Bennie, DB, Miami 1988–
Blair, T.C., TE, Tulsa 1974
Bland, Carl, WR, Virginia Union 1984–88
Blessing, Paul, E, Nebr. St. Tchrs. 1944

Blue, Luther, WR, Iowa State 1977–79
Boadway, Steve, LB, Arizona 1987
Boden, Lynn, T, S. Dakota St. 1975–78
Bodenger, Maurice,* G, Tulane 1934
Bolinger, Russ, G, Long Beach St. 1976–82
Bolton, Andy, RB, Fisk 1976–78
Booth, Richard, B, W. Reserve 1941, 45
Bostic, John, DB, Bethune-Cookman 1985–87
Bouwens, Shawn, G, Nebraska-Wesleyan 1991–
Bowman, William, B, Wm. & Mary 1954,56
Box, Cloyce, E, W. Texas St. 1949–50,52–54
Boyd Thomas, LB, Alabama 1987
Bradley, Danny, WR, Nebraska 1987
Bradley, Luther, DB, Notre Dame 1978–81
Bradshaw, Charlie, T, Baylor 1967–68
Brettschneider, Carl, LB, Iowa St. 1960–63
Briggs, Paul, T, Colorado 1948
Brill, Howar, B, Wichita 1939
Brim, Michael, CB, Virginia Union 1989
Briscoe, Marlin, WR, Neb-Omaha 1975–76
Britt, Maurice, E, Arkansas 1941
Brock, Lou, DB, Southern California 1988
Brock, Willie, C, Colorado 1978
Brooks, Jon, LB, Clemson 1979
Brooks, Kevin, DE, Michigan 1989–90
Brown, Arnold, DB, N. Carolina Central 1985–86
Brown, Charlie, WR, N. Arizona 1970
Brown, Howard, G, Indiana 1948–50
Brown, Lomas, T, Florida 1985–
Brown, Mark, LB, Purdue 1989–91
Brown, Marvin, B, East Texas St. 1957
Brown, Roger, T, Maryland St. 1960–66
Brumley, Robert, B, Rice 1945
Bulger, Chester, T, Auburn 1950
Bundra, Mike, T, USC 1962–63
Bunz, Dan, LB, Cal State-Long Beach 1985
Burns, Mike, DB, USC 1978
Burton, Leonard, C, South Carolina 1992–
Busich, Samuel, E, Ohio 1943
Bussey, Dexter, RB, Texas Arlington 1974–84
Butcher, Paul, LB, Wayne State 1986–88

C

Caddel, Ernie,* B, Stanford 1934–38
Cain, James, E, Alabama 1950–55
Cain, Pat, C-G, Wichitat State 1987
Callahan, J.R., B, Texas 1946
Callihan, William,* B, Nebraska 1940–45
Callicutt, Ken, RB, Clemson 1978–82
Calvelli, Anthony, C, Stanford 1939–40
Campbell, Jeff, WR, Colorado 1990–
Campbell, Mike, RB, Lenoir Rhyne 1968
Campbell, Stanley, G, Iowa St. 1952,55–58
Cappleman, Bill, QB, Florida State 1973
Capria, Carl, DB, Purdue 1974
Cardwell, Lloyd, B, Nebraska 1937–43
Carpenter, Lewis, B, Arkansas 1953–55
Carr, Carl, LB, North Carolina 1987
Carrington, Darren, CB, Northern Arizona 1990
Carter, Pat, TE, Florida State 1988
Cassady, Howard, B, Ohio St. 1956–61,63

Caston, Toby, LB, LSU 1989–
Caver, James, WR, Missouri 1983
Cesare, Billy, DB, Miami 1982
Chadwick, Jeff, WR, Grand Valley St. 1983–88
Chandler, Karl, C, Princeton 1978
Chantiles, Thomas, T, USC 1942
Chapman, Clarence, DB, Eastern Michigan 1985
Chase, Benjamin, G, Navy 1947
Cherry, Raphel, DB, Hawaii 1987–88
Christensen, Frank, Utah 1934–37
Christensen, George,* T, Oregon 1934–38
Christiansen, Jack,* B, Colorado A&M 1951–58
Cifelli, August, T, Notre Dame 1951–53
Cifers, Robert, B, Tennesse 1944–46
Clark, Al, DB, Eastern Michigan 1971
Clark, Dexter, DB, Toledo 1987
Clark, Earl "Dutch,"* B, Colorado 1934–38
Clark, Ernie, LB, Mich. St. 1963–67
Clark, Jessie, RB, Arkansas 1988
Clark, Robert, WR, N. Carolina Central 1989–91
Clark, Wayne, E, Utah 1944–45
Clay, William, DB, Georgia Tech 1992–
Clemons, Raymond,* G, Cen. Okla. St. 1939
Cline, Jackie, DE, Alabama 1990
Cline, Ollie, B, Ohio St. 1950–53
Clowes, John, T, Wm. & Mary 1951
Cobb, Garry, LB, USC 1979–84
Cody, Bill, LB, Auburn 1966
Cofer, Michael, DE-LB, Tennessee 1983–
Cogdill, Gail, E, Wash. St. 1960–68
Cole, Eddie, LB, Mississippi 1979–80
Colella, Thomas, B, Canisius 1941–43
Colon, Harry, DB, Missouri 1992–
Compton, Dick, B, McMurry 1962–64
Concannon, Jack, QB, Boston Col. 1975
Conlee, Gerald, C, St. Mary's 1943
Conover, Scott, T, Purdue 1991–
Cook, Gene, E, Toledo 1959
Cook, Ted, E, Alabama 1974
Cooke, Bill, DT, Massachusetts 1978

With 5,220 receiving yards, Gail Cogdill is first on that all-time Detroit list.

Cooper, Harold,* B, Detroit 1937
Corgan, Michael, B, Notre Dame 1943
Cotton, Craig, TE, Youngstown 1969–72
Conttrell, Bill, T, Delaware Valley 1967–70
Crabtree, Clement, T, Wake Forest 1940–41
Craig, Paco, WR, UCLA 1988
Creekmur, Louis, T, Wm. & Mary 1950–59
Cremer, Theodore, E, Auburn 1946–48
Cribbs, James, Memphis State 1989
Crockett, Ray, CB, Baylor 1989–
Croft, Don, DT, UTEP 1976
Cronin, Gene, G, Coll. of Pacific 1956–59
Crosby, Ron, LB, Penn State 1977
Crosswhite, Leon, RB, Oklahoma, 1973–74
Culp, Curley, DT, Arizona State 1980–81
Cunningham, Leon, C, South Carolina 1955
Curley, August, LB, USC 1983–86

D
D'Addio, Dave, FB, Maryland 1984
D'Alonzo, Peter, B, Villanova 1951–52
Dallafior, Ken, G, Minnesota 1989–92
Danielson, Gary, QB, Purdue 1976–84
Darby, Byron, DE, USC 1989
David, James, B, Colorado A&M 1952–59
Davis, Ben, DB, Defiance 1974–76
Davis, Glenn, E, Ohio State 1960–61
Davis, Jerome, NT, Ball State 1987
Davis, Milt, HB, UCLA 1956
Dawley, Frederick, B, Michigan 1944
Dawson, Mike, DT, Arizona 1983
Daykin, Tony, LB, Georgia Tech 1977–78
DeCorrevont, William, B, Northwestern 1946
DeFruiter, Robert, B, Nebraska 1947
Delaney, Jeff, DB, Pittsburgh 1981
DeMarco, Mario,* G, Miami 1949
Dennis, Guy, G, Florida 1973–75
DePoyster, Jerry, K, Wyoming 1968
Derby, John, LB, Iowa 1992–
DeShane, Charles, B, Alabama 1945–49
Dibble, Dorne, E, Mich. St. 1951,53–57
Dickel, Dan, LB, Iowa 1978
Diehl, David, E, Michigan St. 1939–40,44–45
Dieterich, Chris, T, N. Carolina St. 1980–86
Diorio, Jerry, TE, Michigan 1987
Dodge, Kirk, LB, UNLV 1984–85
Doig, Steve, LB, New Hampshire 1984–85
Doll, Donald, B, USC 1949–52
Dollinger, Tony, FB, Evangel 1987
Doran, James, E, Iowa State 1951–59
D'Orazio, Joseph,* T, Ithaca 1944
Dorney, Keith, T-G, Penn State 1979–87
Dove, Robert, E-G, Notre Dame 1952–54
Dozier, D.J., RB, Penn State 1991
Dublinski, Thomas, QB, Utah 1952–54
Dubzinski, Walter, G, Boston College 1941
Dubish, Andrew, C, Georgia 1948
Duckens, Mark, DE, Arizona State 1990
Dudley, William, B, Virginia 1947–49
Dugger, John, E, Ohio State 1947–48
Duncan, James, E, Wake Forest 1950
Duncan, Rick, P, East Montana St. 1969
Dunlap, Leonard, DB, N. Texas St. 1975

E
Earon, Blaine, E, Duke 1952–53
Ebding, Harry,* E, St. Mary's 1934–37
Eddy, Nick, RB, Notre Dame 1968–72
Edwards, Stan, FB, Michigan 1987

Ehrmann, Joe, DT, Syracuse 1981–82
Eiden, Edmund, B, Scranton 1944
Elam, Cleveland, DT, Tennessee St. 1979
Elder, Donnie, DB, Memphis State 1986
Elias, Homer, G, Tennessee State 1978–84
Ellerson, Gary, RB, Wisconsin 1987
Ellis, Ken, DB, Southern 1979
Ellis, Lawrence,* B, Syracuse, 1948
Emerick, Robert, T, Miami (O.) 1934
Emerson, Grover, Texas 1934–37
Engebretson, Paul, T, N'western 1934
English, Doug, DT–NT, Texas 1975–79,81–85
Enke, Fred, QB, Arizona 1948–51
Erxleben, Russell, P, Texas 1987
Evans, Leon, DE, Miami 1985–87
Evans, Murray, B, Hardin-Simmons 1942–43
Evey, Dick, DT, Tennessee 1971

F
Fanning, Mike, DT, Notre Dame 1983
Fantetti, Ken, LB, Wyoming 1979–85
Farkas, Andrew, B, Detroit 1945
Farmer, George, WR, UCLA 1975
Farr, Mel, RB, UCLA 1967–73
Farr, Miller, DB, Wichita 1973
Farr, Mike, WR, UCLA 1990–92
Federico, Creig, DB, Illinois State 1987
Feldhaus, William,* T, Cincinnati 1937–40
Felton, Joe, G, Albion, 1987
Felts, Bob, HB, Florida A&M 1965–67
Fena, Thomas,* G, Colorado 1937
Fenenbock, Charles, B, UCLA 1943–45
Ferguson, Joe, QB, Arkansas 1985–87
Ferguson, Keith, DE, Ohio State 1985–
Fichman, Leon, T, Alabama 1946–47
Fields, Anthony, DB, Eastern Michigan 1987
Fields, Edgar, DT, Texas A&M 1981
Fifer, William, T,West Texas State 1978
Fisk, William, E, USC 1940–43
Flanagan, Ed, C, Purdue 1965–74
Flanagan, Richard, LB, Ohio State 1950–52
Folmar, Brendon, Claifornia (PA) 1987
Ford, Darryl, LB, New Mexico State 1992–
Ford, John, WR, Virginia, 1989
Forte, Aldo, G, Montana 1946
Fortin, Roman, T, San Diego State 1991
Fowler, Amos, C, S. Mississippi 1978–84
Franklin, Dennis, WR, Michigan 1975–76
Franks, Dennis, C, Michigan 1979
Freitas, Rockne, T, Oregon State 1968–77
French, Barry, G, Purdue 1951
Friede, Mike, WR, Indiana 1980
Frizzell, William, DB, N. Carolina Central 1984–85
Frohbose, Bill, DB, Miami (Fla.) 1974
Frutig, Edward, E, Michigan 1945–46
Fucci, Dominic,* B, Kentucky 1955
Furness, Steve, DT, Rhode Island 1981
Furst, Anthony, T, Dayton 1940–41,44

G
Gagliano, Robert, QB, Utah State 1989–90
Gagnon, Roy, G, Oregon 1935
Gaines, Lawrence, FB, Wyoming 1976–79
Gallagher, Dave, DT, Michigan 1978–79
Gallagher, Frank, G, N. Carolina 1967–72
Gambol, Chris, T, Iowa 1989
Gambrell, Bill, E, South Carolina 1968
Gandee, Sherwin, E, Ohio State 1952–57

Gatski, Frank, C, Marshall 1957
Gaubatz, Dennis, LB, LSU 1963–64
Gay, William, DE, USC 1978–87
Gedman, Gene,* B, Indiana 1953,56–58
Geile, Chris, C, Eastern Illinois 1987
George, Ray, T, USC 1939
Geremsky, Thad, E, Pittsburgh 1951
Germany, Willie, DB, Morgan State 1973
Gibbons, James, E, Iowa 1958–68
Gibbs, Sonny, QB, TCU 1964
Gibson, Dennis, LB, Iowa State 1987–
Giles, Jimmie, TE, Alcorn State 1986
Gill, Sloko, G, Youngstown 1942
Gillette, Jim, B, Virginia 1948
Gilmer, Harry, QB, Alabama 1955–56
Ginn, Tommie, G, Arkansas 1980–81
Gipson, Paul, RB, Houston 1971
Girard, Earl, B, Wisconsin 1952–56
Glass, William, DE, Baylor 1958–61
Glover, Kevin, C-G, Maryland 1985–
Goich, Dan, DE, California 1969–70
Goldman, Samuel, E, Howard 1949
Golsteyn, Jerry, QB, N. Illinois 1979
Gonzaga, John, T, (No College) 1961–65
Goodman, Henry, T, W. Virginia 1942
Goovert, Ron, LB, MSU 1967
Gordon, John, DT, Hawaii 1972
Gordy, John, G, Tennessee 1957,59–67
Gore, Gordon, B, Okla. S.W. Tchrs. 1939
Graham, Lester,* G, Tulsa 1938
Graham, William, DB, Texas 1982–87
Gray, Dan, DE, Rutgers 1978–79
Gray, Hector, DB, Florida St. 1981–83
Gray, Mel, WR-KR, Purdue 1989–
Greco, Don, G, Western Illinois 1982–85
Green, Curtis, DE-NT, Alabama St. 1981–89
Green, Donnie, T, Purdue 1978
Green, Willie, WR, Mississippi 1991–
Greene, John, E, Michigan 1944–50
Greer, Albert, E, Jackson State 1963
Greer, Terry, WR, Alabama St. 1990
Grefe, Theodore, E, Notre Dame 1945
Griffin, James, DB, Middle Tenn. St. 1986–89
Grigonis, Frank, B, Chattanooga 1942
Grimes, George, B, Virginia 1948
Grymes, Darrell, WR, Central State 1987
Groomes, Melvin, B, Indiana 1948–49
Grossman, Rex, B, Indiana 1950
Grottkau, Robert, G, Oregon 1959–60
Gutowsky, "Ace,"* RB, Okla. City U. 1934–38

H
Hackenbruck, John,* T, Oregon State 1940
Hackney, Elmer,* B, Kansas St. 1942–46
Hadd, Gary, DT-NT, Minnesota 1988
Hafen, Bernard, E, Utah 1949–50
Haggerty, Mike, T, Miami (Fla.) 1973
Hall, Alvin, DB, Miami (OH) 1981–85,87
Hall, John, B, TCU 1942
Hall, Tom, E, Minnesota 1962–63
Hamilton, Raymond, E, Arkansas 1939
Hamlin, Gene, C, Western Michigan 1972
Hand, Larry, DE, Appalachian St. 1964–77
Hanneman, Chuck, E, Mich. Normal 1937–41
Hansen, Dale,* T, Mich. State 1944; 1948–49
Hanson, Jason, K, Washington State 1992–
Harder, Pat,* B, Wisconsin 1951–53
Harding, Roger, C, California 1948
Hardy, James, QB, USC 1952

Harrell, James, LB, Florida 1979–83; 1985–86
Harrison, Granville, E, Miss. State 1942
Hart, Leon, E, Notre Dame 1950–57
Harvey, Maurice, DB, Ball State 1983,87
Haverdick, Dave, DE, Morehead St. 1970
Hayworth, Tracy, LB, Tennessee 1990–
Hekkers, George, T, Wisconsin 1947–49
Held, Paul, B, San Jose State 1955
Helms, John, E, Georgia Tech 1946
Henderson, John, E, Michigan 1965–67
Hennigan, Mike, LB, Tenn. Tech 1973–75
Hertwig, Craig, T, Georgia 1975–77
Heywood, Ralph, E, USC 1947
Hickman, Donnie, G, USC 1978
Hicks, Ivan, DB, Michigan 1987
Hicks, Mark, LB, Arizona State 1987
Hicks, R.W., C, Humboldt State 1975
Hightower, John, E, Sam Houston 1943
Hilgenberg, Wally, LB, Iowa 1964–66
Hilger, Rusty, QB, Oklahoma State 1988
Hill, David, TE, Texas A&I 1976–82
Hill, Harlon, E, Florence State 1962
Hill, J.D., WR, Arizona State 1976–78
Hill, James, B, Tennessee 1951–52
Hill, Jimmy, DB, Sam Houston 1965
Hill, Rod, DB, Kentucky State 1986
Hillman, Bill,* B, Tennessee 1946
Hilton, John, TE, Richmond 1972–73
Hinchman, Hubert, B, Butler 1934
Hinnant, Mike, TE-G, Temple 1992
Hipple, Eric, QB, Utah State 1980–1989
Hirsch, Steve, DB, Northern Illinois 1987
Hoernschemeyer, Robert,* B, Indiana 1950–55
Hogland, Doug, G, Oregon State 1958
Holaar, John, B, Appalachian State 1949
Holmes, Jerry, CB, West Virginia 1988–89
Hons, Todd, QB, Arizona State 1987
Hooks, Jim, RB, Cent. St. (Okla.) 1973–76
Hoopes, Mitch, P, Arizona 1977
Hoover, Mel, WR, Arizona State 1987
Hopp, Harry,* B, Nebraska 1940–43
Howard, Billy, DT, Alcorn A&M 1974–76
Howard, William, B, USC 1939
Hubbard, Marv, FB, Colgate 1977
Huffman, Vernon, B, Indiana 1937–38
Hughes, Chuck,* WR, Tex. El Paso 1970–71
Hunter, Herman, RB, Tennessee St. 1986
Hunter, James, DB, Grambling 1976–82
Hunter, Jeff, DE, Albany St. 1990–92
Hunter, Scott, QB, Alabama 1979
Hupke, Thomas,* G, Alabama 1934–37
Hutchison, Elvin, B, Whittier 1939

I

Irvin, LeRoy, CB, Kansas 1990
Isselhardt, Ralph, G, Franklin 1937
Ivory, Bob, G, Detroit 1947
Izo, George, QB, Notre Dame 1965

J

Jackson, Cedric, RB, Texas Christian 1991
Jackson, Ernie, DB, Jackson St. 1979
James, Garry, RB, LSU 1986–88
James, John, P, Florida 1982
James, June,* LB, Texas 1985–86
Jamison, George, LB, Cincinnati 1987–
Jarvis, Ray, WR, Norfolk State 1974–78
Jaszewski, Floyd, T, Minnesota 1950–51

Jauron, Dick, DB, Yale 1973–77
Jefferson, William, B, Mississippi St. 1941
Jenkins, Ken, RB, Bucknell 1983–84
Jenkins, Leon, DB, West Virginia 1972
Jenkins, Melvin, CB, Cincinnati 1991–92
Jenkins, Walter, E, Wayne State 1955
Jessie, Ron, WR, Kansas 1971–74
Jett, John, E, Wake Forest 1941
Johnson, Demetrious, DB, Missouri 1983–86
Johnson, Gilvanni, WR, Michigan 1987
Johnson, James, LB, San Diego St. 1985–86
Johnson, Jimmie, TE, Howard 1992–
Johnson, John "Jack,"* T, Utah 1934–40
Johnson, John Henry, B, Ariz. St. 1957–59
Johnson, Levi, DB, Texas A&I 1973–77
Johnson, Richard, WR, Colorado, 1989–90
Johnson, Rick, T, Grand Valley St. 1987
Johnson, Troy, WR, Southern 1989
Johnson, Troy, LB, Oklahoma 1992
Jolley, Gordon, T, Utah 1972–75
Jones, A.J., RB, Texas 1985
Jones, Andre, LB, Notre Dame 1992
Jones, David, C–G, Texas 1984–85
Jones, Doug, DB, S. Fernando Valley 1979
Jones, Elmer, G, Wake Forest 1947–48
Jones, James, FB, Florida 1983–88
Jones, James, B, Union Tenn. 1946
Jones, Jimmie, RB, UCLA 1974
Jones, Ralph, E, Alabama 1946
Jones, Victor, LB, Virginia Tech 1989–
Junker, Steve, E, Xavier 1957, 59–61
Jurkiewicz, Walter, C, Indiana 1946

K

Kab, Vyto, TE, Penn State 1987–88
Kacmarek, Jeff, NT, Western Michigan 1987
Kamanu, Lew, DE, Weber State 1967–68
Kane, Rick, RB, San Jose State 1977–83,85
Kaporch, Albert, T, St. Bonaventure 1943–45
Karlis, Rich, K, Cincinnati 1990
Karlivacz, Carl,* B, Syracuse 1953–57
Karpinski, Keith, LB, Penn State 1989
Karras, Alex, DT, Iowa 1958–62; 1964–70
Karras, Ted, G, Indiana 1965
Karstens, George, C, Indiana 1949
Kaska, Anton, B, Illinois Wesleyan 1935
Kearney, Jim, DB, Prairie View 1965–66
Keene, Robert, B, Detroit 1943–45
Kennedy, William, E, Mich. St. 1942,44
Kenney, Steve, G, Clemson 1986
Kent, Greg, DT, Utah 1968
Kercher, Richard, B, Tulsa 1954
Ketkzo, Alexander,* T, Michigan St. 1943
King, Angelo, LB, S. Carolina St. 1984–87
King, Horace, RB, Georgia 1975–83
Kinzer, Matt, P, Purdue 1987
Kipp, James, T, Montana State 1942
Kiser, Paul, G, Wake Forest 1987
Kizzire, Lee,* Wyoming 1937
Klewicki, Edward, E, Michigan St. 1935–38
Kmetovic, Peter, B, Stanford 1947
Knorr, Lawrence, C, Dayton 1942–45
Knox, Sam,* G, New Hampshire 1934–36
Komlo, Jeff, QB, Delaware 1979–81
Kopay, Dave, RB, Washington 1968
Kopcha, Joseph,* G, Chattanooga 1936
Kostiuk, Michael, T, Detroit 1945
Kowalkowski, Bob, G, Virginia 1966–76
Kowgios, Nick, FB, Lafayette 1987

Bobby Layne owns virtually every Lions passing record.

Krall, Gerald, B, Ohio State 1950
Kramer, Erik, QB, N. Caroilina St. 1991–
Kramer, Ron, E, Michigan 1965–67
Kring, Frank, B, TCU 1945
Krol, Joseph, B, W. Ontario 1945
Krouse, Raymond,* T, Maryland 1956–57
Kuczinski, Bert, E, Pennsylvania 1943

L

LaLonde, Roger, DT, Muskingum 1964
Landry, Greg, QB, Massachusettes 1968–78
Lane, Dick, DB, Scottsbluff JC 1960–65
LaRose, Dan, T, Missouri 1961–63
Lary, Yale, DB, Texas A&M 1952–53,56–64
Larson, Bill, TE, Colorado State 1977
Laslavic, Jim, LB, Penn State 1973–77
Laster, Don, T, Tennessee State 1984
Latimer, Al, DB, Clemson 1982–84
Lawless, Burton, G, Florida 1980
Lay, Russell, B, Michigan State 1934
Layne, Robert,* QB, Texas 1950–58
Lear, Leslie, B, Manitoba 1947
LeBeau, Dick, DB, Ohio State 1959–72
Lee, Edward, WR, So. Carolina State 1983
Lee, Gary, WR, Georgia Tech 1987–88
Lee, Ken, LB, Washington 1971
Lee, Larry, C, UCLA 1981–85
Lee, Monte, LB, Texas 1963–64
LeForce, Clyde, QB, Tulsa 1947–49
Leonard, Tony, DB, Viriginia U'n 1978–79
Lewis, Dan, HB, Wisconsin 1958–64
Lewis, David, TE, California 1984–86
Lewis, Eddie, DB, Kansas 1979–80
Lewis, Mark, TE, Texas A&M 1987–88
Liles, Alva, DT, Boise State 1980
Liles, Elvin, G, Okla. A&M 1943–45
Lindon, Luther, T, Kentucky 1944–45
Lininger, Jack, C, Ohio State 1950–51
Linn, Jack, G-T, West Virginia 1992–
Lio, Augustino, G, Georgetown 1941–43
Little, David, TE, Mid. Tennessee St. 1991
Lloyd, Dave, C, George 1962
Lockett, Danny, LB, Arizona 1987–88
Lomakoski, John, T, W. Michigan 1962
Long, Chuck, QB, Iowa 1986–89,91
Long, Ken, G, Purdue 1976
Long, Robert, E, UCLA 1955–59
Looney, Joe Don,* HB, Oklahoma 1965–66
Lowe, Gary, B, Michigan State 1957–64
Lowther, Jackie,* B, Detroit 1944
Lucci, Mike, LB, Tennessee 1965–73
Luce, Derrel, LB, Baylor 1980

Lumpkin, Roy,* B, Georgia Tech 1934
Lusk, Bob, C, Wm. & Mary 1956
Lynch, Eric, RB, Grand Valley State 1992–

M
Machurek, Mike, QB, Idaho State 1982–84
Mackenroth, John, C, N. Dakota 1983
Madarik, Elmer,* B, Detroit 1945–47
Maggiolo, Chick, B, Illinios 1949
Magnani, Dante, B, St. Mary's 1950
Maher, Bruce, Detroit 1960–67
Mains, Gilbert, T, Murray State 1952–61
Malinchak, Bill, E, Indiana 1966–69
Mandley, Pete, WR, Northern Arizona 1984–88
Mann, Errol, K, North Dakota 1969–76
Mann, Robert, E, Michigan 1948–49
Manzo, Joseph, T, Boston College 1945
Margucci, Joseph, B, USC 1947–48
Markovich, Mark, G, Penn State 1976–77
Maronic, Stephen, T, N. Carolina 1939–40
Marsh, Amos,* FB, Oregon State 1965–67
Martin, James, G, Notre Dame 1951–61
Martin, Robbie, WR, Cal Poly SLO 1981–84
Martinovich, Philip, G, C.O.P. 1939
Matheson, Jack, E, Western Mich. 1943–46
Matheson, Riley, G, Texas Mines 1943
Matthews, Aubrey, WR, Delta St. 1990–
Mathews, Ned, B, UCLA 1940–43
Mathewson, Morley, E, California 1941
Matich, Trevor, C, BYU 1989
Matisi, Tony,* T, Pittsburgh 1938–39
Matson, Ollie, FB, San Francisco 1963
Mattiford, John, G, Marshall 1941
Maves, Earl, B, Wisconsin 1948
Maxwell, Bruce, RB, Arkansas 1970
Maxwell, Vernon, LB, Arizona State 1985–87
Mazza, Vincent, E, (No College) 1945–46
Mazzanti, Jerry, DE, Arkansas 1966
McCall, Reese, TE, Auburn 1983–85
McCambridge, John, DE, NWU 1967
McClung, Willie, T, Florida A&M 1960–61
McCord, Darris, DE, Tennessee 1955–67
McCoy, Joel, B, Alabama 1946
McCoy, Mike, DT, Notre Dame 1980
McCray, Prentice, DB, Arizona State 1980
McCullouch, Earl, E, USC 1968–73
McDermott, Lloyd, T, Kentucky 1950
McDonald, James, B, Ohio State 1938–40
McDonald, James, TE, USC 1985
McDonald, Keith, WR, San Jose St. 1989
McDonald, Mike, LS-LB, Southern California 1992
McDonough, Bob, DB, California (PA) 1987
McDuffie, George, DE, Findlay 1987
McElhenny, Hugh, HB, Washington 1964
McGee, Willie, WR, Alcorn State 1978
McGraw, Mike, LB, Wyoming 1977
McGraw, Thurman, T, Colo. A&M 1950–54
McIlhenny, Donald, B, SMU 1956
McInnis, Hugh, E, Miss. Southern 1964
McKalip, William, E, Oregon St. 1934, 1936
McKnight, Dennis, C-G, Drake 1990,92
McLemore, Thomas, TE, Southern 1992–
McLenna, Bruce,* HB, Hillsadale 1966
McMakin, John, TE, Clemson 1975
McNorton, Bruce, DB, Georgetown, Ky. 1982–90
McWilliams, William, B, Jordon 1934
Meade, Mike, FB, Penn State 1984–85
Melinkovich, Mike, DE, Gray Harbour JC 1967
Mello, James, B, Notre Dame 1949

Mendenhall, John, DT, Grambling 1980
Meska, Richard, T, St. Mary's 1945
Messner, Max, LB, Cincinnati 1960–63
Middleton, David, E, Auburn 1955–60
Mike–Mayer, Steve, K, Maryland 1977
Miketa, Andrew, C, N. Carolina 1954–55
Miklich, William, B, Idaho 1948
Milano, Arch, E, St. Francis 1945
Milburn, Darryl, DE, Grambling 1991
Milinichik, Joe, G-T, N. Carolina St. 1987–89
Miller, Blake, C, Louisiana State 1992
Miller, John, S, Michigan State 1989–90
Miller, Robert, T, Virginia 1952–58
Miller, Terry, LB, Illinois 1970
Mills, Dick, G, Pittsburgh 1961–62
Misko, John, P, Oregon State 1987
Mitchell, Devon, DB, Iowa 1986–88
Mitchell, Granville,* E, Davis–Elkins 1934
Mitchell, Melvin, C, Tennessee St. 1977
Mitchell, Jim, DE, Virginia St. 1970–77
Mitrick, Frank, T, Oglethorpe 1945
Mobley, Stacey, WR, Jackson State 1989
Mohring, John, LB, C.W. Post 1980
Momsen, Robert, G, Ohio State 1951
Monahan, Regis,* B, Ohio State 1935–38
Montgomery, James, T, Texas A&M 1946
Montgomery, Wilbert, RB, Abilene Christian 1985
Montier, Mike, C, Colorado 1978
Mooney, Ed, LB, Texas Tech 1968–71
Moore, Alvin, RB, Arizona State 1985–86
Moore, Denis, T, USC 1967–69
Moore, Herman, WR, Virginia 1991–
Moore, Paul,* B, Presbyterian 1940–41
Moore, William, E, No. Carolina 1939
Morlock, John, B, Marshall 1940
Morrall, Earl, QB, Michigan State 1958–64
Morris, Glen,* E, Colorado State 1940
Morris, Jon, C, Holy Cross 1975–77
Morris, Randall, RB, Tennessee 1988
Morrison, Don, T, Texas Arlington 1979
Morse, Raymond, E, Oregon 1935–38,40
Moscrip, James, E, Stanford 1938–39
Moss, Martin, DT-NT, UCLA 1982–85
Mote, Kelly, E, Duke 1947–49
Mott, Steve, C, Alabama 1983–88
Mugg, Garvin, T, N. Texas State 1945
Munson, Bill, QB, Utah State 1968–76
Murakowski, Art, B, Northwestern 1951
Murray, Eddie, K, Tulane 1980–91
Myers, Tom, QB, Northwestern 1965–66

N
Nardi, Richard, B, Ohio State 1938
Naumoff, Paul, LB, Tennessee 1967–78
Nelson, Reed, C, Brigham Young 1947
Nelson, Robert, C, Baylor 1941, 1945
Nichols, Mark, WR, San Jose St. 1981–87
Ninowski, Jim, QB, Mich. State 1960–61
Niziolek, Bob, TE, Colorado 1981
Noga, Niko, LB, Hawaii 1989–91
Noppenberg, John, B, Miami 1941
Nori, Reino, B, N. Illinois State 1937
Norris, Ulysses, TE, Georgia 1979–83
Nott, Douglass, B, Detroit 1935
Nowatzke, Tom, FB, Indiana 1965–69

O
Oates, Brad, T, Brigham Young 1978
Obee, Duncan, C, Dayton 1941

Eddie Murray scored a club-best 1,113 points in his Lions career.

O'Brien, Jim, WR, Cincinnati 1973
O'Brien, William, B, (No College) 1947
Odle, Phil, E, BYU 1968–70
Office, Anthony, LB, Illinois State 1987
Ogle, Rick, LB, Colorado 1972
Oldham, Chris, DB, Oregon 1990
Oldham, Ray, DB, Middle Tennessee 1980–82
Olenski, Mitchell, T, Alabama 1947
Olszewski, John, FB, California 1961
O'Neil, Ed, LB, Penn State 1974–79
O'Neil, Bill, HB, Detroit 1935
Opalewski, Edward, T, Mich. N. 1943–44
Orton, Greg, G, Nebraska 1987
Orvis, Herb, DT, Colorado 1972–77
Overton, Don, RB, Fairmont St. 1991–92
Owens, Dan, DE, Southern California 1990–
Owens, Steve, RB, Oklahoma 1970–75

P
Paige, Tony, FB, Virginia Tech 1987–89
Painter, Carl, RB, Hampton Inst. 1988–89
Palmer, Paul, RB-WR, Temple 1989
Panciera, Donald, B, San Francisco 1950
Panelli, John, B, Notre Dame 1949–50
Paolucci, Ben, T, Wayne State 1959
Paris, Bubba, T, Michigan 1991
Parker, Raymond,* B, Centenary 1935–36
Parker, Willie, G, North Texas St. 1980
Parkin, Dave, DB, Utah State 1979
Parson, Ray, T, Minnesota 1971
Parsons, Lloyd, B, Gust. Adolphus 1941
Patt, Maurice,* E, Carnegie Tech 1938
Patterson, Don, DB, Georgia Tech 1979
Pavelec, Theodore, G, Detroit 1941–42
Payton, Eddie, RB, Jackson State 1977
Pearson, Lindell, B, Oklahoma 1950
Peete, Rodney, QB, USC 1989–
Perriman, Brett, WR, Miami 1991–
Perry, Gerald, T, California 1954,56–59
Pesuit, Wally, C, Kentucky 1979–80
Pete, Lawrence, NT, Nebraska 1989–
Peters, Floyd, T, San Francisco St. 1963
Peterson, Ken, B, Gonzaga 1936
Phillips, Jason, WR, Houston 1989–90
Picard, Bob, WR, East. Washington 1976
Pickard, Bob, WR, Xavier 1974
Piepul, Milton, B, Notre Dame 1941
Pierson, Reggie, DB, Oklahoma State 1976
Pietrosante, Nick,* B, Notre Dame 1959–65
Pifferini, Robert, C, San Jose State 1949
Pingel, John, B, Michigan State 1939

In just four seasons, Barry Sanders has become Detroit's all-time leading rusher.

Pinkney, Reggie, DB, E. Carolina 1977–78
Plum, Milt, QB, Penn State 1962–67
Polansky, John,* B, Wake Forest 1942
Poole, Oliver, E, Mississippi 1949
Porcher, Robert, DE, South Carolina 1992–
Porter, Ricky, RB, Slippery Rock St. 1982
Porter, Tracy, WR, LSU 1981–82
Potts, Charles, DB, Purdue 1972
Prchlik, John, T, Yale 1949–53
Pregulman, Mervin, G, Michigan 1947–48
Prescott, Harold, E, Hardin-Simmons 1949
Presnell, Glenn, B, Nebraska 1934–36
Price, Charles, B, Texas A&M 1940–41,45
Price, Ernest, DT, Texas A&I 1973–78
Prindle, Mike, K, Western Michigan 1987
Pringle, Alan, K, Rice 1975
Pritchett, Kelvin, DE, Mississippi 1991–
Pureifory, Dave, DE, E. Michigan 1978–82

Q
Quaerna, Jerry, G–T, Michigan 1987
Quinlan, Bill, DE, Michigan State 1964

R
Rabb, Warren, QB, LSU 1960
Rabold, Mike,* G, Indiana 1959
Radovich, William, G, USC 1938–41,45
Ramsey, Derrick, TE, Kentucky 1987
Randolph, Al, DB, Iowa 1972
Randolph, Clare,* C, Indiana 1934–36
Ranspot, Keith, E, SMU 1941
Rasley, Rocky, G, Oregon State 1969–73
Rasmussen, Wayne, DB, S. Dakota St. 1964–73
Reckmack, Raymond, B, Syracuse 1937
Redmond, Rudy, DB, Pacific 1972–73
Reeberg, Lucien,* T, Hampton Inst. 1963
Reed, Joe, QB, Mississippi State 1975–79
Reese, Lloyd, B, Tennessee 1947
Reichow, Jerry, QB, Iowa 1956–59
Rexer, Freeman, E, Tulane 1944
Reynolds, Robert, T, Stanford 1937–38
Rhodes, Bruce,* DB, S. Francisco St. 1978

Ricardo, Benny, K, San Diego St. 1976–79
Ricca, James, T, Georgetown 1955
Rich, Randy, DB, New Mexico 1977
Richards, Perry, E, Detroit 1956
Richards, Ray, G, Nebraska 1934
Richins, Aldo, B, Utah 1935
Rifenberg, Richard, E, Michigan 1950
Riley, Eugene, TE, Ball State 1991
Riley, Lee, B, Detroit 1955
Ritchart, Delbert,* C, Colorado 1936–37
Robb, Joe,* DE, TCU 1968–71
Robertson, Lake, E, Mississippi 1945
Robinson, Bo, FB, W. Texas St. 1979–80
Robinson, John, DB, Tenn. State 1966–67
Robinson, Junior, DB, East Carolina 1992–
Robinson, Shelton, LB, North Carolina 1986–88
Rockennbach, Lyle, G, Michigan St. 1943
Rogas, Daniel, G, Tulane 1951
Rogers, Reggie, DE, Washington 1987–88
Rogers, William,* T, Villanova 1938–40
Roskie, Kenneth, B, E. Carolina 1948
Ross, Tim, LB, Bowling Green St. 1987
Rosteck, Ernest, C, (No College) 1944
Rote, Tobin, QB, Rice 1957–59
Rothwell, Fred, C, Kansas State 1974
Roundtree, Ray, WR, Penn State 1988
Rouse, Stillman, E, Missouri 1940
Roussos, Michael, T, Pittsburgh 1949
Rowe, Robert, B, Colgate 1934
Rubick, Rob, TE, Grand Valley State 1982–88
Rubino, Anthony, G, Wake Forest 1943–46
Rush, Jerry, DT, Michigan State 1965–71
Russas, Albert, T, Tennessee 1949
Russell, Kenneth, T, Bowling Green 1957–59
Ryan, David, B, Hardin-Simmons 1945–46
Ryan, Kent, B, Utah State 1938–40
Rychiec, Tom, E, Am. Int'l 1958
Ryder, Nick, FB, Miami 1963–64

S
Saleaumua, Dan, NT, Arizona State 1987–88
Salem, Harvey, G, California 1986–90
Salsbury, James, G, UCLA 1955–56
Sanchez, John, T, San Francisco 1947
Sanders, Barry, RB, Oklahoma St. 1989–
Sanders, Charlie, TE, Minnesota 1968–77
Sanders, Daryl, T, Ohio State 1963–66
Sanders, Eric, T-G, Nevada–Reno 1986–92
Sanders, Ken, DE, Howard–Payne 1972–79
Sandifer, Daniel,* B, LSU 1950
Sanzotta Dominic, B, W. Res. 1942,46
Sarratt, Charles, B, Oklahoma 1948
Sarringhaus, Paul, B, Ohio State 1948
Sarton, Lawrence, G, Fordham 1942,45
Schibanoff, Alexander, T, Frank–Marsh 1942
Schiechi, John, C, Santa Clara 1942
Schmidt, Joseph, LB, Pittsburgh 1953–65
Schmiesing, Joe, DT, New Mexico St. 1972
Schneller, John,* E, Wisconsin 1934–36
Scholtz, Bob, C, Notre Dame 1960–64
Schottel, Ivan, B, NW Mo. St. 1946,48
Schroll, Charles, B, LSU 1950
Scott, Clyde, B, Arkansas 1952
Scott, Fred, WR, Amherst 1978–83
Scott, Kevin, CB, Stanford 1991–
Scott, Perry, E, Muhlenberg 1942
Scroggins, Tracy, LB, Tulsa 1992–
Self, Clarence, B, Wisconsin 1950–51

Seltzer, Harry, B, Morris-Harvey 1942
Sewell, Harley, G, Texas 1953–62
Sheffield, Chris, DB, Albany State 1987
Shepherd, William,* B, W. Maryland 1935–40
Shoals, Roger, T, Maryland, 1965–70
Siegert, Wayne, T, Illinois 1951
Sieminski, Chuck, DT, Penn State 1968
Sigillo, Dominic, T, Xavier 1945
Simmons, Davie, LB, N. Carolina 1980
Simmons, John,* C, Detroit 1949–50
Simon, Jim, G–T, Miami (Fla.) 1963–65
Simonson, Dave, T, Minnesota 1977
Sims, Billy, RB, Oklahoma 1980–84
Singer, Curt, T, Tennessee 1988
Sinkwich, Frank, B, Georgia 1943–44
Sirochman, George, G, Duquesne 1944
Skladany, Tom, P, Ohio State 1978–82
Slaby, Lou, LB, Pittsburgh 1966
Sloan, Dwight, B, Arkansas 1939–40
Small, John, DT, Citadel 1973–74
Smith, Bobby, DB, UCLA 1965–66
Smith, Harry, T, USC 1940
Smith, J.D., T, Rice 1964–66
Smith, J. Robert, HB, Iowa 1949–54
Smith, Oscar, RB, Nicholls State, 1986
Smith, Ricky, DB, Alabama State 1980–82
Smith, Robert L., B, Texas A&M 1953–54
Smith, Wayne, DB, Purdue 1980–82
Sneddon, Robert, B, St. Mary's 1945
Snell, Ray, G, Wisconsin 1985
Soboleski, Joseph, T, Michigan 1950
Sokolosky, John, C, Wayne St. 1978
Spangler, Eugene, B, Tulsa 1946
Souders, Cecil, E, Ohio State 1947–49
Speelman, Harry,* T, Michigan State 1940
Spencer, Oliver, T, Kansas 1953,56,59–61
Speth, George, T, Murray State 1942
Spielman, Chris, LB, Ohio State 1988–
Spindler, Marc, DE, Pitttsburgh 1990–
Stacco, Edward, T, Colgate 1947
Stacy, James, T, Oklahoma 1935–37
Staggers, Jon, WR, Missouri 1975
Stanfel, Richard, G, San Francisco 1952–55
Stanley, Walter, WR, Mesa College 1989
Starring, Stephen, WR, McNeese State 1988
Steele, Chuck, C, California 1987
Steen, James,* T, Syracuse 1935–36
Steffen, Jim, B, UCLA 1959–60
Stephens, Hal, DE, East Carolina 1985
Stevenson, Mark, G–C, Western Illinois 1985
Stewart, Jim, DB, Tulsa 1979
Stits, William, B, UCLA 1954–56
Stokes, Lee,* C, Centenary 1937–39
Stovall, Richard, C, Abilene Christian 1947–48
Stradford, Troy, RB, Boston College 1992
Strauthers, Tom, DE, Jackson State 1988
Strenger, Rich, T, Michigan 1983–87
Stringfellow, Joseph, E, Miss. So. 1942
Stuart, Roy, T, Tulsa 1943
Studstill, Pat, WR, Houston 1961–67
Sucic, Stephen, B, Illinois 1947–48
Sugar, Leo, E, Purdue 1962
Sully, Ivory, DB, Delaware 1987
Sumler, Tony, DB, Wichita State 1978
Summers, Wilbur, Louisville 1977
Summerall, George, E, Arkansas 1952
Sunter, Ian, K (No College) 1976
Swain, Bill, LB, Oregon 1968–69
Sweetan, Karl, QB, Wake Forest 1966–67

Swiacki, William, E, Columbia 1951–52
Swider, Larry, P, Pittsburgh 1979
Szakash, Paul, B, Montana 1938–42
Szymanski, Frank,* C, Notre Dame 1945–47

T
Tassos, Damon, G, Texas A&M 1945–46
Tatarek, Bob, DT, Miami (Ohio) 1972
Tautolo, Terry, LB, UCLA 1981–82,84
Taylor, Altie, RB, Utah State 1969–76
Taylor, Terry, CB, Southern Illinois 1989–91
Teal, Jim, LB, Purdue 1973
Tearry, Larry, C, Wake Forest 1978–79
Ten Napel, Garth, LB, Texas A&M 1976–77
Tennell, Derrick, TE, UCLA, 1991
Terry, Nat, DB, Florida State 1978
Tharpe, Larry, T, Tennessee State 1992–
Thomas, Bob, K, Notre Dame 1982
Thomas, Calvin,* G, Tulsa 1939–40
Thomas, Russell,* T, Ohio State 1946–49
Thomason, James, B, Texas A&M 1945
Thompson, Bobby, RB, Oklahoma 1975–76
Thompson, Bobby, DB, Arizona 1964–68
Thompson, Dave, C, Clemson 1971–73
Thompson, Jesse, WR, California 1978–81
Thompson, Leonard, WR, Okla. St. 1975–86
Thompson, Robert, LB, Michigan 1987
Thompson, Vince, RB, Villanova 1981–83
Thrower, Jim, DB, East Texas St. 1973–75
Thuerk, Owen, E, St. Joseph (Ind.) 1941
Tillison, Ed, RB, NW Missouri State 1992–
Todd, Jim, HB, Ball State 1966
Tolle, Stuart, NT, Bowling Green 1987
Tomasetti, Louis, B, Bucknell 1941
Tonelli, Anthony,* C, USC 1939
Topor, Ted, LB, Michigan 1955
Torgeson, LaVern, C, Wash. St. 1951–54
Tracy, Thomas, B, Tennessee 1956–57
Treadway, John, T, Hardin-Simmons 1949
Trebotich, Ivan, B, St. Mary's 1944–45
Tressa, Thomas, G, Davis-Elkins 1942
Triplett, Bill, RB, Miami (Ohio) 1968–72
Triplett, Wallace, B, Penn State 1949–50
Tripson, John, T, Mississippi State 1941
Tripucka, Frank, QB, Notre Dame 1949
Truvillion, Eric, WR, Florida A&M 1987
Tsoutsouvas, John, C, Stanford 1940
Tuinei, Tom, DT, Hawaii 1980
Tully, Darren, B, E. Texas Teachers 1939
Turner, Harold, E, Tennessee State 1954
Turnure, Tom, C-G, Washington 1980–83,85–86
Tyler, Maurice, Morgan State 1976

U
Uremovich, Emil, T, Ind. 1941–42,45–46
Utley, Michael, G, Washington State 1989–91

V
Van Horn, Doug, G, Ohio State 1966
Van Tone, Arthur, B, So. Mississippi 1943–45
Vanzo, Frederick,* B, Northwestern 1938–41
Vargo, Larry, E, Detroit 1963
Vaughn, Charles,* B, Tennessee 1935
Vaughn, Tom, DB, Iowa State 1965–71
Vezmar, Walter,* T, Michigan State 1946–47

W
Wagner, Sidney,* G, Mich. State 1936–38
Wagoner, Dan, DB, Kansas 1982–84

Walker, Doak, B, SMU 1950–55
Walker, Wayne, LB, Idaho 1958–72
Walker, Willie, WR, Tennessee St. 1966
Walters, Rod, G, Iowa 1979
Walton, Chuck, G, Iowa State 1967–74
Walton, Larry, WR, Arizona State 1969–76
Ward, Elmer, C, Utah State 1935–36
Ward, Paul, C, Whitworth 1961–62
Ward, William, G, Washington St. 1947–49
Ware, Andre, QB, Houston 1990–
Warne, Jim, T, Arizona State 1987
Washington, Dave, LB, Alcorn St. 1978–79
Washington, Gene, WR, Stanford 1979
Watkins, Bobby, DB, Southwest Texas St. 1982–88
Watkins, Larry, RB, Alcorn A&M 1969
Watkins, Tom, HB, Iowa State 1962–67
Watson, Joseph, C, Rice 1950
Watt, Joseph, B, Syracuse 1947–48
Weatherall, Jim,* T, Oklahoma 1959–60
Weaver, Charlie, LB, USC 1971–81
Weaver, Herman, P, Tennessee 1970–76
Webb, Ken, HB, Presbyterian 1958–62
Weber, Richard, B, St. Louis 1945
Welch, Herb, S, UCLA 1990–91
Weger, Mike, DB, Bowling Green 1967–75
Weiss, Howard, B, Wisconsin 1939–40
Weithe, John, G, Xavier 1939–42
Welch, Jim, RB, SMU 1968
Wells, Warren, E, Texas Southern 1964
West, Charlie, DB, Texas El Paso 1974–77
Wester, Cleve, RB, Condordia 1987
Westfall, Robert,* B, Michigan 1944–47
Wetterlund, Chet,* B, Ill. Wesleyan 1942
Wheeler, Mark, TE, Kentucky 1987
White, Bryon, B, Colorado 1940–41
White, Daryl, G, Nebraska 1974
White, Sheldon, CB, Miami (Ohio) 1990–92
White, Stan, LB, Ohio State 1980–82
White, Wilbur, HB, Colorado A&M 1936
White, William, S, Ohio State 1988–
Whited, Mike, T, Pacific 1980
Whitlow, Bob, G-C, Arizona 1961–65
Whitsell, Dave, DB, Indiana 1958–60
Wiatrak, John, C, Washington 1939
Wickert, Tom, T, Washington State 1977
Wickett, Lloyd, T, Oregon State 1943,46
Wiese, Robert,* B, Michigan 1947–48
Wilder, James, RB, Missouri 1990
Williams, Bobbby, DB, Central St. 1969–71
Williams, Eric, DT-DE-NT, Wash. St. 1984–89
Williams, Eric T, DB, North Carolina St. 1987
Williams, Gardner, DB, St. Mary's 1984
Williams, Jimmy, LB, Nebraska 1982–90
Williams, Michael, WR, Northeastern 1989
Williams, Ray, WR, Washington State 1980
Williams, Rex, C, Texas Tech 1945
Williams, Sam, DE, Michigan St. 1960–65
Williams, Scott, FB, Georgia 1986–88
Williams, Walt, DB, New Mexico St. 1977–81
Wilson, Camp, B, Tulsa 1946–49
Winkler, Randy, T, Tarleton State 1967
Winslow, Robert, E, USC 1940
Witkowski, John, QB, Columbia 1984,88
Witte, Mark, TE, North Texas St. 1987
Wojciechowicz, Alex,* C, Fordham 1938–46
Woit, Richard, B, Arkansas State 1955
Womack, Bruce, G, W. Texas State 1951
Woodcock, John, DT, Hawaii 1976–80
Woods, Jerry, DB, Northern Michigan 1989

Wayne Walker played in more games (200) than any other Lion.

Woods, Larry, DT, Tennessee State 1971–72
Woods, Robert, WR, Grambling 1979
Woolfolk, Butch, RB, Michigan 1987–88
Wright, John, WR, Illinois 1969
Wyatt, Doug, DB, Tulsa 1973–74
Wyche, Sam, QB, Furman 1974

Y
Yarbrough, Jim, T, Florida 1969–77
Yepremian, Garo, K, (No College) 1966–67
Young, Adrian, LB, USC 1972
Yowarsky, Walter, E, Kentucky 1955

Z
Zatkoff, Roger, G, Michigan 1957–58
Zawadzkas, Jerry, E, Columbia 1967
Zimmerman, Leroy, B, San Jose St. 1947
Zofko, Mickey, RB, Auburn 1971–74
Zuzzio, Anthony, G, Muhlenberg 1942

* deceased

DETROIT LIONS YEAR-BY-YEAR RESULTS

Year	Coach	Regular Season			Pct.	Lions Points	Opp. Points	Home			Away			Post Season		Pre Season		
1934	P.Clark	10	3	0	.769	238	59	6	2	0	4	1	0					
1935	P.Clark	7	3	2	.700	191	111	5	0	1	2	3	1	1	0			
1936	P.Clark	8	4	0	.666	235	102	5	1	0	3	3	0					
1937	E.Clark	7	4	0	.636	180	105	4	2	0	3	2	0					
1938	E.Clark	7	4	0	.636	119	108	4	3	0	3	1	0					
1939	Henderson	6	5	0	.545	145	150	4	2	0	2	3	0					
1940	P.Clark	5	5	1	.500	138	153	3	3	0	2	2	1					
1941	Edwards	4	6	1	.400	121	195	3	2	0	1	4	1					
1942	Karcis#	0	11	0	.000	38	263	0	7	0	0	4	0					
1943	Dorais	3	6	1	.333	178	238	2	2	1	1	4	0					
1944	Dorais	6	3	1	.667	216	151	3	2	0	3	1	1					
1945	Dorais	7	3	0	.700	195	194	3	1	0	4	2	0					
1946	Dorais	1	10	0	.091	152	310	1	5	0	0	5	0					
1947	Dorais	3	9	0	.250	231	305	2	4	0	1	5	0					
1948	McMillin	2	10	0	.167	200	407	2	4	0	0	6	0					
1949	McMillin	4	8	0	.333	237	259	2	4	0	2	4	0			3	2	0
1950	McMillin	6	6	0	.500	321	295	4	2	0	2	4	0			2	3	0
1951	Parker	7	4	1	.636	336	259	3	3	1	4	1	0			4	1	1
1952	Parker	9	3	0	.750	344	192	5	1	0	4	2	0	2	0	6	0	0
1953	Parker	10	2	0	.833	271	205	5	1	0	5	1	0	1	0	4	1	1
1954	Parker	9	2	1	.818	337	189	5	0	1	4	2	0	0	1	6	0	0
1955	Parker	3	9	0	.250	230	275	2	4	0	1	5	0			4	2	0
1956	Parker	9	3	0	.750	300	188	5	1	0	4	2	0			4	2	0
1957	Wilson	8	4	0	.667	251	231	5	1	0	3	3	0	2	0	3	3	0
1958	Wilson	4	7	1	.364	261	276	2	4	0	2	3	1			3	3	0
1959	Wilson	3	8	1	.213	203	275	2	4	0	1	4	1			4	2	1
1960	Wilson	7	5	0	.583	235	212	5	1	0	2	4	0			2	3	1
1961	Wilson	8	5	1	.615	270	258	2	5	0	6	0	1			4	1	0
1962	Wilson	11	3	0	.786	315	177	7	0	0	4	3	0			4	1	0
1963	Wilson	5	8	1	.385	326	265	3	3	1	2	5	0			2	3	0
1964	Wilson	7	5	2	.583	280	260	3	3	1	4	2	1			3	1	1
1965	Gilmer	6	7	1	.462	257	295	2	4	1	4	3	0			1	4	0
1966	Gilmer	4	9	1	.308	206	317	3	4	0	1	5	1			0	4	1
1967	Schmidt	5	7	2	.417	260	232	3	4	0	2	3	2			3	2	0
1968	Schmidt	4	8	2	.333	207	246	1	4	2	3	4	0			2	3	0
1969	Schmidt	9	4	1	.692	259	193	5	2	0	4	2	1			5	1	0
1970	Schmidt	10	4	0	.714	347	202	6	1	0	4	3	0	0	1	4	2	0
1971	Schmidt	7	6	1	.583	341	286	3	4	0	4	2	1			3	3	0
1972	Schmidt	8	5	1	.607	339	290	5	2	0	3	3	1			4	2	0
1973	McCafferty	6	7	1	.464	271	247	4	3	0	2	4	1			4	2	0
1974	Forzano	7	7	0	.500	256	270	5	2	0	2	5	0			2	4	0
1975	Forzano	7	7	0	.500	245	262	4	3	0	3	4	0			2	4	0
1976	Hudspeth*	6	8	0	.429	262	220	5	2	0	1	6	0			3	4	0
1977	Hudspeth	6	8	0	.429	183	252	5	2	0	1	6	0			3	3	0
1978	M.Clark	7	9	0	.438	290	300	5	3	0	2	6	0			2	2	0
1979	M.Clark	2	14	0	.125	219	365	2	6	0	0	8	0			2	2	0
1980	M.Clark	9	7	0	.563	334	272	6	2	0	3	5	0			3	1	0
1981	M.Clark	8	8	0	.500	397	322	7	1	0	1	7	0			1	3	0
1982	M.Clark	4	5	0	.444	181	176	2	3	0	2	2	0	0	1	2	2	0
1983	M.Clark	9	7	0	.563	347	287	6	2	0	3	5	0	0	1	2	2	0
1984	M.Clark	4	11	1	.281	283	408	2	5	1	2	6	0			2	2	0
1985	Rogers	7	9	0	.438	307	366	6	2	0	1	7	0			1	2	1
1986	Rogers	5	11	0	.313	277	326	1	7	0	4	4	0			2	2	0
1987	Rogers	4	11	0	.267	269	384	1	6	0	3	5	0			2	2	0
1988	Rogers@	4	12	0	.333	220	313	2	6	0	2	6	0			0	4	0
1989	Fontes	7	9	0	.438	312	364	4	4	0	3	5	0			0	4	0
1990	Fontes	6	10	0	.375	373	413	3	5	0	3	5	0			4	0	0
1991	Fontes	12	4	0	.750	339	295	8	0	0	4	4	0	1	1	2	3	0
1992	Fontes	5	11	0	.313	273	332	3	5	0	2	6	0			1	3	0
TOTALS		**364–393–25**			.481	14,875	14,706	216–171–10			148–222–15			7–5		120–100–7		

ALL-TIME RECORD (including post-season): 371–398–25, .483

\# Karcis (0–8) replaced Edwards who began 1942 season with a 0–3 record

* Hudspeth (5–5) replaced Forzano who began 1976 season with a 1–3 record

@ Fontes (2–3) replaced Rogers who began 1988 season with a 2–9 record

LIONS' HEAD COACHES

Coach	Years	Total	Games*	Won	Lost	Tied
Potsy Clark	1934–36, '40	4	49	31	15	3
Dutch Clark	1937–38	2	22	14	8	0
Gus Henderson	1939	1	11	6	5	0
Bill Edwards	1941–42	1+	14	4	9	1
John Karcis	1942	1–	8	0	8	0
Gus Dorais	1943–47	5	53	20	31	2
Bo McMillin	1948–50	3	36	12	24	0
Buddy Parker	1951–56	6	76	50	24	2
George Wilson	1957–64	8	106	55	45	6
Harry Gilmer	1965–66	2	28	10	16	2
Joe Schmidt	1967–72	6	85	43	35	7
Don McCafferty	1973	1	14	6	7	1
Rick Forzano	1974–76	2+	32	15	17	0
Tommy Hudspeth	1976–77	1+	24	11	13	0
Monte Clark	1978–84	7	107	43	63	1
Darryl Rogers	1985–88	3+	58	18	40	0
Wayne Fontes	1988–92	4+	71	33	38	0
Totals	**1934–92**	**59**	**794**	**371**	**398**	**25**

*Includes Regular Season and Post-Season Games

Potsy Clark

Dutch Clark

Gus Henderson

Bill Edwards

John Karcis

Gus Dorais

Bo McMillin

Buddy Parker

George Wilson

Harry Gilmer

Joe Schmidt

Don McCafferty

Rick Forzano

Tommy Hudspeth

Monte Clark

Darryl Rogers

Wayne Fontes

LIONS' INDIVIDUAL RECORDS

CAREER — SERVICE

Most Seasons
15 by Wayne Walker, 1958–72
14 by Dick LeBeau, 1959–72
13 by Joe Schmidt, 1953–65
    by Darris McCord, 1955–67
    by Larry Hand, 1964–77
12 by Alex Karras, 1958–62, 1964–70
    by Paul Naumoff, 1967–78
    by Leonard Thompson, 1975–86
    by Ed Murray, 1980–91

Most Games
200 by Wayne Walker, 1958–72
185 by Dick LeBeau, 1959–72
175 by Leonard Thompson, 1975–86
174 by Ed Murray, 1980–91
168 by Darris McCord, 1955–67
     by Paul Naumoff, 1967–78
164 by Larry Hand, 1964–77
161 by Alex Karras, 1958–62, 64–70

CAREER — RUSHING

Most Attempts
1,203 by Dexter Bussey, 1974–84
1,189 by Barry Sanders, 1989–92
1,165 by Altie Taylor, 1969–76
1,131 by Billy Sims, 1980–84
  960 by James Jones, 1983–88
  938 by Nick Pietrosante, 1959–65
  739 by Mel Farr, 1967–73
  693 by Ace Gutowsky, 1934–38
  651 by Dan Lewis, 1958–64

Most Yards Gained
5,674 by Barry Sanders, 1989–92
5,106 by Billy Sims, 1980–84
5,105 by Dexter Bussey, 1974–84
4,297 by Altie Taylor, 1969–76
3,933 by Nick Pietrosante, 1959–65
3,452 by James Jones, 1983–88
3,072 by Mel Farr, 1967–73
2,698 by Dan Lewis, 1958–64
2,451 by Steve Owens, 1970–76

CAREER — PASSING

Most Attempts
2,193 by Bobby Layne, 1950–58
1,747 by Greg Landry, 1968–78
1,684 by Gary Danielson, 1976–84
1,546 by Eric Hipple, 1980–89
1,315 by Milt Plum, 1962–67
1,314 by Bill Munson, 1968–76

Most Completions
1,074 by Bobby Layne, 1950–58
  957 by Greg Landry, 1968–78
  952 by Gary Danielson, 1976–84
  830 by Eric Hipple, 1980–89
  716 by Bill Munson, 1968–76
  671 by Milt Plum, 1962–67

Most Yards Gained
15,710 by Bobby Layne, 1950–58
12,457 by Greg Landry, 1968–78
11,885 by Gary Danielson, 1976–84
 8,787 by Eric Hipple, 1980–89
 8,536 by Milt Plum, 1962–67
 8,451 by Bill Munson, 1968–76

Most Touchdown Passes
118 by Bobby Layne, 1950–58
 80 by Greg Landry, 1968–78
 69 by Gary Danielson, 1976–84
 56 by Bill Munson, 1968–76
 55 by Milt Plum, 1962–67
    by Eric Hipple, 1980–89
 53 by Earl Morrall, 1958–64

Most Passes Intercepted
142 by Bobby Layne, 1950–58
 87 by Milt Plum, 1962–67
 81 by Greg Landry, 1968–78
 71 by Gary Danielson, 1976–84
 70 by Eric Hipple, 1980–89
 42 by Bill Munson, 1968–76
 41 by Earl Morrall, 1958–64

CAREER — RECEIVING

Most Passes Received
336 by Charlie Sanders, 1968–77
325 by Gail Cogdill, 1960–68
287 by Jim Gibbons, 1958–68
285 by James Jones, 1983–88
277 by Leonard Thompson, 1975–86
245 by David Hill, 1976–82
227 by Terry Barr, 1957–65
223 by Fred Scott, 1978–83

Most Yards Gained
5,220 by Gail Cogdill, 1960–68
4,817 by Charlie Sanders, 1968–77
4,682 by Leonard Thompson, 1975–86
3,810 by Terry Barr, 1957–65
3,651 by Fred Scott, 1978–83

CAREER — INTERCEPTIONS

Most Passes Intercepted
62 by Dick LeBeau, 1959–72
56 by Lem Barney, 1967–77
50 by Yale Lary, 1952–53, 1956–64
46 by Jack Christiansen, 1951–58
36 by Jim David, 1952–59

Most Yards Gained
1,051 by Lem Barney, 1967–77
787 by Yale Lary, 1952–53, 1956–64
762 by Dick LeBeau, 1959–72
719 by Bob Smith, 1949–53
717 by Jack Christiansen, 1951–58

CAREER — SCORING

Most Points
1,113 by Ed Murray, 1980–91
636 by Errol Mann, 1969–76
534 by Doak Walker, 1950–55
345 by Wayne Walker, 1958–72
342 by Barry Sanders, 1989–92
282 by Billy Sims, 1980–84
259 by Jim Martin, 1951–61

Most Touchdowns (Total)
57 by Barry Sanders, 1989–92
47 by Billy Sims, 1980–84
38 by Terry Barr, 1957–65
     by Leonard Thompson, 1975–86
36 by Mel Farr, 1967–73
34 by Doak Walker, 1950–55
33 by James Jones, 1983–88
32 by Cloyce Box, 1949–50, 1952–54
31 by Leon Hart, 1950–57
30 by Nick Pietrosante, 1959–65
     by Gail Codgill, 1960–68
     by Altie Taylor, 1969–76

Most Touchdowns (Rushing)
52 by Barry Sanders, 1989–92
42 by Billy Sims, 1984–84
28 by Nick Pietrosnate, 1959–65
26 by Mel Farr, 1967–73
24 by Altie Taylor, 1969–76
23 by James Jones, 1983
20 by Steve Owens, 1970–76
19 by Greg Landry, 1968–78
18 by Dexter Bussey, 1974–84

Most Touchdowns (Receiving)
35 by Leonard Thompson, 1975–86
     by Terry Barr, 1957–65
32 by Cloyce Box, 1949–50, 1952–54
31 by Charlie Sanders, 1967–77
28 by Gail Cogdill, 1960–68
26 by Larry Walton, 1969–76
25 by Leon Hart, 1950–57

Most Touchdowns (Returns)
11 by Jack Christiansen, 1951–58
10 by Lem Barney, 1967–77

Most Extra Points
384 by Eddie Murray, 1980–91
213 by Errol Mann, 1969–76
183 by Doak Walker, 1950–55
172 by Wayne Walker, 1958–72
91 by Jim Martin, 1951–61

Most Field Goals
244 by Eddie Murray, 1980–91
141 by Errol Mann, 1969–76
56 by Jim Martin, 1951–61
53 by Wayne Walker, 1958–72
49 by Doak Walker, 1950–55

CAREER — PUNTING

Most Punts
503 by Yale Lary, 1952–53, 56–64
464 by Jim Arnold, 1986–92
436 by Herman Weaver, 1970–76
268 by Tom Skladany, 1978–82
266 by Mike Black, 1983–86

Best Average
44.2 by Yale Lary, 1952–53, 1956–64
42.8 by Bob Smith, 1949–54
42.4 by Jim Arnold, 1986–92
       by Tom Skladany, 1978–82
       by Pat Studstill, 1961–67

CAREER — PUNT RETURNS

Most Returns
143 by Pete Mandley, 1984–1988
      by Lem Barney, 1967–77
126 by Yale Lary, 1952–53, 1956–64
118 by Robbie Martin, 1981–84

Most Return Yardage
1,360 by Pete Mandley, 1984–88
1,312 by Lem Barney, 1967–77
1,118 by Robbie Martin, 1981–84
1,084 by Jack Christiansen, 1951–58

CAREER — KICKOFF RETURNS

Most Returns
143 by Mel Gray, 1989–92
122 by Alvin Hall, 1981–85
91 by Tom Watkins, 1962–67
75 by Pat Studstill, 1961–67

Most Return Yardage
3,514 by Mel Gray, 1989–92
2,714 by Alvin Hall, 1981–85
2,262 by Tom Watkins, 1962–67
1,924 by Pat Studstill, 1961–67

SEASON — RUSHING

Most Attempts

342 by Barry Sanders, 1991
313 by Billy Sims, 1980
312 by Barry Sanders, 1992
296 by Billy Sims, 1981
280 by Barry Sanders, 1989
255 by Barry Sanders, 1990
252 by James Jones, 1986
246 by Steve Owens, 1971
225 by Dexter Bussey, 1978
220 by Billy Sims, 1983
206 by Mel Farr, 1967
201 by Nick Pietrosante, 1961

Most Yards Gained

1,548 by Barry Sanders, 1991
1,470 by Barry Sanders, 1989
1,437 by Billy Sims, 1981
1,352 by Barry Sanders, 1992
1,304 by Barry Sanders, 1990
1,303 by Billy Sims, 1980
1,040 by Billy Sims, 1983
1,035 by Steve Owens, 1971
  924 by Dexter Bussey, 1978
  903 by James Jones, 1986
  886 by James Jones, 1985
  872 by Nick Pietrosante, 1960

Most Rushing TDs

16 by Barry Sanders, 1991
14 by Barry Sanders, 1989
13 by Barry Sanders, 1990
   by Billy Sims, 1980, 1981
 9 by Greg Landry, 1972
   by Mel Farr, 1970
   by Barry Sanders, 1992
 8 by James Jones, 1986
   by Nick Pietrosante, 1960
   by Steve Owens, 1971
 7 by Billy Sims, 1983
   by Bob Hoernschemeyer, 1953
   by Gene Gedman, 1956

SEASON — PASSING

Most Attempts

417 by Gary Danielson, 1980
416 by Chuck Long, 1987
410 by Gary Danielson, 1984
406 by Eric Hipple, 1985
387 by Eric Hipple, 1983
368 by Jeff Komlo, 1979
351 by Gary Danielson, 1978
336 by Bobby Layne, 1950
332 by Bobby Layne, 1951
179 by Milt Plum, 1962

Most Completions

252 by Gary Danielson, 1984
244 by Gary Danielson, 1980
232 by Chuck Long, 1987
223 by Eric Hipple, 1985
204 by Eric Hipple, 1983
199 by Gary Danielson, 1978
192 by Eric Hipple, 1986
183 by Jeff Komlo, 1979
181 by Bill Munson, 1968

Most Yards Gained

3,223 by Gary Danielson, 1980
3,076 by Gary Danielson, 1984
2,952 by Eric Hipple, 1985
2,621 by Earl Morrall, 1963
2,598 by Chuck Long, 1987
2,577 by Eric Hipple, 1983
2,403 by Bobby Layne, 1951
2,378 by Milt Plum, 1962
2,358 by Eric Hipple, 1981
2,323 by Bobby Layne, 1950

Most Touchdown Passes

26 by Bobby Layne, 1951
24 by Earl Morrall, 1963
19 by Bobby Layne, 1952
18 by Gary Danielson, 1978
   by Greg Landry, 1972
   by Milt Plum, 1964

Most Passes Intercepted

23 by Jeff Komlo, 1979
   by Bobby Layne, 1951
21 by Bobby Layne, 1953
20 by Chuck Long, 1987
   by Milt Plum, 1962
   by Bobby Layne, 1952
   by Clyde LeForce, 1947
   by Frank Sinkwich, 1943–44

Fewest Passes Intercepted

3 by Dwight Sloan, 1939 (102 att.)
4 by Harry Gilmer, 1955 (122 att.)
5 by Fred Enke, 1949 (142 att.)
6 by Chuck Long, 1988 (141 att.)
7 by Bill Munson, 1974 (292 att.)
  by Greg Landry, 1977 (240 att.)
  by Joe Ferguson, 1986 (155 att.)

SEASON — RECEIVING

Most Passes Received

77 by James Jones, 1984
70 by Richard Johnson, 1989
69 by Brett Perriman, 1992
67 by Pat Studstill, 1966
66 by Terry Barr, 1963
   by Bob Mann, 1949
64 by Richard Johnson, 1990
62 by Fred Scott, 1979
58 by Pete Mandley, 1987
57 by Terry Barr, 1963
54 by Ron Jessie, 1974
   by James Jones, 1986
   by Tom Nowatzke, 1966
53 by Fred Scott, 1981
   by David Hill, 1978
   by Jeff Chadwick, 1986

Most Yards Gained

1,266 by Pat Studstill, 1966
1,091 by Richard Johnson, 1989
1,086 by Terry Barr, 1963
1,030 by Terry Barr, 1964
1,022 by Fred Scott, 1981
1,014 by Bob Mann, 1949
1,009 by Cloyce Box, 1950

Most Receiving TDs

15 by Cloyce Box, 1952
13 by Terry Barr, 1963
12 by Leon Hart, 1951
11 by Cloyce Box, 1950
10 by Gail Cogdill, 1963

SEASON — INTERCEPTIONS

Most Passes Intercepted

12 by Jack Christiansen, 1953
    by Don Doll, 1950
11 by Don Doll, 1949
10 by Jack Christiansen, 1957
    by Lem Barney, 1967

Most Yards Gained

301 by Don Doll, 1949
238 by Jack Christiansen, 1953
232 by Lem Barney, 1967
218 by Bob Smith, 1949
208 by Dick Jauron, 1973

SEASON — SCORING

Most Points

128 by Doak Walker, 1950
121 by Eddie Murray, 1981
116 by Eddie Murray, 1980
113 by Eddie Murray, 1983
109 by Eddie Murray, 1985
106 by Doak Walker, 1954
103 by Errol Mann, 1971
102 by Barry Sanders, 1991
101 by Errol Mann 1969, 1970

Most Touchdowns (Total)

17 by Barry Sanders, 1991
16 by Barry Sanders, 1990
16 by Billy Sims, 1980
15 by Billy Sims, 1981
    by Cloyce Box, 1952
14 by Barry Sanders, 1989
13 by Terry Barr, 1963

Most Touchdowns (Returning)

4 by Jack Christiansen, 1951
3 by Lem Barney, 1967

Most Extra Points

46 by Eddie Murray, 1981
43 by Doak Walker, 1951, 1954
41 by Errol Mann, 1970
40 by Eddie Murray, 1991
38 by Eddie Murray, 1983
    by Errol Mann, 1972
    by Doak Walker, 1950
37 by Wayne Walker, 1962
    by Errol Mann, 1971

Most Field Goals

27 by Eddie Murray, 1980
26 by Eddie Murray, 1985
25 by Eddie Murray, 1981, 1983
    by Errol Mann, 1969
23 by Errol Mann, 1974
22 by Errol Mann, 1971
21 by Jason Hanson, 1992
20 by Benny Ricardo, 1978
    by Errol Mann, 1970, 1972
    by Eddie Murray, 1984, 1987, 1988
    by Eddie Murray, 1989

Consecutive Field Goals

19 by Eddie Murray, from 11–13–88 (vs. Tampa Bay) to 11–12–89 (at G.B.)

SEASON — PUNTING

Most Punts

97 by Jim Arnold, 1988
93 by Wilbur Summers, 1977
88 by Larry Swider, 1979
86 by Tom Skladany, 1978
83 by Herman Weaver, 1976
82 by Jim Arnold, 1989
80 by Herman Weaver, 1975
78 by Pat Studstill, 1965
76 by Mike Black, 1984
75 by Jim Arnold, 1991
73 by Mike Black, 1985
72 by Tom Skladany, 1980
    by Herman Weaver, 1974

Best Gross Average

48.9 by Yale Lary, 1963
48.4 by Yale Lary, 1961
47.1 by Yale Lary, 1959

Best Net Average

39.6 by Jim Arnold, 1987

SEASON — PUNT RETURNS

Most Returns

52 by Robbie Martin, 1981
43 by Pete Mandley, 1986
38 by Pete Mandley, 1985
37 by Pete Mandley, 1988
36 by Walter Stanley, 1989
34 by Mel Gray, 1990
32 by Tom Watkins, 1963
29 by Pat Studstill, 1962

Most Yards Returned

496 by Walter Stanley, 1989
457 by Pat Studstill, 1962
450 by Robbie Martin, 1981
403 by Pete Mandley, 1985
399 by Tom Watkins, 1963
385 by Mel Gray, 1991
362 by Mel Gray, 1990
343 by Jack Christiansen, 1951

SEASON — KICKOFF RETURNS

Most Returns

48 by Herman Hunter, 1986
42 by Mel Gray, 1992
41 by Mel Gray, 1990
39 by Alvin Hall, 1985
38 by Jimmie Jones, 1974
36 by Mel Gray, 1991
32 by Gary Lee, 1987
29 by Pat Studstill, 1964
26 by Mickey Zofko, 1972
25 by Lem Barney, 1968
    by Bobby Williams, 1970

Most Yards Returned

1,007 by Herman Hunter, 1986
1,006 by Mel Gray, 1992
  939 by Mel Gray, 1990
  929 by Mel Gray, 1991
  927 by Jimmie Jones, 1974
  886 by Alvin Hall, 1985
  719 by Gary Lee, 1987
  708 by Pat Studstill, 1964
  670 by Lem Barney, 1968
  640 by Mel Gray, 1989
  616 by Mickey Zofko, 1972

Index

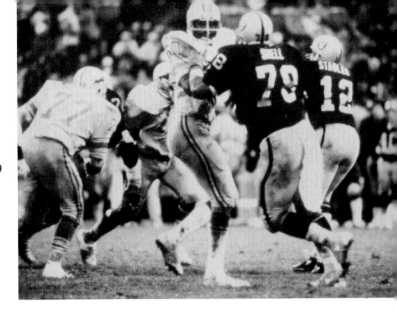

Postscript

by Joe Falls
The Detroit News

They have frustrated us. They have infuriated us. How many times have we seen them play and said: "Never again!"

But we are always there, the next game, the next week, the next month, the next season. We cannot stay away from them. They are like our children. They make us mad and they make us glad. They know how to bring out all the emotions in us. They are very much like our own children. They are the Detroit Lions. They get to us like no other team in town.

It's been like this with me: I've followed this team for 40 years. I'd like to say I covered all the games but that would not be true. For a time, I was a baseball writer. Other times I was sent out on other assignments. Sometimes I would stay away on my own, saying to myself: "Never again."

Who was I kidding? In my own way, I have not missed a game in all of these 40 years. By four o'clock on a Sunday afternoon, I know how they've come out. Maybe I don't know all the details, but I know if they've won or lost. This hasn't changed in these four decades.

Maybe our other teams play too much. Their games do not seem to carry the same urgency as the Lions. The Tigers go on from late in February until early in October. The Red Wings go from mid-September until May and are back at it four months later. Pro basketball and the Pistons begin in mid-October and never end. What does another win or loss mean anyway?

Football is different. They play once a week — mostly on Sunday — just 16 times a year. That means eight at home and eight on the road. Every game has a special meaning.

But it is more than that. It is a clear case of success or failure. There seems to be no middle ground for this football team. Either they thrill us or anger us. Football can do that to you like no other sport. The Lions can do it like no other team.

I can tell myself I'm taking this Sunday off — I've had enough and I'm taking my family to eat out at the Edison Inn in Port Huron. We'll drive up in the middle of the afternoon, with the sun shining down on the flat fields around us, and I'll tell myself this is the way to live.

Sure. When nobody is paying attention, I'll flip on the radio and try to tell from Mark Champion's voice whether the Lions are ahead or behind. I can do that, you know. I did it with Van Patrick and now I can do it with Champion.

I had to know what's going on, which means that every Sunday for the past four decades — from one o'clock until four — my mind, my heart and I guess part of my soul is wherever the Lions are, guessing, wondering how they're going to come out.

My memories of this team may be a little different than yours. I remember the memorable playoff game against the San Francisco 49ers in 1957 when we stayed at the sumptuous Rickey's Motel in Palo Alto and how head coach George Wilson introduced me to screwdrivers at breakfast and guess who was singing with the band by lunchtime? I remember those great games from the West Coast, when the TV pictures were first coming into our living rooms, and how the Lions would play in Los Angeles and San Francisco on back-to-back Sundays and it would be getting dark outside and we would lay on the floor and watch the glorious pictures from the LA Coliseum and Kezar Stadium. Who could ever forget those pigeons on the field at Kezar? How come they never got in the way?

I remember the hot tomato soup on Thanksgiving Day in the press box at snowy Tiger Stadium and the violent battle going on down there against the Green Bay Packers . . . and going over to Wrigley Field in Chicago for the final game of the season on those biting cold Sundays in the middle of December and the windows of the press box becoming so covered with ice that we were scrape, scrape, scraping the ice all through the game but still could not see the entire field.

I remember Eric Hipple's stunning debut on Monday Night Football, and getting a call on the Sunday afternoon that Don McCafferty, the head coach, had suddenly died. I remember seeing Buddy Parker sitting in his seat in the plane carrying us back from a road loss,

just sitting there and staring straight ahead, a drink in his hand and his tie cut in half.

I will never forget Billy Sims on those mad dashes to the outside or Yale Lary dancing in front of the receiver and picking the ball off and returning it 45 yards to get the Lions out of a jam. And, hey, how lucky we've all been to see this little man, Barry Sanders, do his stuff like no other back in football.

They have frustrated us. They have infuriated us. But we are always there, the next game, the next week, the next month, the next year. They have made us mad and they have made us glad. They know how to bring out all the emotions in us. They are like our children.

They are the Detroit Lions.
They are *ours*.

Dan,
Merry Christmas
1993

Love Always Your
Best Friend

Stephanie